IN A TROUBLED AGE

Dina Weil

MINERVA PRESS
LONDON
MONTREUX WASHINGTON SYDNEY

IN A TROUBLED AGE
Copyright © Dina Weil 1997

All Rights Reserved

No part of this book may be reproduced in any form,
by photocopying or by any electronic or mechanical means,
including information storage or retrieval systems,
without permission in writing from both the copyright owner
and the publisher of this book.

ISBN 1 86106 123 4

First Published 1997 by
MINERVA PRESS
195 Knightsbridge
London SW7 1RE

2nd Impression 1998

Printed in Great Britain for Minerva Press

IN A TROUBLED AGE

For My Daughters and Their Families

*In Memory of My Parents
Esther and Julius Berlowitz*

and

My Husband Josef Weil

Contents

PART I: AND DON'T FORGET US

Earliest Memories	11
Cousins	25
Ille	28
Fräulein Feinberg	31
Florence	34
When in Rome	39
From 'Juden Unerwünscht' to 'Juden Verboten' and Killed, 1938/1941...	48
The Last Year in Germany, 1942	65
Hilma	71
The Deportation	73
Life Goes On	76
The Escape	78
At the Police Station	89
Alingsås	91
The Next Refugee Camp	93
Norrköping	97
Stockholm	103
Marianne	111
An Odd Invitation	112
Erich	113
The Aftermath	115
Youth Aliyah	119
Hillel Storch	121

Looking For Greener Pastures	124
Travel	127
Basel	128
France	130
Living it up in a Hotel	133
Youth Aliyah in Paris	135
Working with Akiba	137
My Boss, Meta	139
Life in Paris, Winter 1947/48	141
Falling in Love Again	145

PART II: ALIYAH

Aliyah, February 1948	151
A New Beginning	158
Life on a Kibbutz	161
Weddings	176
A Journey to the United States	185
Back in Ma'ayan	191
Town Life	196
Reserve Duty	203
Moving Again	205
June 1967: the Six Day War	209
A Last Visit	213
A Wedding in Kabul	214
Our Trip Abroad	219
1973	221

PART III: THE CHILDREN GREW UP AND BECAME PEOPLE

Letters from Israel to Friends in Sweden	227
A Great Sorrow	258
More Letters	264
Epilogue	302
Glossary	304
Appendix	306

Part I
AND DON'T FORGET US

Earliest Memories

Sitting on my potty at a tender age I yelled with conviction:
"I don't want to be Jewish. I want to be like Fräulein Heti!"
Heti, our nursemaid was a devout Catholic. I probably did not know that word and certainly could not pronounce it, but it was the first time in my life that I expressed an opinion about religion, although not necessarily my own.

Living in Berlin with my parents and my brother in comfort, and after Heti had been followed by a series of other Kinderfräuleins who were not interested in saving my soul, I forgot about religious strife. I was Jewish, and that was that.

At an early age I was taken to the temple for Simchat Torah, but since I cried all the time I had to be taken home again. I was usually a quiet child but it seems that religion did not bring out the best in me.

A Christmas tree for the maids and a Menorah for the family often stood peacefully together. Until 1933. Then the Christmas tree vanished and Chanukah was a festive occasion only when my brother Bill came home from his school in France.

My father regarded religion as nonsense but wanted his children to feel and be Jewish. Pessach seemed to be the ideal occasion, the Seder was the big event in our house and uncles, aunts and cousins were invited.

My mother invaded the kitchen and cooked gefillte fisch with pike for everybody and a Polish carp with raisins for herself. She made Charimsel and Mazzeklösse. For Purim too she would be busy in the kitchen and prepared huge amounts of Kreppchen on a big white scoured wooden board which covered almost the whole kitchen table. We would eat them with chicken soup as fast as we could.

For the rest of the year the kitchen belonged to the maid, unless it was her day off. Then my mother quite often reached gleefully for the scrubbing brush, scrubbed the white tiles whiter, and Bill and I would get cocoa and rolls with butter for our supper.

Uncle Adolf, Mother's eldest brother, led the Seder. He was tall, broad, mostly bald, with a big belly and a booming voice. His wife was thin and quiet and had a crooked spine. She had taught my mother how to cook before her marriage. Mother used to tell us how good looking Aunt Jenny had been. Uncle Adolf treated her always with tenderness and care. With the rest of the Kupferberg family he used his resounding voice to interfere whenever possible in the unshakeable belief that he was right. They had one son, who was the apple of their eyes. He played the piano bouncing up and down like a ball; the family suffered but his parents expanded with pride.

Since nobody understood what was being read at the Seder, my uncle, to catch his breath from singing and reading, told jokes in between. He was a travelling salesman and had an inexhaustible stock and a captive audience. My father who had heard those stories a hundred times before, would be waiting impatiently for my uncle to finish, but as host he could hardly say anything.

Mother used to sing the old melodies, usually a little out of tune. I would sometimes try to stop her, though my singing was no better than hers. During my first years in school I was not allowed to sing and had to sit with two other girls on the bench of the buzzers for children with low voices who were not allowed to sing with the rest of the class. But there was not much wrong with my hearing. When I learned modern Hebrew our pronunciations clashed as well.

As the years went by in Nazi Germany, the circle around the Seder table became smaller and the rooms were kept darker.

Bill was sent away to school, the cousins emigrated, and the grown-ups spoke in hushed voices.

I used to go to the synagogue on Yom Kippur with my mother and fasted for the first time when I was eleven. We remained most of the day there and drank a cup of coffee together on our way home. When I was recruited for forced labour and we got extra heavy work on holidays, I stopped fasting. I never started again, since I felt that whatever sins I might have committed could hardly be compared to those of the world around me.

II

When I escaped from Germany I had only a few pictures of my family and friends which I took with me, but slowly, with the help of all my relatives, I collected more.

There they are in my album, my great grandmother Johanna Berlowitz from Schmalleningken who lived from 1818 to 1902, wore a Scheitel, had a very long nose and is said to have tyrannised the whole family with her religious beliefs. There is her son, my grandfather, with sideburns and a moustache growing into each other, quite handsome, and his wife Fanny, looking elegant with and without her daughters, my father and Uncle Paul in uniform, Walter Schaal, my cousin, as a baby.

There is a picture of Meir and Minna Kupferberg, Mother's parents, at the end of their lives, sitting on a bench in the park, she somewhat taller than her husband, still good looking, he kind and relaxed, Mother as a child, very dark, with big eyes... her youngest brother, her eldest sister holding a baby, cousin Josef... some distant cousins on a visit from Vienna...

There is my father holding his infant son proudly on his arm. Bill's first school day and other pictures from our childhood...

A family of Jews in Germany living a very ordinary middle-class life, seemingly secure.

III

My maternal grandfather, Meir Kupferberg, had been very fond of my brother. This gratified my mother. She was sometimes mortified by the way other little boys and girls were preferred to her own unique children, because we had no curls. Not only didn't we have curls, but Bill's hair stood upright unless carefully slicked down, and my hair looked like some particularly straight chives. To make up for this blemish I had a collection of white and pink ribbons, which I had to wear till Mother decided that they made me look too babyish. I had no red ribbons, since my mother had had to wear so much red as a child that she never touched it again. Only a few times did I get a red or a blue dress. I preferred those to the pink ones with little flowers, which always showed whether we had been riding the banister from the third floor down.

I was not allowed to let my hair grow, no plaits, no parting in the middle.

"That's the way hypocrites wear theirs!" was Mother's judgement.

When the time came that I could decide for myself, I had my hair cut short like a boy's. Ille, my best friend, had the same haircut and we agreed that it had only one drawback, one's ears had to be clean at all times. I was well into middle age before straight hair became all the rage.

I remember my maternal grandmother living with Aunt Bertha, a widow with three sons; the youngest was sent to an orphanage after his father's death. This seems to have been the accepted custom at the time, because the same happened to a great cousin whose father died early.

My grandmother would sit in Aunt Bertha's apartment in a rocking chair, unable to talk after a stroke. She had been a tall woman, and when as a young girl she was told that one day she would be as tall as her own father, she would cry. She had three sons and three daughters.

The family was devout and bought only bread at the bakery.

"Because", said grandmother to my mother, "all those pastries you see are made with pork fat and are not kosher."

But whenever Mother got one of them as a present because she was a pretty little girl, she had to eat it. Grandmother would not allow the baker's wife to be put to shame by refusing her gift. She would not allow my mother to throw food away, either.

If I complained as a kid about chores my mother would say:

"You should thank your lucky stars that I am your mother! Grandmother was much stricter: Imagine, I even had to go out into the street and collect horse manure for her geraniums!"

Mother was the youngest. I met her second sister only when she came to visit my sick mother. To my great astonishment, I was told at the age of fifteen that the lady sitting next to Mother's bed was my aunt. Both had tears in their eyes and my aunt was patting my mother's hand. Aunt Selma was soft spoken, like my mother, Aunt Bertha and Uncle Max. Uncle Adolf and Uncle Jacques, the youngest brother, were the ones with the overriding voices.

Mother's explanation for the long silence was that her sister had been a wild young girl but turned out all right, which in those years probably meant that she had married. Wild was not defined more closely. A cousin's version was that my father had first been interested in my aunt until she brought her younger sister along. Both versions of the quarrel sound a bit odd.

Uncle Max and his wife had six children, four daughters and two sons.

My uncle came to visit in the mornings when Father was out. He and Mother would sit quietly and talk, almost whisper, over a cup of coffee. Sometimes he brought his sons, Ferry and Horst, both younger than I. They had slicked-down blond hair, no curls there either, and after a shy: "Good day!" vanished behind their father's back. There they remained during the rest of the visit. Senta, their sister, came regularly to our house to play with us. She was very nice, and I don't remember that we ever quarrelled.

Not so our elders; one could never be quite sure as to who was talking to whom. Usually, when sick, one was reunited with the family. Like my mother and her elder sister. Father did not talk to either Uncle Max or his wife. Mother talked only to her brother not her sister-in-law.

Everybody talked to everybody's children. A real blessing that children were never included in these hostilities. My father's favourite niece was Edith, Uncle Max's eldest daughter.

When Uncle Jacques was ill in hospital and no one was talking to him at the time, the family was worried. He was, after all, their brother. The family council decided that somebody had to find out how sick he was. The somebody turned out to be my mother, the youngest and most biddable. Naturally, once she had visited Uncle Jacques in hospital she continued talking to him. He was nearest her in age and probably her favourite brother. Logic being absent in these squabbles the family decided not to talk to her either.

IV

My paternal grandfather, Wolf Berlowitz, lived and died in London and is buried there like Karl Marx before him. There the similarity ends. He had lived with his family in Danzig, had speculated, went broke and left, and was never mentioned in our hearing. A great pity; it would have been interesting to know what kind of a man he was. Bill, when he wrote the family history, discovered that Grandfather had lived under another name in London, had died intestate and his possessions should have gone to the Crown, but the Crown generously waived its right and they went to his landlady. On the death certificate it said that he was "a bastard and a bachelor". Actually he was, of course, neither. His family had visited him now and then in England.

My father, as the eldest, took on the responsibility of the family. He moved to Berlin with his younger brother, Paul, his three sisters Martha, Irma, and Trude, and his mother. Father and his brother Paul built up a shoe business which enabled them to give decent dowries to their sisters and keep their mother in the style to which she had been accustomed. My father left Danzig with a heavy heart, he had loved the city. The whole experience made a deep impression on him and ultimately influenced all our lives. He never speculated and refused to emigrate without sufficient funds to avoid being a burden to his son.

Although Mother believed that some money had remained after the bankruptcy, Aunt Martha's wedding had to be postponed. Mother said that she was very unhappy and cut her wrists because she was afraid that her future husband did not love her without her dowry. Luckily she was saved and got married shortly afterwards.

By the time Father could marry, World War I broke out and my mother, who was an accountant, worked in his store till the end of the war. The engagement took place after the war and Walter, my cousin, remembered the following lines that were recited at the engagement party:

> Sie sietzten bis zuletzt sich gar,
> Auch blieb man fern sich manches Jahr.
> Inzwischen brach der Krieg herein
> Und unser'n Julius zog man ein.

Uncle Paul was the first to be called up in 1914, but he sprained his ankle and was sent home. He stopped limping when the war ended. We are not a war loving family. Then my father was called up, among other things he accompanied prisoners of war to Romania and visited his sister in Budapest. He was already too old for active duty.

When my parents finally married in 1919 Father was forty-three, and Mother was seventeen years his junior.

While they were engaged they used to go rowing together:

"You row", Father would say, "because I'll have to work for you all my life!"

I did not see much of my paternal grandmother although we lived in the same house. My only real memory of her is that when Bill and I once rang her doorbell, she came to the door and said:

"Here is a mark for hot dogs for you, now go away!"

Once I was allowed to enter her apartment when my aunt Trude from Budapest and my cousin Cuni came to visit. I was given a big chocolate cigar, and told to give it to Cuni. My heart almost broke and when she opened the door for me I gave her the cigar with the words:

"This is for you, but you have to share it with me!" We were very young.

Grandmother was finicky and did not eat at everybody's house. She would sometimes hide cookies in her purse and throw them away the minute she left. For a time she also refused to eat bread, as she could see into a bakery and watch the unhygienic habits of the bakers.

Bill, Cuni, her younger sister, Lisi, and I were the youngest grandchildren. Grandmother seemed to have spent most of her grandmotherly love on her four elder grandchildren, the children of her two eldest daughters. But I may be wronging her, she died when I was not yet five.

My father's eldest sister and my mother did not talk, because when Father and Mother visited Aunt Martha during the war she offered her brother a cup of cocoa but none to his fiancée. Maybe there were weightier reasons that were not deemed appropriate for my ears.

My father was a quiet man who loved to tell jokes and challenge us to impossible bets. Then, as now, I never agreed to bet, but Bill did. He accepted a dare to have his ear pulled for one hour. Bill would not give up so my father stopped pulling after fifty minutes and told my brother that he had lost, but Mother made him pay up. Once he offered ten marks for anyone who would eat a live tadpole. That time there were no takers.

He always had his small change loose in his pockets and walked up and down with his hands on his back playing with the money. We used to walk behind him since any money that fell to the floor was ours. Once a five mark coin fell and within seconds my father and Bill were on the floor trying to get it from under the sideboard where it had rolled. Neither could reach it and Bill yelled for me to help him. I raced from the room and came back with an umbrella. Bill picked up the coin and we shared the money triumphantly.

We had a joint piggy bank and Mother would see to it that Father made regular contributions. For one of her birthdays she emptied it, bought a big purse and said proudly to relatives and friends, "Look what wonderful children I have. Look what a lovely present they gave me."

V

Father liked to explain things. From family outings in the Grunewald I tried to walk back with him alone, so that nobody could disturb us. Since he was capable of walking the whole way in silence, I prepared questions that needed long answers. How does an aeroplane fly? How does a light bulb glow? The answers to these questions would absorb both of us. If he did not know, he would look up the subject in the Brockhaus and tell me about it later. When we reached Halensee, my patience and my love for my father's voice gave out and I would ask for and get money for ice cream.

Seeing my father and me from the vantage point of a mother and grandmother, I suppose he was quite as glad as I was when we reached the ice cream parlour.

Father was superstitious. None of his superstitions brought any luck and many things were forbidden; such as sleeping with one's head to the door, walking under ladders, taking a ring off someone else's hand, and having birthday parties before the exact date. Cats that crossed your way were unlucky and he would spot them even in the dark. Not going back through the same door or crossing the street at some other point on the way back was unlucky. The last two were fortunately not required of us. Going back into the house was not good either but apparently only for my parents, because we children were sent back for whatever it was they had forgotten.

Uncle Paul was a bachelor, the family, mainly my father, not having allowed him to marry his gentile girlfriend. Although they never married she remained Aunt Paula for my elder cousins and at my uncle's funeral my father admitted that if he had known what a decent person she was he would not have opposed the marriage. Uncle Paul lived many years with his sister, Irma, and her family. He was hard of hearing and would always cup his hand around his ear and ask us to repeat what we had said.

Uncle Paul had a motorboat in Oberschönweide which had been built to his specifications. It was named *Pan* and he travelled quite far with it even to the sea, much against Grandmother's wishes, but he always had a machinist with him. He would invite members of the family for outings on Sunday. We would take the train with the rest of the Berliners who fled the city on a hot summer day. Memory being what it is, I remember the train ride and having to lie down for a nap, being able to watch the trees waving a pattern of light and dark green above me through the cabin door.

Once Uncle Paul gave me a very big doll with a porcelain head. These porcelain heads were a curse, since they were so easily broken. My dolls spent much time in the doll clinic, and in one of my mother's cupboards under lock and key. Once when Bill and I were alone at home we opened the cupboard with another key and broke the lock. Playing somewhat roughly with the doll, we broke its head too.

After Grandmother died Uncle Paul sold the boat to a famous actor and the family was quite proud of the fact and mentioned it occasionally.

We stayed with Aunt Irma for a week when our family moved from the Schönhauser Allee to the Dahlmannstrasse. Uncle Paul would see to it that we got enough to eat and heap our plates with food in spite of our weak protests which he could not hear. I found that the only way not to overeat and be sick was to stop eating. That would convince him that I, for one, had had enough. But Bill, older and more responsible, felt obliged to finish and would then chide me:

"You stupid goose, you always manage! You just leave the food and I have to eat up everything."

No use telling him to follow my example.

Aunt Irma had a potato peeler in her kitchen. One set it up at the kitchen table, put a potato on a spit and turned a lever. The potato would go round and round and slowly advance while a knife on the side peeled it. We thought this the height of sophistication and would take turns peeling the potatoes.

In later years my mother and Uncle Paul quarrelled. Here too children were exempted from enmity. When Uncle Paul was sick in hospital, my mother, true to Kupferberg tradition, went and visited him at once and he was very content and pleased to see her. She also told me to go: "He is your uncle!"

VI

When I think about my childhood, memories come floating into my mind. I am never quite sure how old I am, I see the events but not myself.

Among my earliest memories is one in the Münzstrasse, where I was born and where we lived till I went to school. I was standing in the middle of the dining room; my mother was at the window looking out. Somebody yelled at her and told her to move away from the window or he would shoot. She didn't, but hid behind the curtains. In spite of diligently asking everybody who might remember what that shooting was about, I never found out.

I also remember running after Bill around the table in the same dining room with the head of a dead chicken in my hand. He escaped, screaming. It was thus I learned that heroes may have feet of clay, because Bill was certainly the greatest hero in my life.

When one of the maids threatened me at the age of three with the black man outside the back door, Bill, although he was only three years older, took me to the door and showed me that no black man was waiting to take me away.

Bill was only a little kid when he fell downstairs at our shoe store. He fell badly and bit half his tongue off. He was taken to our family doctor and had it stitched back on. A few years later when we were again playing in the store I was swinging back and forth with one hand on my father's desk and the other on his armchair, a favourite occupation of mine. I also fell badly. Bill picked me up, put his dirty hand over my chin where the blood gushed out and brought me to our father. I was taken to the same doctor who put a clamp in to hold the wound together. Of course I cried when I was sat down in the doctor's chair. But these tears were nothing to the screams I emitted when the doctor, by way of consolation, told me that I was sitting in the very same chair where a few years back he had sewed my brother's tongue back in.

Once my mother fell while crossing the busy Schönhauser Allee, where we lived at that time. Bill took me by the hand and crossed with me to the other side, leaving my mother to fend for herself. Since he could not help her, he saw no sense in standing around and possibly being run over. I have always been grateful that he thought highly enough of me to take me with him! I would have followed him anywhere on earth without question.

As a very little girl I had to be told to eat and chew and swallow and again to eat and chew and swallow: "Gerda, don't forget to chew! Gerda, don't forget to swallow!" I was told to chew not because I had a tendency to swallow my food without chewing, but because I sat around drearily with my food in my mouth, not doing anything about it. Very often by the time I finished with 'long teeth', as it was called, the food would be ice cold and quite often I had an upset stomach.

I was skinny with too long legs and my heels would hit my behind when I was running. I also fell a lot and my knees were permanently scabby.

Of all the Fräuleins we had, Fräulein Grethe was the one we liked least. She was not only very unpleasant about my slow eating, and caused most of my stomach upsets during her reign, but also tried to alter my sleeping habits. When I moved around too much during my afternoon nap, she scolded me for not sleeping, and finally I really did not sleep, lying perfectly still as best I could. Once I saw a mouse cross the room and, not unnaturally, screamed, which brought one more scolding on my head.

"You should have had your eyes closed!" she said. "Then you would not have seen the mouse." How true.

Fräulein Grethe was with us in Altheide, where my mother had to go for a health cure. As far as I remember, I was sick on alternate days and had porridge in between, which I ate quite fast. On those days I usually fell.

Once, when out with Fräulein Grethe I fell again and bloodied my knees. I was told to sit quietly next to her and Bill was told to go and play. He took pity on me and tried to entertain me. In the meantime Fräulein Grethe amused herself with her boyfriend.

Before going home she threatened us not to tell Mother, but she mistook at least my character, because that was the first thing I did on entering the apartment. This took care of Fräulein Grethe who was dismissed because she had not had the ability to make herself loved.

She also quarrelled with the maid time and again when the four of us played 'Mensch ärger Dich nicht'. We felt above such things and found the quarrel between the maid and Fräulein Grethe more amusing than the game itself.

The minute we were old enough to travel without a Fräulein, we travelled alone with my mother and the three of us had a lot more fun.

My childhood ended abruptly when I was less than ten. It was then that my father sent us to Italy for a longer period and we started to learn Italian. Bill was much better at it than I was, and I felt frustrated. When a friend wrote my mother that she had seen Father with his secretary in a fur coat on the Kurfürstendamm, we returned on the next train. My mother and the friend never talked again.

Hitler came to absolute power in March 1933, and Father asked Bill and me whether we wanted to be baptised. He said when asked that he and Mother would remain Jewish but that we had to decide our own future. He did not know then that there was no choice for Jews. Bill decided against baptism and I agreed, stunned by the question and the seriousness of the occasion. Bill was sent to school in France, I was sent to the Theodor Herzl School although my parents were anything but Zionists.

When it became clear that the Hitler regime was there to stay for the foreseeable future, my mother was desperate to emigrate and would rush around Berlin from consulate to consulate often in a taxi, to follow up any kind of rumour, whether about immigration to Italy, Chile or Australia.

Cousins

Aunt Trude, Father's youngest sister, married her cousin Hermann Berlowitz, who had emigrated to Hungary before the First World War. They lived in Budapest where their two daughters were born. The whole family was baptised for practical reasons, which my mother said was understandable but visiting the Pope in Rome and kissing his ring was overdoing piety.

My mother took me to Budapest on a long visit when I was barely five and did not need a ticket. Not many memories remain but I remember that Cuni was taken to the kitchen by the cook and given huge amounts of noodles which were stuffed into her mouth. I looked on horror stricken. She too was on the skinny side and the cook probably thought that it reflected badly on her cooking.

We visited the chocolate factory my uncle managed. It was the day before we left and at the end of our tour I was given a little basket with chocolates. I wanted to eat those on our trip home but Mother put her foot down. I was supposed to sleep on the night train. I yelled and that is one of the few times that she slapped me.

Cuni's grandfather had been betrothed to their grandmother's sister, but when the date of the wedding neared he was told that he would have to marry the elder sister, who was not only older than her sister but also older than her future husband. He accepted the deal. Since she was neither very young nor beautiful it was thought in the town that he must have received a very large dowry and his credit jumped sky high.

Cuni's grandmother became a tough old widow who emigrated to Israel in the Thirties and lived to be over ninety.

Cousin Hertha, whom we called Aunt, was a favourite cousin of my father's. She was a tall good looking woman of majestic proportions. She too had wanted to marry one of her cousins but her family had not let her do so. She was married to an equally tall and good looking man who did not talk much. His name was Sigismund Basch. They had a son and a daughter; the son was Bill's age, the daughter a few years older. We often played with Heinz, and when Bill was at school abroad Heinz used to take me to those movie houses where my parents would not let me go alone.

Mother gave bridge parties and always prepared appetising titbits for the players. Bill and I would look at them with longing but were only allowed to eat any after the guests had left. There was one exception and we used to ask, "Is Aunt Hertha coming?" because if she was among the guests, we ate sweets before she came. There was never anything left after she had gone.

Cousin Emmy, whom I also called Aunt, lived in Chemnitz and I doubt if she was anybody's favourite. She came to live with us for a time after my mother fell ill, to manage the household. She had a sour face and for the good of my soul demanded that I wash my underwear and my handkerchiefs in the basin in my bedroom. I would plaster my washed and wet handkerchiefs on the mirror so that at least I would not need to iron them too. There was no reason for this. I brought the bulk of the washing, the bed linen, towels and underwear to the laundry. The lady there seeing a fifteen year old girl with the heavy load was indignant:

"Don't you have a brother or a father to do this?" I did not tell her that we were Jewish, that my brother had emigrated and my father was over sixty.

I did not like the food Aunt Emmy cooked. Neither apparently did my father and one day she went too far. She made Hefeklösse (yeast dumplings) and my father, who had dentures, could not eat them. They were rubbery and bounced back and Father's dentures with them. Aunt Emmy was sent away and for a time I did the cooking according to my mother's instructions with a wooden spoon in one hand and a book, and not a cookbook either, in the other.

Ille

Ille played mostly with boys, her brother and her cousins. When her mother decided that she must have a girlfriend, she picked me and we became best friends. Her parents, her uncles and aunts were good friends of our parents and we spent winter vacations together in Spindlermühle, Czechoslovakia and once a summer holiday in Denmark.

The family would be called by my parents collectively 'The Baums'. My father, who was somewhat older than the Baums but up to anything they might do, like walking, climbing or chin-ups, was called Uncle B. My father did not mind, but the Baums then called my mother, who was so much younger, Tante B and she was appalled.

Ille and I slept over at each other's houses; we went to the movies and raced each other home. By the time the maid had opened the door, we had already yelled, "Front!" which meant that whoever said it first could use the bathroom near the front door, the other had to run to the one near the bedrooms. Every second was precious.

I was taller than Ille, but very quiet. Whenever I was teased by the grown-ups, Ille would protect me and hold forth to all and sundry that I could and did talk when alone with her. I was very glad about her intervention. It saved me from stupidly saying: "I can talk". The things children have to put up with! One of those was Ille's Uncle Siegbert. He used to pinch our cheeks in a way that really hurt, and we ran away or hid whenever we saw him.

Ille's Aunt Betty had a house in Mellensee and we would both be invited there. It was a lovely place and we had a marvellous time. Sometimes we earned money by putting manure on the raspberry bushes.

Once we were sent to buy eggs. We set forth in good spirits, bought the eggs and proceeded homewards. After five minutes the eggs changed hands and unfortunately cascaded down. We picked them up, since it was not quite clear who was to hold them, they fell again... and a third time. The few eggs that had remained whole at first were now broken. We brought the slippery mess home to Ille's aunt, giggling all the way. Only when we could be seen, did we stop and try to look serious.

We went fishing with the boys. I don't remember actually holding a fishing rod, but we were allowed to put the worms on the hook and Ille became quite proficient.

In the Grunewald we played Indians. There were eight boys, including my brother. Sometimes one or the other of the boys would sulk and not play. We two girls could always be depended upon, although I was never very happy hiding behind bushes in the woods.

Stealing fruit in gardens was a legitimate pursuit, stealing a banana in a shop as one of the boys once did was not. In Denmark we would don leather jackets in summer, lie on top of thorny hedges and pick whatever fruit we could reach. I don't know why we did that because for the smallest sum we could go inside and eat as much as we wanted. They seemed to be tastier the harder they were to get.

In Denmark we visited a youth who was there to learn agriculture before going to Palestine and he taught us how to milk a cow. It was my first and last opportunity but I still remember his words, "Do it as if you were playing a scale on the piano!" Fortunately this was one of the things I had been taught.

I have before me a picture that Ille gave me long after the war was over. My father is sitting on a snowy mountain, surrounded by some of the Baums, Ille is standing next to him with a big smile on her face and her hands in her pockets.

Between my father's feet there is an extra pair of shoes. Ille's Uncle Siegbert had complained to my father that the shoes he had bought from him twelve years before were not watertight any more and he was not satisfied. My father asked him how much he had paid for them and then said:

"If you take your shoes off now, I'll return your money."

Siegbert Baum did, my father paid and the picture was taken of him and the shoes he had so suddenly acquired. Gerhart, one of Ille's cousins, was sent to the hotel to bring up another pair of shoes. He received five marks as an incentive, but with the money in his pocket, Gerhart ate lunch first. In the meantime Siegbert got cold feet and asked to be drawn home on a toboggan.

Our parents used to go on walking tours and my mother and my father were usually well in advance of the Baums. They would meet at a restaurant, and once my father told the waiter about the friends that would be coming and asked him to go around and offer everybody as much food as they could eat. He would pay for it after the meal. The Baums who liked to eat big portions were astonished, but well satisfied and decided to go to the restaurant again.

Another time my father being first at the restaurant ordered extra portions of potatoes for which he paid, and for some time to come everybody talked about that restaurant and those enormous plates of potatoes.

We skated, skied and tobogganed together. We swam and ran and laughed. Those were the happy days.

Fräulein Feinberg

Jenny Feinberg came to our house to supervise Bill's homework. She was thirty-two or three, not pretty but friendly and good humoured and very conscientious. Bill and I liked her and we never gave her any trouble.

Our parents sent us with her on a walking tour through the Sächsische Schweiz for a week. Her shoes were not sturdy and we bought and ate lots of chocolate so she could put the cardboard from the chocolate into her shoes and would not feel the stones we were walking on. We had a marvellous time with her.

When Bill was twelve he was sent to Rabbi Dr Joachim Prinz to study for his Bar Mitzvah. Unfortunately there were another ninety-nine boys who were also supposed to study with him and nothing came of it. Fräulein Feinberg came from a religious home and she prepared him for his great day. She was more than competent to do so.

That same year our parents sent us with her to Denmark for the summer vacation. We stayed in a pension in Taarbeck near Klampenborg and quite a few parents there were pleased and kept sending their children on walks with us. She never complained. On one such outing Bill, who was ahead of everybody, found some red berries and proceeded to eat them. When Fräulein Feinberg arrived with the other children she was upset, not recognising the berries, and reprimanded Bill for having eaten them without first asking. Bill became frightened that the berries might be poisonous and lay down on his bed, waiting to die. Fortunately, although wild, the berries were not harmful.

Fräulein Feinberg could not swim but was persuaded to go into the water and try. She immediately swallowed sea water and started to cry so that she swallowed even more water and became hysterical. Helpful hands drew her out of the water and people tried to calm her. When the commotion had subsided Bill was asked what he would have done, had she drowned. Bill's answer, given without hesitation, was:

"I would have cancelled her breakfast for tomorrow morning!"

After Bill had left for France my parents were loath to let Fräulein Feinberg go and retained her to do my homework with me every afternoon. I was not pleased, I felt capable of doing it as before, on my own. Now I had to sit all afternoon and study and only rarely would we go out for a walk. Sometimes, especially before a Hebrew test, I was so tired that I cried when I finally went to bed. But I seldom made a mistake in writing. It was a pity that having shed so many tears over my Hebrew studies nothing much was left in my head by the time I came to Israel.

Fräulein Feinberg also went to my school to listen to my teachers' appraisal of me and reported to my mother. The teachers usually complained:

"Gerda pays attention, but does not participate during lessons."

There were always so many children who had their hands up as soon as the teacher asked a question. They liked showing off.

Mother asked Fräulein Feinberg to tell me the facts of life. Not being married and not having children of her own, she expressed herself so cautiously that she only confused me. Conception was not mentioned, neither was sex, of course. It was just as well that our school was a modern one and we were taught where babies come from in two special lessons. The first for girls and boys separate, the second all together. Here too sex was not mentioned, we were not as modern as all that. Some kids knew more about the subject and emitted a few giggles. I was not really interested in the reproduction of the human species and the relevant organs at that time and my ideas remained vague.

Jenny Feinberg had a good affidavit, a guarantee from relatives in the US. She became engaged to a man who had a low number at the American consulate and chances of an early emigration. They married and left Germany together. When I asked about him she told me:

"Oh, he is very nice and we play chess together in the evenings!"

It sounded neither exciting, nor romantic, and in retrospect I hope she knew more about marriage and sex than she told me.

When I started going out with boys at the age of sixteen, my mother gave me a few warnings expressed in such general terms that they lost their meaning. Of course, I knew I was not supposed to come home expecting a baby. The trouble was, I had only the foggiest idea how one gets pregnant.

Florence

Bill spent two years in school in France. Then my parents decided to send us together to Italy because they could transfer the school fees from Germany there. We received a brochure from a Landschulheim in Florence with glowing promises about the studies and general modern aspects of its education. The school was the joint venture of several German Jewish refugees and almost all the children and teachers came from Germany and were Jewish. Robert Kempner, who later became very well known as a lawyer at the Nürnberg trials was one of the directors.

Since Bill had been travelling to France and back by himself it was not deemed necessary for anybody to accompany us. We would be put on the train in Berlin and met at the station in Florence. It was spring 1936, I was twelve going on thirteen, Bill was fifteen going on sixteen.

I was a bit apprehensive but as always took things in my stride. When passports were asked for at the frontier, my brother was asleep and rather than wake him, I handed the passports over since I knew where he kept them. I felt very grown up.

We were collected at the station by two elderly ladies who both looked and were older than my mother. Our hearts sank. One was the white-haired frail-looking mother of a teacher, who himself had a son our age. The other was the grey-haired robust widow of a doctor of medicine, who earned her living by dispensing medical care at the school like the blindfolded goddess of justice. She resembled an automaton, one put one's penny in and took one's chance. If lucky, one might get the right medicine for whatever ailed one. Fortunately we were quite healthy and had outgrown our tendency to ear infections. When this unqualified lady admitted to being out of her depth, an Italian doctor would be called in.

I still have a scar from breaking a window with an unfamiliar Italian lock with my elbow, while trying to shut it during a very bad thunderstorm. I admired the beautiful colouring of the lightning while unsuccessfully trying to reach the shutters outside. There were no curtains and no teachers either. Most of the girls had their heads on their arms on the table and were moaning or crying. When I finally succeeded, my hand slipped and my elbow went through the glass. I tried to stop the blood with my other none-too-clean hand and went in search of Schatulle, which was Mrs Borchard's nickname. She put a thin bandage on my elbow, and as I walked out of her office, blood from the deep cut was already dripping on to the floor.

The day after we arrived we were asked a few questions so that we could be assigned to our classes. We were, of course, asked our names and age. It was then that Bill prodded me with his elbow and asked behind his hand:

"Gerda, how old am I?"

He had expected more momentous inquiries. One of the questions I still remember: we were asked where South, North, East and West were. We knew.

The main issue was to find the right Italian classes for us. Bill was sent to a class that had started studying two months earlier and was given extra tuition in the afternoons so he could keep up with the others. I studied with two children, neither of them overly bright, and was easily the best pupil. After some time it was decided to put me in my brother's class, but without the extra lessons that he had received. The only younger boy in the class was as bored as I was. He because he was a little genius, I because I could not cope. So we sat there and ate our copybooks. We had no chewing gum.

It took the teacher a while to discover that I did not fit into his class. In the meantime new children had arrived and I was assigned to their class, unfortunately only after they had already been studying for a few weeks. This finished any interest I had in learning Italian and I copied everything from Hans, a nice boy who sat next to me.

I can't remember ever learning or not learning any other subjects. But I suppose we did. Sometimes we jumped out of the window a minute before the teacher arrived and roamed through the Podere, the farmland that surrounded the three houses which constituted our school. It was worked by different farmers and we were allowed to walk there though not allowed to steal fruit, which we did whenever the occasion arose. Once when a bunch of us were harvesting apples, a farmer came shouting and let his dogs loose on us. We all ran away as fast as our feet would carry us. The only one who did not was Moura, who had collected the fruit in her skirt. She slowly let it down and apples cascaded in all directions. In the seconds before I took to my heels I saw the falling apples and Moura as if turned to stone, looking terrified at the farmer and his dogs. Then she must have run too, but I never looked back.

I lodged with two girls, one much younger, only eight, one a little older, in a pleasant room. We had to go through another room where the two oldest girls, eighteen and seventeen, lived. One was the girlfriend of a young Italian teacher who taught at our school and who visited her frequently. They spent their time together on her bed unless they were downstairs, where he would prepare her for her matriculation. I walked through the room with my head held high and my eyes averted. They never noticed any of us, coming or going.

During the summer months the school moved to Forte dei Marmi where we all lived in small houses, congregating at the main house for meals. As in Florence we were pretty free to do what we wanted. There Moura and I shared a room with two or three other girls. I saw Moura again more than fifty years later in Canada, when Bill, his wife, Shirley, and I visited her and her husband and memories came back to us thick and fast.

One of the girls who roomed with us was Italian. Her name was Isotta and she usually went out after 'lights out' and crept back at ungodly hours through the open window. She used a lot of make up and hardly any soap. She did not stay long with us.

That summer the Olympic Games were held in Berlin. The older kids went to the nearest Trattoria to listen to the reports on the radio. They drank wine and my brother, who had once drunk too much, almost fell into a brook, crossing a bridge without rails on his way home. He described this adventure to a girlfriend at the school in a letter, but forgot to give it to her. My mother, who was visiting at the time, found it in his pocket and read it. It did not improve her opinion of the Landschulheim.

I had learned to ride Bill's bike in a little wood near the house where I lived and when an excursion was organised and announced on the board in the dining hall, Bill consented to give me his bike. The trip was 'kid's stuff' to him, and proudly I signed my name. I had no fears, not having fallen off his bike even once. Unfortunately I had hurt my right hand and could not close it. The bike had felloe brakes and the right handle was for the back wheel.

We started out on a beautiful clear morning with the sun shining on the lovely landscape. Our destination was Lucca, and the surrounding countryside. At first everything went well, till we had to go down some steep inclines. Not being able to use the back wheel brake and discovering quickly that it was inadvisable to use the front brake I took my long legs off the pedals and put my big feet on the road. This did not do much for my sandals but braked the bike nicely. I was always the first to be at the bottom of any hill. Nobody knew why I was in such a hurry and nobody asked.

By the time we came to Lucca I was pretty sure of myself. It was then that I got my bike into the tram rails. Naturally I fell and when I got the bike and myself out and up I saw that the handle bar was crooked. The teacher came over to see if I was hurt and proceeded to bend it back into its original position. I was quite contrite about being so much trouble to Schöpfchen, our teacher. I told her how sorry I was, but that I had been riding a bike for just two weeks. Her face turned ashen, she gave me a stricken look, but did not reprove me. She was glad that I was still in one piece. Nobody had ever asked me how much experience I had riding a bike. The school was not the kind where anyone paid attention to such little details.

I did learn one other practical thing in Florence. One of the older girls taught me how to wash my hair as my mother had done that at home. This came in very handy when I was in Rome in a convent school where the nuns washed our hair only once a month.

When my mother came to see how her children were doing, she was told that I was stupid and lazy, which Mother did not believe for a moment and we were taken out of the school. My brother was sent to Meran to learn the hotel business and I was taken home, back to the Herzl School where studying was taken more seriously and where my mother told all her troubles at the school in Florence to the headmistress, Mrs Fürst.

When in Rome

When Bill had finished his studies in Meran, he got a job in a hotel in Rome. In the summer of 1937 my parents and I travelled to Italy and they decided to leave me there with Bill. Mother started looking for a school. She used to talk easily to people whom she met. When she was travelling back from Épinal after taking my brother to his boarding school, she had met a Jewish lady on the train who lived in Épinal, and after hearing how sad my mother was about leaving her son alone in France, promised to look after him. She took him into her home and her family, so that he spent every Sunday with them, as long as he stayed in France.

This time Mother met a nice man in the hotel and confided in him. She had had, she said, a very bad experience with a school in Florence and now wished to find a boarding school in Rome where the supervision of the children would be stricter, and where her daughter would be taught Italian. Could he help? The man recommended the French convent school of Notre Dame de Sion. My mother, who in her youth had danced at Zionist's balls, liked the name. I don't think she would have sent me to the convent if its name had been Holy Mary. We both went there and Mother approved of what she saw. I did not, but was persuaded to give it a try. I was such a reasonable child.

"We are Jewish", she said, "but not religious." Mother Superior regretted that we were not devout:

"One of the sisters could take your daughter to the synagogue every Saturday, should you wish it."

This sounded ominous in my ears. But nothing further was said.

I had to have special clothing, a blue dress which the dressmaker, a lay nun, made for me. She was Austrian and so pleased that she could talk to me in German that she made me extra wide sleeves, which the other girls envied. I already had a blue winter coat and although the lapels were too broad and modern this was generously overlooked. I required two black cotton coveralls to keep the dress from getting dirty, and a blue hat.

I had a blue hat, Mother had insisted that I needed one in Rome. It had formerly often resided, slightly dusty, underneath my bed till my father saw it and demanded that I wear it; his reason was that, although he did not see the necessity of my having a hat at all, if I kept it under the bed, he rather thought that my head was the better place for it. I had hoped that Father would be against a hat, as once before he had saved Bill and me from unnecessary paraphernalia. The then reigning power in the nursery had insisted that we wear gloves on a trip. When we made a big fuss Father asked about it. He got the explanation that we should wear gloves because the train was dirty and they could be washed.

Father looking somewhat astonished said: "So can their hands!" in a tone that brooked no contradiction.

On my first evening in the convent school I met a Spanish girl who knew German. Pilar and her sister, Carmen, had long blonde plaits. They had gone to a German school in Barcelona, their mother was in Rome, their father back in Spain fighting. I told Pilar that I was Jewish and this was so unexpected to her that, misunderstanding me, she said: "We'll eat soon." I explained and while this was of the utmost importance in my life, it made no impression on her at all. Having cleared up the first obstacle to any friendship in the convent, Pilar and I started talking.

Not all the girls boarded at the convent. Many lived with their families in the city. The others slept in two big dormitories, the older ones in a dormitory that had cubicles – three wooden walls and a curtain in front. The curtain was opened by a nun when we were in bed, so that she could see us when she made the rounds at night. I was deemed too tall to sleep or study with my peers and was given a cubicle next to the two oldest girls in whose class I was also put.

Underneath the bed was a basin which would be filled with warm water in the evening to wash our feet. A smaller basin on a table was for our other ablutions.

We had our meals silently in a small refectory. Pilar and I were allowed to sit next to each other, but not for long because we whispered too much and were separated. The same nun always sat on a dais in front of us, busy with her rosary, moving her lips and watching us like a hawk. We all faced her and when the lay sister came in with the food she nodded to two of us, who got up and handed out the food which the sister put on plates. We were allowed to whisper how much we wanted and the air was full of 'Issimos', 'Pochissimo', 'Moltissimo'. Neither of the nuns talked to us.

If there were ants about they would be sprayed immediately and vigorously with a poisonous substance right in front of our faces, although they too were God's creatures.

Our days were monotonous. We got up, washed and dressed. The other girls went to chapel; I ate chocolate if I had any since everybody else was praying and I could not be detected. When Bill gave me chocolate or my mother sent food parcels to him after she had returned to Berlin, I hid the sweets in my cupboard to eat at my leisure, instead of handing them over to be distributed in very small quantities by the nuns at the four o'clock break. Our repast at this hour consisted of white bread and water.

After breakfast, school, lunch, a one hour recreation break which in good weather we spent in the garden with our teacher playing ball, and studies until the evening.

We sat almost all day.

Once a week we had gymnastics, fully dressed in uniforms and coveralls, and changed only our shoes. I did not like to do chin-ups especially not fully dressed and excused myself on the grounds that my dress was too tight. The excuse was accepted.

We were called up for bathing or hair washing in the afternoon by a lay nun who would prepare the bath. She came into the classroom where we studied and nodded her head silently at a girl, who would close her book, get up and follow the nun out of the room. Quite often, if the girl had a lot of homework she would shake her head emphatically and remain seated. The nun would then nod to another girl. I was always longing to be called up, not only because I wished to be clean but to move my limbs. The first time Mother came to visit I asked her to arrange this for me.

Our mail was, of course, read. Bill, experienced in the ways of boarding schools, wrote me a postcard in German but with Hebrew letters. I was summoned to the office.

"What language is this?" I was asked. "We gave the card to a priest who has studied Hebrew but he couldn't understand the writing."

After a lame explanation about modern Hebrew and a statement that my brother and I always corresponded like this, I was allowed to leave. The postcard had taken a week to reach me.

Apart from not being allowed to talk at meals and during lessons, we were not supposed to talk during our afternoon study periods or when we went to bed. Still, we all talked in undertones or murmured, and my Italian improved greatly.

Each class had different coloured ribbons with crosses around their necks and belts to match. It was the only coloured item we were allowed. Our colours were purple and white but I refused to wear a cross and was told to sew my small Magen David on to the ribbon. I refused that too, it was too small and would have looked ridiculous. So I walked about with an undecorated ribbon which curved upwards at all times.

The girls did not mind my being Jewish. Some, although they admired Hitler, could not understand why he persecuted the Jews. They also asked me if I was waiting for the Messiah and laughed heartily when I said yes. What else could I say?

I was taught how to behave in front of the venerable priest who visited the convent once a month to distribute prizes to those who had earned them. I usually got one for good behaviour, seldom one for effort. We had to walk up to him, our hands in white gloves clutched together in front of us, and bend so he could hang the sash, which was the prize, around our necks. We were then supposed to kiss his ring and retire backwards. The nun who instructed me was shocked at the thought that I might kiss his hand or show him my behind. In any event I kissed neither ring nor hand, since he could hardly see or feel that, and I always retired in good order. We would then go about with the sash for a whole month, gym lessons included, when the procedure would be repeated.

Our teacher was also the needlework teacher and when she went out to buy yarn she would take her class of three boarders, Elena, Adelaide and me, with her. On my first outing we met Mother Superior who immediately confiscated the red brooch I had on my coat.

"It is not seemly for a convent girl to go out adorned like this," Mother Superior said.

I doubt if she knew that we were sometimes goosed on the buses we took when out decorously dressed, which was even less seemly and had never happened to me in Berlin.

Elena came every night to give me a chaste kiss. She liked me and seemed to feel that in spite of my height I needed mothering. I had never even kissed my relatives at home and among my friends kissing was certainly not the custom. Adelaide, although very nice to me, refrained from kissing. She was the studious type.

Once I did not feel well, stayed in bed and discovered that the food for the sick was better and more plentiful. So occasionally I would claim to be sick and get my food on a tray. I would finish every bit of it and the sister would look at the tray silently, only once did she remark drily:

"Well, at least your appetite hasn't suffered."

My curriculum was different from that of my classmates. They learned Latin and Greek, I did not; I had English lessons, they didn't. I also had piano lessons and periods of practise to fill in the time. I studied algebra together with them and became quite good at it, learning everything by heart, never understanding what I was doing. Nobody ever explained the Italian words to me.

Bill got the Jüdische Rundschau from home. I would take part of the paper to the convent and copy a long series of articles about famous people in Jewish history, printing them into a copybook. My studies never occupied me for the whole afternoon but I had to sit there. Copying Jewish articles helped me keep my balance in this all too Catholic environment. I also had a Jewish calendar with the picture of a pretty boy at which I would look fondly when nothing better occurred to me.

Prayers on Sunday mornings were longer than on weekdays and I stood around waiting anxiously for the girls to come to breakfast. The first Sunday I stood near the chapel door. All the nuns came out first with folded hands and bowed heads, looking down and passing silently through the hall. I curtsied politely and said: "Good morning!" to every one of them. Nobody answered. I had an eerie feeling that I did not exist outside my own imagination. The second Sunday standing in a corner I averted my face, the third Sunday I hid. The girls always came last.

I was afraid to hide too well, because Bill took me out on Sundays and it would have been unbearable if the nun in quest of me could not find me. If we left before I had eaten I would get breakfast at the hotel, which I loved.

When Bill and I walked away from the convent, the girls stood at a window if they could and waved and called. I was instructed to turn, wave back and take my time about it. My brother, impatient because we might miss our bus, would say:

"Come on, I've got to get back to work. You see this crowd all week, what do you want to stand there waving at them for?"

It never occurred to him that the waving and calling was for his benefit and that he was supposed to turn around and look at the girls. In a society starved of everyday contact with males even a look was a sensation. My brother looked plenty but not at convent girls.

Bill went back to Reception, where he worked and I strolled around Rome. The girls in the convent knew that I walked about Rome on my own most of the day. They had asked. The nuns didn't and would probably have fainted at the idea. To me it seemed the natural thing to do. I needed no chaperone in Berlin, why in Rome? I have sometimes wondered if my parents ever gave it a thought. I have a letter from my mother where she enjoined us to have fun together the next Sunday. Did she realise that since Bill worked on Sundays, we were only together on the bus?

I would eat a hot lunch at the hotel restaurant where I had my own table and the waiters treated me royally. There I would sit in lonely splendour in my blue convent dress with the white collar and consume my food with no nun fingering her rosary in front of me.

Once a month I had to sign a money order for the school fees. Bill took me to the bank on his free day, he paid the fees and kept what was left of the money. On this day we ate together in his room. The first time we bought too much food and had a huge parcel, which Bill carried high above his head like an extremely proficient waiter, through the lobby of the hotel. The sauce was dripping from one corner but he went on unperturbed.

After finishing our lunch he hurriedly brought me back to the convent. The convent was on the other side of the Tiber and once or twice that winter there was danger of the bus not getting through because of flooding. When I came the next Sunday Bill asked me to clear things away, he had pushed all the remnants into his cupboard. I did so hurriedly, as a mouse jumped at me when I opened the door.

The second time we bought less. We had one knife, one spoon, one fork and managed nicely, washing these before we ate. My housewifely habits have since improved.

All the convent girls were taken to a theatre performance during that term. There were no male actors, everything was clean and proper. It was probably the worst performance I have ever seen in my life; strictly amateur. But I sat there spellbound and drank it all in. Stage lights and colours, women in pretty dresses, so different from our daily lives where everyone wore black. The garden around the convent was colourful enough but we were not allowed to go out on our own.

In the spring of 1938 my passport expired and although I could renew it in Rome I would have been unable to go home again. My parents did not want that.

My cousin Josef, Aunt Bertha's son, was sent from Berlin with clothes for my brother, to take me back to Berlin. Many of my friends had emigrated by now, and I refused to go back to the Herzl School and start all over, making up for lost time again as I had after I came back from Florence.

One of my friends was going to a Handelsschule and I asked my mother to let me go to the same school. Her answer was:

> I have enrolled you in the Handelsschule in the Joachimsthalerstrasse, which is the best in Berlin without consideration to where your friends may be. Many kisses, lovingly your mother.

Growing up was not easy.

The leave taking was sad. My brother envied me that I could go back to our parents, he was heavy hearted that he would stay alone in Italy. And though the convent held no attractions for me, neither did Germany. I would be lonely at home and without a future. Before boarding the train I asked my brother to kiss me. He was embarrassed and gave me a slight peck on the cheek. As the train pulled out of the station I saw him standing there, my big brother, a lonely boy of seventeen, slender and serious, and I thought back to our childhood days in the nursery when he had promised to marry me because, as he said: "You I already know!" When we saw each other again sixteen years later in the US he embraced and kissed me without prompting. By then we were both married and had children of our own.

My cousin and I travelled through Switzerland as Austria had just returned to the greater Reich, and the borders were closed. It was a long and dreary train ride.

When we travelled with my parents, father used to tell us often that we were running out of money. At the frontier he would have to declare the real state of affairs and we would prick up our ears and find that there was always money left.

My cousin on the other hand, had developed running out of money into a fine art. He had spent all the Italian money in Italy, all the Swiss money in Switzerland, where he bought me chocolate, and when we arrived in Germany his first words to my father were: "Uncle Julius, can you give me a groschen to phone my wife, I haven't got a penny!"

From 'Juden Unerwünscht' to 'Juden Verboten' and Killed, 1938/41

In 1938, 20,000 so-called Polish Jews were driven over the frontier into Poland. Uncle Max was among them. He had been born in what was at that time Austria, served in the German Army and opted for Germany but remained stateless. His wife who had converted to Judaism, lost her German citizenship when she married him. She was able to rescue their son Ferry, who was fourteen, from being deported with his father and remained behind with her six children. Uncle Adolf, also born in Austria, had a German passport and stayed. The youngest brother, Jacques, had already emigrated to Chile with his family.

That same year the Italian government decreed that all Jews who had come to Italy after the First World War had to leave. My brother had to find another haven in a hurry, any country but Germany. My father would not allow him to come back. Cuba became a possibility but only with two hundred dollars in his pocket and no money could be sent from Germany. Apart from that he needed a visa to another country and could not receive a work permit.

Bill had an affidavit for the US from distant relatives which meant that they would be financially responsible for him when he came. My cousin Walter, who had emigrated to Palestine with my father's help, sent the necessary funds to him. When Bill arrived in Cuba, he was put into a prison for immigrants, because he needed our parents' permission for his immigration. They cabled their agreement to the Cuban authorities.

It was a time of intense agitation and stress for my parents. Phone calls, letters and cables went back and forth between Palestine, Italy, Germany, and later Cuba.

My mother, who in spite of a heart condition had always been vivacious and enterprising, was now told to rest and stop running around in her efforts to emigrate. She did not listen. One day that autumn I found her on the floor of our living room. I helped her up and walked with her to my parents' room and put her to bed. The doctor was called and diagnosed an embolus in her head; she was paralysed on one side. With my help she had walked to her room at the other end of the apartment. Now she could hardly talk, and was unable to walk.

After Mother had been made comfortable with a night nurse at her side, Father sat down in the living room and cried and I stood helpless and frightened by his side. My mother was only forty-six years old.

II

When I came back from Rome I had started classes at the Jewish Commercial school. As soon as I had finished the half year course, I got an order to attend a German trade school and had to go there once a week together with Ruth, a girl from my class. We were the only Jews in the class, maybe in the school, a bureaucratic error overruling state policy.

On the 6th of November, 1938 Ernst von Rath was shot in Paris by a young Jew whose parents had also been deported to Poland. A well prepared 'spontaneous' pogrom three days later, on the 9th, was the consequence. It was the night of the burnt out synagogues, the arrests and beatings of thousands of Jews, some beaten to death; the night of the broken glass and the plundered shops.

On the morning after the so-called Kristallnacht, Ruth and I were sitting in the classroom when our teacher arrived. When she saw us, she called us out and asked urgently:

"Are your fathers at home?"

We both nodded.

"Don't you know what happened last night?"

We shook our heads.

I could see that she was concerned but did not wish or dare to say more. Without any further explanation, she said:

"You had better go straight home."

We did, but with an unexpected free morning, decided to walk instead of taking the train and find out what new disaster had befallen the Jewish community. We walked for the better part of an hour but did not see much. Berlin is a big city. We saw smoke here and there in the distance. Only when we were back in our own neighbourhood did we see several shuttered shops that should have been open. The glass had been cleared away and we were not especially worried, still not knowing the full extent of what had happened. It took a few days for all the terrible news about the pogrom to reach us and sink in.

The men who had not been arrested during the first night tried to hide, sleeping wherever they could. At first we did not tell Mother because she was too ill to be able to bear more excitement and my father stayed home hoping for the best.

I used to bring my mother flowers every day and went to do her errands. She often sent me to shops that had been looted and shut. Sometimes I found what she wanted in another shop, often I made feeble excuses. When we finally told her about the pogrom, Mother cried. She cried often now, her nerves could take no more. She was frightened by the threat that lay over us all and felt trapped by her illness. Only very slowly, while my father cared for her, did her health improve and she learned to walk and talk again.

III

Trudi had been my companion for years in the Herzlschule, we had studied and played together. She did not look Jewish and we went swimming again, after I returned from Rome, in places where it was not explicitly forbidden. We often played ball and on one occasion I jumped backwards into a jar of potato salad that someone had broken and left. I cut my foot badly. Several people came to help and my foot was bandaged. The problem was getting home. It was a long bus ride and I would have to walk quite a bit. I doubted if I would be able to sit on the bus without arousing unfavourable comment, which was the last thing we wanted. I had ten marks in my pocket for emergencies and suggested to Trudi that we take a taxi to my home, which was two minutes from the S-Bahn station and the train would take her home in ten minutes. I thought I had handled the situation rather well. Not so my parents who were annoyed and told me that this had not been the emergency they had envisioned when giving me ten marks.

My father had left the shoe store some years before the November pogrom and my two uncles, Paul and Ferdinand, Aunt Irma's husband, managed it. The store was on the first floor and had not been broken into. My father told me that I could go and take any shoes I liked as the store would be closed. I invited Trudi to share with me the pleasure of getting new shoes. We were the only shoppers and both my uncles did everything in their power to satisfy their unusual customers. I found four or five pairs of shoes, Trudi took two pairs and we decided that since her mother had the same size, she should take two more pairs for her. This was not what my father had had in mind. As he had nothing to do with the store any more, he received a considerable bill. He generously paid for all the shoes, suspecting that Trudi's parents could not afford them.

Many Jews in Germany were poor, too poor to emigrate. Trudi and her parents were among them. They perished in the Holocaust.

IV

I did not go back to the trade school which I was now forbidden to attend, and started looking around for something to do. For a few months I worked in a Jewish kindergarten as a trainee, eight hours and no pay but I got a hot lunch. Then the lady who owned it emigrated to England. Before she left she gave me fifteen marks and I bought a wristwatch. The golden one that had been my mother's had been confiscated with the rest of the gold and silver we had owned.

A friend from school told me about an opportunity to go to Palestine and I hinted to my Mother that I might still have a chance to get out with Youth Aliyah. With tears in her eyes she begged me not to leave her and I gave up the idea.

The next step was a Jewish Kinderhort, where the oldest children were only two years younger than I was. I was not a success, especially after I twisted the arm of a fourteen year old boy to make him obey me. With the smaller children we went for walks. There were special corners in some parks with yellow benches with the words "For Jews only!" My mother used to rest on these on her walks with my father. Once, when alone, she got a proposal of marriage from the man sitting next to her, which she found very flattering.

Then I started to learn photography. My teacher went with me for nature walks. We took pictures and talked English now and then as the man had just come back from the States, God knows why, and occasionally we played football. He complimented me on my talent for football, never on my English or my photography.

This interlude lasted only a few weeks and then my parents decided to send me back to school. I took a nine months course in a nursery teachers' seminar and learned the rudiments of education for pre-school children with practical work at a Jewish communal kindergarten where children were combed and searched for lice as soon as they entered. We never found any and I had to come to Israel to make their acquaintance. For one month we became so-called social workers and had to clean apartments for the sick, the elderly or families with many children. Once a week that month I was shown how social cases were handled at the community centre.

My first assignment was to clean the home of four people: three sisters and their brother, who looked all equally ancient to me. I had no idea how to go about cleaning anybody's flat. So I put on my best smile and told the lady who opened the door and seemed the most mobile that I would like to do the work as she wished and the best thing would be if she told me exactly what she wanted. She did and I did and she was so enthusiastic about me that she promised to sing my praise at her next interview at the centre and tell them what a "pearl" I was.

Next day I came to a family with a bedridden husband and a wife who worked; the two kids went to a kindergarten. With my experience from the day before, my cleaning methods were acceptable. This was another family who could have no hope of emigrating.

In the Jewish community office I had an open file in front of me, so that people who came in would think I was busy and not taking any notice of them. Even so it was embarrassing to listen to their many problems. Not only did these people have no money, they could neither emigrate, nor did they have a chance of getting any work.

V

On the 1st of September, 1939, Germany started the war. I locked myself into the toilet and cried. There seemed to be no more hope. My brother had written repeatedly to my parents to send me to Cuba, that he would take care of me. But they would not let me go. I was a girl and I was too young. Like Bill, I had an affidavit for the United States, a guarantee from another family of distant relatives. But I was way at the end of the waiting list, like Bill who had to spend two years in Cuba waiting to get to the US. Once I went to the consulate to see what my chances were. The scene there was indescribable. People outside were yelling, pushing, and brandishing papers and guarantees in the air. The door was closed with an embassy official standing outside waving people away. I left immediately, seeing no chance even to get inside.

Many years later I read in the German magazine *Kultur – Chronik* to my great astonishment that "during the years 1930–1939 only 119,107 Germans went to the US, and that included the German Jews. The German quota had been fixed at double that number". The *Lexicon des Judentums* writes that "the US at that time did not want immigrants and certainly not Jews. Roosevelt was a decided opponent of Jewish immigration and tried to convince other countries to take them in". It was undeniably the United States' policy to keep the Jews at bay.

The other day a journalist, who is a very distant member of our family, said to Bill and me:

"I can't even say that I am sorry for those of my relations who perished in the Holocaust. It was their own fault for not getting out in time! They had the money!"

This thought about the German Jews and how much they had loved Germany, not wanting to leave, and never really believing in the murderous intentions of the Nazis, has been expressed again and again, although seldom so crassly.

There were many reasons why people could or did not emigrate: a sick member of the family who could not immigrate into any country, and whom the family would not leave behind, lack of funds or closed frontiers around the world were powerful reasons.

VI

The Jewish communities were ordered to make lists of all the Jews within three days. Our seminar, the Handelsschule, the students from the Leo Baeck seminar and others were recruited to help. Every community would send its lists to Berlin. We worked in shifts and I opted for night work, because I could type and there were not enough typists for the second shift. Mrs Fürst, the headmistress of the Herzl School, who was also there at night, recognised me immediately and remembered my mother and her complaints about the Landschulheim in Florence.

"What is your mother going to say?" She asked quite upset. I was not worried. I was not going to tell anybody that I had volunteered.

For three nights I typed what the young man next to me dictated. We were thorough and conscientious. When the deportations started and became prominent in our lives I thought back to those lists. We could so easily have left out a few names. Would it have made a difference to anybody?

In due time I finished the seminar, but there was, of course, no work.

I got a new photography teacher who was supposed to teach me the technical side of his profession. When he tried to take and pat my hand during lessons, I did what I could to avoid him in the dark. He complained that I would not learn anything at the other end of the room with my hands in my pockets. Mother's answer when I told her was:

"Father would wish you to go on. Whatever you can learn may be useful."

And so I learned how to avoid unpleasant and pushy married men. I was too shy to tell my father.

The commercial school opened a two year course for English and Spanish, with stenography and bookkeeping. I went back there. Afternoons and evenings I had extra lessons in English, Italian, and for a short time even French. The English lessons I earned by giving Spanish lessons. What I learned in the mornings I taught a Russian lady with a Nansen passport in the afternoon. Eventually even my parents had to admit that I needed breathing space now and then and photography was put on the shelf.

I was so busy that, following in my mother's footsteps, I took taxis from one place to another. I seldom ate my midday dinner at home. My mother could not do any housework and we had a very nice woman, who also cooked, who came in every day. My father had never known what went on in our household, now he did the shopping. They could not wait till I came home at odd hours.

I was given lunch money which I secretly spent quite often on a book. We could not go to the public library and the Jewish one at the corner had been closed down. I needed to read, but Father maintained with reason:

"This is not the time to acquire a library!"

Bill had taught me that collecting books was more important than food. When our parents had taken us to Venice in the thirties, we had been sent daily to the beach by ourselves with one lira for ice cream, while they rested. Bill had discovered that one could buy a small Italian children's book for seventy centesimi and still get two miniature ice creams for 15c each. Left to myself I would have preferred more ice cream, but he got the money and was handling our finances.

It was in Venice too, that my father wished to eat a clear meat soup with a raw egg. But instead of using the internationally known word 'Boullion' my father used the German word 'Brühe'. The waiter looked astonished and asked again whether Father really wanted them together. "Of course!" Father said. After a while the waiter, shaking his head, brought a bottle of beer in one hand and a raw egg in the other.

As long as I still had Bill's bike I now went swimming by myself very early on Sunday mornings before people were up and before raids by the Gestapo could be expected. Later on bikes, radios, electrical appliances, furs, and a lot of other possessions were confiscated. They took pets too.

Sometimes I had a short break, and without telling anyone that there were two unused hours in my life, I went to the movies. When my Italian teacher told me very tactfully that he was not allowed to teach Jews any more, I was quite relieved. I had been going there to different courses three evenings a week.

My father knew that the only thing he could give me and I could count on keeping, was a good schooling, so that no matter what work I was required to do, I would always be ready.

VII

I had made friends at school and met new people during the nights when we wrote the lists. Herbert Strauss became a good friend, he had a fiancée waiting in England, a girlfriend in Berlin, and told me that he was married. My parents immediately forbade me to see him. They did not know about the girlfriend and when he invited me to go to Potsdam for a walk I went.

I had other dates with other young men and the day came when I fell in love for the first time in my life.

Günter, one of Herbert's friends, was tall and good looking but somewhat superficial. His gentile mother went to court to swear that both her sons were not her husband's. She stated that they were the sons of the Aryan German whom she brought with her. Quite a few Germans were prepared to swear, for a suitable sum of money, that they had children from a woman married to a Jew. Günter was overjoyed. Mainly it seemed because he could now walk along the Kurfürstendamm and sit in any of the famous cafes. I felt like my mother before me: that saving oneself from persecution was one thing, being glad to be freed of the burden of being a Jew so one could sit in a Berlin coffee house was overdoing the delight. I ended our relationship and cried, but my sorrow did not last long.

My other friends had more profound thoughts. Lutz Ehrlich, whom I also met through Herbert, was and still is a very good friend. We walked a lot, since we were not allowed to sit anywhere, and had endless discussions, we read novels and poetry and any other books we could get hold of. Many were forbidden and had been burnt or taken out of circulation.

Years later I learned how much had been missing from my early education, when I got to know the writers, painters and musicians that had been banned at the time I was growing up.

Herbert and Lutz studied together with Leo Baeck to become rabbis. Had they had an option, they would have chosen a different profession, but nothing else was available. Although they were committed Jews they were hardly religious and Herbert delivered his first sermon on Yom Kippur after eating a raw egg so his voice would ring better. Fasting was a secondary consideration.

We listened to music on Herbert's record player in his rented room. His was also the bread I ate when I was hungry and had spent my money on a book or did not feel like eating alone in a Chinese restaurant in the Kantstrasse. All of us went to Jewish community concerts or plays whenever we could. Once I went with Lutz to the Gedächtniskirche to listen to Bach's *Mattheus Passion* and as a prospective rabbi he forgot to take his hat off as we entered. I dug my elbow into his ribs and hissed at him. Calming as it was to sit quietly and listen to those beautiful sounds, I had no intention of going to prison, or worse!

VIII

After the war started, many Jewish families were evicted from their homes. We were among them. One could only rent a room or an apartment in a Jewish house, which meant that it had been owned by Jews before October 1938 when they had been expropriated. My father rented two rooms from an elderly Jewish widow in Halensee. We moved. We moved from a six room apartment to two furnished rooms and had to sell the furniture in a hurry and too cheaply. Some of it was put in storage by my father's secretary under her name. It was later bombed. The secretary had been the subject of many a quarrel between my parents, but now they had made their peace.

My relations with my parents at that time became strained. Even the curfew for Jews became a problem since I did not always get home on time and my father was furious with me. It was not a suitable time for teenage rebellion. Not that I had ever heard the expression, or that in our family children were granted that right.

I never finished my language course because in May, 1941 Jewish trade and professional schools were closed down; only the elementary schools were still allowed to operate and we were assigned to different factories for forced labour. My friend, Lotte, with whom I had studied languages for the past year, and I were sent to the same factory. Deutsche Telephonwerke und Kabelindustrie in the Zeughofstrasse, entrance for Jews – Wrangelstrasse – no mixing with Aryans. It was a long way from home. Our wages were minimal. I never got more than nineteen marks a week and usually less. A certain percentage was taken off for the Judenabgabe that had been decreed after the November pogrom. Paying for the sick fund without being able to consult any of its doctors, we nevertheless got glasses when we needed them like the rest of the population for twenty-five pfennigs.

For my eighteenth birthday I asked if I could invite three friends, Lotte, Lutz and Herbert. The answer was no. I related my troubles to Herbert who took me out in his girlfriend's paddleboat on the Havel as a birthday present. When I came home several aunts and uncles were visiting and offended that I had not been in.

In those years I developed a passion for walking alone in the rain through dark and empty streets whenever I felt stifled by our lives. It was not a very safe habit.

IX

Lotte, whose twin brother had been sent to Holland, lived with her parents near the Tiergarten. We rode the S-Bahn together to work; I lived three stations further down the line and she would board my train at her station. Shortly after my birthday a young blond, blue-eyed man boarded the train one Saturday noon and showed great interest in us. This was flattering but neither of us had any intention of starting anything with a German. He boarded the same train the following Saturday and the third.

We were extremely surprised to see him again at a Jewish concert sitting two rows in front of us, clapping his hands with unexpected vigour. After the concert he walked behind us for a while but before we separated he vanished. We were not quite sure which of us he was interested in. This became clear the next Saturday when he again boarded our train and asked me for a date.

Joachim and I met frequently and fell quickly and completely in love. We were both doing forced labour but spent as much time together as we possibly could. I lived in Halensee, Joachim in Treptow with his father, at the other end of the city. Joachim's mother, a gentile, had committed suicide several years earlier partly because of the Hitler regime, and partly because of illness.

We walked a lot, sometimes visiting friends and relatives.

X

Kurt Lewin, Joachim's friend, whom I soon got to know, lived with his parents in a very small apartment behind a shop. The shop was shuttered and was used as a room. It was very dark. Kurt and Joachim had come to know each other in a Jewish youth orchestra. Kurt played the violin, Joachim the piano.

When we visited, there were usually other young people sitting around. Kurt's father would stand in a corner watching us with a sardonic eye while we discussed many things but mainly life in the Third Reich and if we still had a future.

His mother bustled around and offered small pieces of cake and cookies. They were very good and once I took the last one off the plate instead of politely refusing it and earned a big smile from Mrs Lewin.

On the 19th of September, 1941, Jews were forced to wear the yellow badge, firmly sewn onto their outer garments. We were also required to have a star next to our name at the front door of our apartment and open the door clearly marked as Jews. We got used to that too, although occasionally one would take off the badge and sew it on again according to one's plans. When once two SS men stopped me in the street to find out with a pencil if the badge was sewn on tight, my heart sank. It was and they let me go. There was one factory where Jewish workers glued yellow stars on to metal plates with needles attached that went into one's clothing and were fastened with cork or a metal stopper. They were used for emergencies, when one was in a hurry. Herbert had given me one, but I seldom used it.

We did not have to see the yellow badge to know who was a Jew, we could recognise our fellow Jews even from behind: the way their shoulders were bent, the way they held their briefcases or purses and hurried, spoke volumes. We were not allowed to stop in the street any more and when questioned had to have a destination.

Once it was bruited about that Jews should not go out the next Sunday. I had planned to go to Treptow where Joachim would be waiting for me and since Jews had no phones, I could not call him. I wanted to be with him and decided to go. I had a five minute walk to the station, a long train ride, and then a ten minute walk from the station and back. For once my prudent father did not object. In fact he went out himself to see what would happen, but he left Mother at home. I was in the street and on the train for more than three hours altogether and saw no other Jews. Nobody gave me a second look, nothing happened to my father either. For some reason the Nazis did not want Jews with yellow badges showing their faces, but could not afford to make it official.

XI

The deportations of the German Jews to the ghettos and concentration camps in the East started in October 1941 and everybody got their deportation order in writing. About a year later when many elderly people had committed suicide and younger people had gone into hiding these written orders were dispensed with and people were taken from their homes at any time in the evening or during the night.

Ever since Uncle Max had been deported, my father had had a small suitcase ready. Deportations or arrests had never been far from our minds. My father took me aside to tell me that if necessary we would separate. If Mother, because of her illness, and he, because of his age, were to be sent to Theresienstadt, a camp for the sick and elderly, I would be on my own. I was confused and hurt. My mother had said she needed me.

Only much later when I was safe in Sweden did I recognise that Father had been right and that it must have been as hard for him to say those words as it had been for me to hear them. It took courage to let me know his intentions. By then I knew that many had perished because their families had insisted on remaining together.

One late afternoon that autumn we met a young man at Kurt's place who had been deported to Lodz, or Lietzmanstadt as the Germans called it, with one of the first transports, and escaped to Berlin where he could hide. He planned to go to Holland and said the to me unforgettable words to all of us:

"Don't imagine that Lietzmanstadt is a work camp! It is nothing of the sort. They're not deporting for that! Believe me!"

We also met his sister who was later implicated in a bomb attack at an anti-Communist exhibition. She was sentenced to seven years of hard labour. After the war I looked for their names on the World Jewish Congress lists of survivors but could not find them.

People disappeared continually, some hid with gentiles or had false papers, most were deported. Often there was no time and no way even to say goodbye. Lotte, my friend, with whom I had shared so many confidences and anxieties, and her parents were deported.

I still have her picture in my album looking young and hopeful. She had just had time to let Herbert know that they would be on the fifth transport, which was said to be going to Kovno. Later it was rumoured that the train never arrived anywhere. The 'Mundfunk' said that the BBC had asked about it. It was assumed that everybody on the train had been killed outright, possibly gassed.

Nobody knew anything for sure. We were surrounded by uncertainty and rumours and lived in terror and despair; sorrow for those who had gone, fear for our own lives.

XII

With all the grief and difficulties around us, Joachim and I decided to get married and be together. My parents liked Joachim but my father tried to persuade him that I was not a suitable person to get married to.

"She is spoilt", he said, "and used to better circumstances. This is not a time to get married with no prospects for any of us."

Joachim convinced my father that his intentions and his love for me were serious. Joachim's father had no objections and preparations were made for our wedding on my mother's birthday.

My father went through the kitchenware and decided which pans and pots I might take with me. My mother gave me her Rosenthal tea service and suitable clothing for the wedding out of her own wardrobe. All strain had gone out of our relationship: in their eyes I had now become a grown woman.

On our wedding day Joachim brought flowers for my mother and fifty lilies of the valley as a bridal bouquet for me.

They were the loveliest flowers I had ever seen. We set out to the registry office with our fathers and in spite of the fearful circumstances I was happy and proud and very much in love.

The Last Year In Germany, 1942

Joachim and I were married on the 2nd of January, 1942. The wedding was on a Friday and Joachim wanted me to take Saturday off, so that we could have a three day honeymoon. He had no difficulty getting one more day off. My request was refused and I was only allowed to stay away on Friday.

"Don't worry," Joachim assured me, "I'll take care of it."

He did. He phoned the head office in the factory and was told that I could stay home on Saturday. What he neglected to tell them on the phone was that I was Jewish and in the forced labour department. When I got back on Monday there was not only Chriskolz, the political leader, but also our work manager, both extremely angry with me. The work manager was angry because we had gone over his head. Chriskolz because of general bloody-mindedness.

"As penalty", I was told, "you will have to make up for the whole time, Friday and Saturday! You will work one hour longer every day!"

We worked till a quarter to four and Jews could only shop between four and five. If I left the factory at a quarter to five I could not get to the stores on time. I had to go and talk to the work manager again. White faced and anxious, with my hands firmly in my pockets to keep them from shaking, I went back.

"I cannot possibly be home in time to do the shopping for my husband and my father-in-law if I have to work that late. We can only shop for one hour. With half an hour longer I could manage."

He looked sharply at me for what seemed ages.

"Okay," he said, "you can work every day till four o'clock."

"Thank you!" I answered with feeling and went quickly to my chair, hearing Chriskolz exclaiming angrily behind my back:

"But that's only a quarter of an hour, it's only a quarter of an hour!" The work manager, who disliked the political leader, paid no attention and for two weeks I remained fifteen minutes longer every day without increasing my output.

Then Chriskolz called me again. "You needn't work overtime any more, but the firm reserves the right to take further measures!"

I did not like the sound of that, but allowed myself only to say, with my hands in their favourite place, my pockets:

"Can I go home today like the others?"

"You can!"

At the first opportunity I asked our forewoman, who was pleasant and sat as often as she could with one of the older women who told her all about the laws against the Jews, what she knew about 'further measures'.

"Nothing," she said, "he just made that up to be nasty. Nothing was said in the office about any further steps." I breathed easier.

II

Now that I was married and had moved to Treptow, I had to cook and clean. For the first two weeks Joachim's father lived and sometimes ate with us. I am afraid that he remained hungry when he did as I had no idea what quantities I should prepare. Once when he saw how little there was he tactfully refrained from eating at all, leaving the food for us. When he married again, he moved to his wife's apartment not far from my parents', where Jenny, his new wife, took better care of him.

My mother had not let me cook anything at home before my wedding for fear that the food would be inedible. Having heard a lot about roux, I thought it would be essential to my future life. One night I got up as quietly as possible to make one. I did not put any liquid in and got a small, unappetising ball of flour and fat which I decided nevertheless to eat. Food was not to be wasted. I then cleaned the pan and went back to bed, hoping that I would be able to fulfil my housewifely duties. When I started cooking in earnest, I used to take the pot off the stove and show it to Joachim for inspection, asking him what he thought of its contents.

At the beginning of 1942 we could still buy some meat, or an egg. Soup bones were cooked several times and sometimes loaned out. Later in the year these things were not available to us any more. We could not get Edelgemüse, literally noble vegetables, which meant all the vegetables apart from white cabbage, some kind of big turnip and carrots. Sometimes there would be fruit or vegetables from France or other countries which the German housewife did not know how to prepare and these we were allowed to buy. Bread was wet and had to be dried over a flame in a pan. We ate Butterschmalz, which was a concoction of some fats mixed with water. Some people made pudding from the water that noodles were cooked in. I never managed it. The noodle water always remained just that. But when we had a little flour, fifty grams, and a few other ingredients, we made cookies, about ten.

A few times Joachim took me out to dinner in posh places, hoping that I would be taken for an Italian. We were risking our lives. I was too dark for an Aryan, Joachim too blond not to be in uniform. Any kind of unpleasantness and a demand for our papers would have landed us with the Gestapo.

During that year we were forbidden to use public transport, unless our work was far enough from home. I had to walk. Only in winter did I take the tram in the morning, standing next to the driver and handing in my fare through a very small window in the door to the conductor. Neither could see me or the yellow badge because of the blackout and the darkness of the early winter mornings.

It was a long way from Treptow to Halensee to see my parents and Joachim's father and Jenny. It had been far enough by train but when we had to march through the whole town, each way took more than two hours fast walking. We became even hungrier than we usually were. My parents gave us all the food they had and Joachim's father and Jenny had something to offer too. They were both doing forced labour in a factory and could not be quite as generous as my parents.

III

Kurt's mother died in Berlin and his father was deported. Mr Lewin had been frightened when he saw that the deportation orders did not include his son and that he had to face the fearful ordeal alone. After his deportation Kurt spent more time with us and we visited him quite often. We went there straight from work and stayed the night because of the curfew at eight o'clock. I would prepare a meal for us. Then we talked for a time and went to bed hoping for a quiet night. Next morning Kurt took me to the tram stop while it was still dark. It was too far to walk from his home to the factory in the morning although after work in the afternoon I had no choice. Kurt had to leave early too, he delivered coal for a coal company which was hard work and especially bad for his violinist's hands. Joachim could sleep a little longer.

One clear Sunday morning we went for a walk with Kurt on the outskirts of Berlin in some woods. Before taking the train back I went to a public WC to sew the yellow stars on to our jackets and found to my horror that we had lost one. So I sewed one on for myself and one for Kurt. We travelled with the jackets folded tightly over our arms, putting them on at a lonely corner. Then we went our separate ways, Joachim without the star could not afford to be seen with me.

We went rowing without stars in a borrowed rowboat. We even took the boat out once for a whole weekend and slept in a barn. The farmer and his wife did not suspect us of being Jewish; they had other worries, but they certainly had doubts about our being married. Still they invited us to share their food. They were an elderly couple and the farmer had few teeth. He kept spitting out what he could not chew or did not like on to the floor. Luckily we were sitting in the yard on benches at a table. I was dismayed, but too hungry not to eat my portion. We stopped taking the rowboat out, because we became so hungry that I cried and even with bread coupons without the J for Jew we could get no food.

IV

During air raids we were not allowed to go to the shelter in our house because there was no special cellar for Jews. We did not mind that, as long as we could remain in our bed. Being hungry and tired, we often failed to hear the alarm next morning and had to put the clock on a china plate inside a metal pail. That noise would have woken the dead.

Coming too late to work was decidedly unpleasant. Chriskolz in his SA uniform would open the iron door and put himself in position. Three or four times I managed to get through with a "Morning!" before he had collected his wits. From then on he would be ready and yell while I was still in front of him. Once I bandaged my knee pretending that I had fallen down some stairs. With the alarm clock going off in the pail, I usually managed to arrive on time, unless the tram was late in winter, an excuse I could not use as I was not allowed to ride on one.

If there was an air raid during the day, the Germans would go to the shelter. We were locked in and told to get on with it. Nobody did any work during air raids. Not a lot of bombs fell that year during daylight hours, and I don't think that any of us were really afraid, but with iron doors and barred windows we were in an unhealthy position in case of fire.

Among our girls was one with a lovely voice but unmusical. During air raids she used to kneel on one of the work tables and sing. She hit the wrong notes and the full alto voice grated on our ears. There were some who encouraged her, but most of us talking quietly were relieved when she stopped. The whole scene in the middle of an air raid was macabre, but if it pleased her nobody was in a mood to argue. There was little enough pleasure for any of us.

Hilma

Hilma, a girl who worked with me at the factory, was a year younger than I was, very pretty with a slight limp that did not seem to bother her. She was good at her work and became forewoman. She used her position to throw small parts into the trash cans. This was quite courageous as we were under the constant supervision of Chriskolz. He was stupid but not blind.

When there were not enough components for the flat relays which we were adjusting, we had to count parts and help with the inventory. This was not very hard, especially if the crates were brought in by workers who were against the regime. Quite often they would bring crates with parts that had already been counted and they brought the chit with the amount. Sometimes if the parts were very small they told us to take a thimble or something similar and just give an estimate of the quantity.

We also had to clean toilets that were being used by Ukrainian girls who had never seen a WC before and stood on them so that there really was something to clean up. We scrubbed stairs and walls that had never been scrubbed before.

Hilma, limping upstairs with two heavy pails of water, fell. One of our own girls said she had done it on purpose and Chriskolz sent her home shouting furiously:

"This is sabotage! It is unheard of! I'll denounce you! You'll hear from the Gestapo!"

The minute I saw Joachim I told him the whole story:

"You've got to get her away before the Gestapo arrests her. Bring her here!"

Joachim went immediately; he looked Aryan enough to take a train but it was some time till he came and brought her with him. I was quite anxious by the time they arrived. Her father had not wanted to let her go. They used to quarrel a lot and then they would not speak to each other for days on end. He was not worried about her.

"She'll be all right," he grumbled. "I was in World War I and it was not that bad, she'll be all right."

Next day Hilma went home to take some more clothes. Her mother saw her as she was leaning over the banister and made signs to her to go away. The Gestapo was there taking her and her husband away.

During her stay with us we took her to Kurt's home. I told her when and where to go and to start peeling potatoes when she got there. The sight I saw when I arrived at Kurt's was Hilma sitting smiling on the table, her long blond hair cascading in front of her, Kurt at her knees playing the guitar and singing, both oblivious to anything else around them.

"Where are the peeled potatoes?" I asked.

"Oh!" was all the answer I got. I was not amused.

Hilma had to stay in our apartment all day, so that people in the house would not know that we were hiding somebody. As soon as we were home she could go out, but she went out in the morning and we had a Gestapo man living in the house. She stayed with us for two weeks, then we had to tell her to find another place.

She found one with other friends and the same happened again. She did not take things seriously enough, and was again asked to leave. Fortunately she had a Christian boyfriend who took her to his relatives and people were told that her home had been bombed and she had nowhere to go. There she remained the whole war and survived. After the war she went to the USA, where she had relatives.

The Deportation

There is no greater sorrow than to recall happiness in times of misery.
                                        Dante, *Inferno*.

What we all were afraid of finally happened that summer. My father wrote us on August 31st, 1942:

> Dear Gerda and Dear Joachim!
>   Just now we received the notice for Theresienstadt and cannot hope for further delay.
>   Sending regards hurriedly,
>   Papi and Mutti

My mother wrote the same day:

> Dear children,
>   Yesterday we were still quietly and almost cheerfully together and today early in the morning before breakfast we received the notice for Theresienstadt. What a blow! Finally a journey, but not to my taste. This time it seems serious.
>   Dear Gerda, after you left I was so pleased with the way the kitchen looked: spick and span. I thank you very much. I hope that we will all be able to be together again with Willi in this life. In spite of everything I still have hopes. Be healthy, have a pleasant time and don't forget us.
>   With love, your Mutti

My father added:

Dear children,
   Think if there is anything to discuss, or if you have any wishes and phone Aunt Bertha immediately. Kindest regards and kisses,
   Papi

My aunt had had a Hungarian passport and so had kept her telephone, when German Jews had none.

Immediately we got the letter in the afternoon, we walked to Halensee to see my parents. We helped them pack. I took my mother in my arms and tried to console her and she cried on my shoulder.

My mother needed me and there was nothing in the world that I could do or even say.

There is no consolation for a sick woman being deported to another country to a concentration camp. Even if Theresienstadt was said to be a better camp than the others. We both knew it.

We were aware that only if a miracle occurred, would we see each other again.

Joachim and I had to leave, we would have to walk all the way back. It would soon be time for the curfew and we did not want to add to my parents' fears and anxiety. They were moved to an old people's home, where they stayed in quarantine for two more weeks because of a typhoid epidemic. We were allowed to visit them once. Joachim sold a Persian carpet that belonged to my parents and when Father came to the door we gave him the money when we shook his hand.

My mother was sitting at a first floor window, unable to walk downstairs. She looked at us with stony eyes that hardly recognised us, as if she had seen and heard things beyond her comprehension.

She was in shock and did not seem to be the woman I had held in my arms a few days earlier. We stood silently with my father at the door. Everything had been said, nothing was left to add. We soon said goodbye with aching hearts and waved to my mother, who did not respond. Then we left. Joachim took my arm; we had a long way to go and I walked blindly through the streets.

Life Goes On

Life went on, difficult as it was. We played *Les Preludes* by Liszt loudly, and opened the windows, imagining all the neighbours rushing to their radios to hear about the latest sea victory. We broke flowerpots and dishes that we did not need, since we had received a printed letter that our property belonged forthwith to the Mayor of Berlin, with orders to handle everything carefully. We had many things that we would never use and invited Kurt when he visited to join us in this relaxing and invigorating sport.

On the 14th of February, 1940, Jewish bank accounts had been closed and the owners were allocated a certain amount to live on. When I started to work at the factory and my earnings were practically nil my father decided that my wages should go to the bank and he would continue to withdraw the sum of money granted to me. After my marriage my father suggested that we go on with this arrangement.

Now that my parents had been deported their bank account was blocked completely and I received no more money from the bank. The factory took no notice of the changed circumstances and sent my wages to the bank who sent the money back. This went on for some months and I was advised to get the necessary papers for the release of my wages from the Jewish Community Centre. I received permission from the factory and left early. I took the S-Bahn, travelling second class without the yellow badge.

Taking a train illegally, second class was advisable, as a meeting with Jewish friends in the third could lead to complications. I sewed the star on shortly before reaching the

Jewish centre. Getting the papers was a mere formality. I left quickly and took the star off and then the train home. I sewed the star on again and at home went to bed for some much needed sleep. Unfortunately I overslept and by the time I awoke it was too late to go back to the factory. Next day Chriskolz, who was in one of his rages, yelled at me again. I took this with equanimity explaining that walking both ways and arrangements there had taken longer than expected. The political leader belonged to the SA and he did not know that after I left the offices of the Jewish Community Centre they had been raided by the Gestapo who had arrested everyone who did not work there. Apparently they had been short of people for a transport. One needed a lot of luck in those days.

My wages were not paid immediately, the firm was short of money they said, and gave me only half the amount. The other half should have been paid at a later date. I never got it because we escaped.

The Escape

These are the times that try men's souls.

Thomas Paine

I met Mr Larsen for the first time when he came to see Joachim and me in 1942 in Berlin. He had taken his family to Denmark away from the Nazis but his business remained in Berlin. So did his rowboat which we had used with his permission on and off. He was a courageous man, which I did not quite appreciate at the time. Not only did he come on business trips to Berlin during the war years, he also visited us regularly when other 'Aryans' avoided us.

He was a tall and lean man who had been badly wounded during the First World War and still bore the signs. A stiff leg and a hoarse voice. His father was a Dane but his mother came from East Prussia, Kreis Gumbinnen, as did my father's family. He used to wonder if my forebears who had owned a hostelry had bought bread at his forebears' bakery.

His mother's family belonged to the Salzburgers; Austrian Protestants who had escaped religious persecution in Austria and gone to East Prussia, where they were welcomed.

When he was a raw army recruit and his sergeant ordered him about, he set down his rifle between his knees and with both hands stretched out towards the sergeant started to argue reasonably: "But sergeant..." We never knew what happened then because we laughed so much. But he always stressed that he had learned arguing from his Jewish friends and was quite proud of it too.

His business was buying and selling veneer. I did not know what veneer was till I met Joachim. It is a thin wooden sheeting that is glued on to furniture.

Mr Larsen had a dry sense of humour and knew how to make the most of life. About flying he would say:

"I'd much rather get off a plane than board one."

Once I asked him if he bought veneer in France because it was cheaper there and his answer was:

"Not really, but I like going to France!"

Being alone in Berlin, he was never in a hurry to leave in the evenings. Neither did he seem worried that the Gestapo or SS might descend upon us. When we finally escaped with his help, he risked his life. He had the courage of his convictions.

Mr Larsen was trying to send his stock out of Germany before it could be bombed. It was Joachim's idea that we should hide underneath a load of veneer being sent to Denmark. Joachim worked with a firm which exported veneer and Mr Larsen wanted to use this firm. One evening he said to us:

"I don't think sending you to Denmark is any good. The Nazis are there too. How about sending both you and the veneer to Sweden?"

While we planned our escape, I started to put things aside that would be needed. Any food that could be kept without spoiling, candles and matches, toilet paper, a battery for a flashlight, newspapers which we were not allowed to buy, string and other necessities. Putting food aside was the hardest of all.

When our plans were taking shape, Joachim asked Kurt if he wanted to come with us.

"You are crazy, you'll never make it!" he answered. But he promised to help us load the wagon.

In time, when he saw how carefully we were preparing everything, he agreed to come, provided we take his violin and his guitar along. Kurt asked his girlfriend and later a friend if they wanted to come with us. Joachim asked his father. None of them would take the risk.

Sometimes we despaired of our plan ever coming off, and wondered if our "See you in a mass grave!" instead of "Goodbye" to friends would not prove too true. Our fears were always stronger and our hope dwindled while we were waiting for Mr Larsen to return from Copenhagen.

II

Finally the day of our departure arrived. It was the 24th of December, 1942. Joachim left early, as usual, I left later. I was a bit nervous about being missed at work and that somebody might try to find out what had happened to me. But so many people were being deported that the same would be assumed for us too. I dressed for the last time in our apartment, putting on as many things as I possibly could, topped by a coat made for me by a seamstress who had been afraid to let a Jewess come and try it on. The material had been meant for my father and was heavy. The coat was a misfit but very warm. I also put on a pair of jackboots like those worn by the Nazis. Kurt and Joachim had the same. When we were later together with Norwegian refugees, this branded us as spies for those who were easily impressed by appearances.

The things we intended to take with us were not in the apartment any more. A friendly neighbour had taken them on a handcart to the goods station.

When I went there I was stopped and asked what I wanted.

"My husband works here. I would like to talk to him."

Naturally I was without the yellow star and was allowed to proceed.

When Joachim saw me, he said immediately:

"You can't get in now, come back in an hour."

What could I do in Berlin on the eve of Christmas with no home to go to? I could not go and have a hot drink somewhere, I could not afford to attract attention. So I walked at a steady pace in a park. Dressed as I was and worried to boot, I began to sweat. An oddly behaving man started to follow me around, and I had to get rid of him before I went back to the station. I walked faster and faster. Mr Larsen was already waiting for me outside:

"You have to go away again for another fifteen minutes. Good luck!"

When I came to the station for the third time everything was empty around the wagon and I could get in. Joachim and Kurt helped me. They had thrown the luggage into our hiding place when it arrived and I was told to tidy up. I crawled to the corner they indicated, arrived at a hole and started to descend. There was no foothold, at least none for jackboots, everything was dark and I was hanging by my fingers, but could not hold out for long, not with my heavy clothes. If I just let myself fall I might make a noise. But I had no choice. To my relief I fell only a few inches. I took out my flashlight, held it in my mouth and steadying myself with one hand, started to clear things away with the other.

Then came the waiting. Time loses its meaning and becomes unreal. After an eternity Kurt arrived. We waited for Joachim who had gone to get a drink of water. We became nervous. Joachim arrived, Larsen shut the doors, wished us a good journey, and took the papers to the station office declaring that the workmen had left, since it was Christmas Eve.

We had the food we had saved, two jerry cans with water, a spirit stove, a pot, a pail, newspapers, some very rare toilet paper, clothing, blankets, a chamber pot and of course Kurt's violin and his guitar. We were thankful that it was neither a piano nor a contrabass. We also had a sleeping bag. It belonged to a German soldier whose mother gave it to us and one of the first things we did in Sweden was to send it back to Berlin.

Kurt had wanted to take his bathrobe with him. I had vetoed this and told him to get some more warm underwear. In time he forgave me. We took our bathing suits though – even in the middle of winter I did not feel that we could go anywhere without one.

III

On the first day, when we were shunted around in Berlin, the veneer started to slide and I was told to get out so that the men could prop it up. We were mostly lying under it, only part of our upper body was completely free.

Naturally I was curious to see where we were and found a hole to look through. At the same moment another wagon bumped into ours, I fell heavily and hit my head. I did not cry out, being afraid that somebody might hear me. Touching my head gingerly, I felt blood. I crawled back into our hiding place, which was now secure. Joachim and Kurt looked at the wound with our flashlight and declared it unimportant. They put my hair over it and my cap on top. It healed nicely.

A little later somebody walked alongside the train and sang:
"It'll all be over in fifty years time..."

A very popular hit that year. We lay down again and waited for things to come.

Water was rationed since it was possible that the trip would take three weeks. At the end of our journey the water was frozen solid. I got the sleeping bag, for which I was thankful but only after I shed a few tears.

We were shunted around in Berlin for three days. And then during the night the train left for Sassnitz. Something must have been wrong with our wagon because every time we stopped somewhere on the line, a railwayman came round to our end of the wagon and started hammering. We became afraid that the veneer would have to be transferred; that would have been the end of us.

As the train was moving through the night and nobody could see us, we stood at the opening, silently looking out at the darkened countryside. It was an eerie sight, not completely dark but no light showing anywhere. We were finally breathing some fresh air and started to hope for a new life.

Every goods wagon has four openings. Two shuttered and two that can be opened and shut completely. Our hiding place was beneath an opening without a shutter and Joachim had measured our heads and our bodies to see whether we would be able to get out that way. We did not intend for anybody to find us in there like trapped mice and the doors were sealed from the outside.

We arrived safely in Sassnitz, having eaten one hot meal on the way. Joachim and Kurt held the cooker and the pot. As I was deemed to be the cleanest, I stirred the food. Green beans from a tin. I also handed out the food which we ate once a day. Since none of us could wash during the whole time, I doubt if I was any cleaner than the other two.

In Sassnitz we were shunted back and forth again. It had started to snow and we could not hear any footsteps. We almost emptied the chamber pot on a passing soldier's head. He did not look up and did not know the danger he had been in. The chamber pot was withdrawn hurriedly, still full. We used the pot only in the evenings so that it could be emptied immediately.

Once Kurt became so thirsty that he had to have something wet. Water was out of the question. He took some cod liver oil and cursed for quite a while, as it did nothing to appease his thirst and left an awful taste in his mouth.

On the 31st of December the door was opened; someone must have glanced fleetingly into the wagon and closed the door again. There were voices, but the only voice I heard was Joachim's saying clearly and loudly:

"Diese Idioten!"

Next we were moved on to the ferry, threw a cautious glance outside and saw that we were standing right above the toilets and the words were in Swedish.

We lay down again and waited.

Joachim was afraid that he would be seasick. Not a nice prospect in our cramped quarters. But when Kurt and I heard by the sound of the motors that the ferry was moving, he did not notice. So neither of us said a word. We had been going for five or ten minutes when Joachim's worries became too much for us and we told him that the ferry was on its way. Only then did he start to feel a little queasy.

IV

The train arrived in Trelleborg and we waited till it was dark to make our next move. We cleaned up with a bottle of cologne smelling vilely of violets. I think my aversion to most perfumes stems from that day. I exchanged my coat for a muskrat jacket which had belonged to my mother and which my father's secretary had stored. Joachim had brought it home triumphantly in spite of the objections of her family.

Apart from the smell I was quite presentable. The men were unshaven. Kurt was the first to leave our goods wagon and then Joachim helped me from the inside and Kurt from the outside and everything went well. After all, I was not only a girl but also the shortest and had had to lie for the whole week in the smallest place. Joachim handed the violin, the guitar and my big handbag to us. The handbag contained almost everything one might need, like Mary Poppins's. Then we waited for Joachim. In the meantime we saw people, soldiers and station personnel, walking about. The soldiers with rifles, the station personnel mostly with a bag or a lamp in one hand. Luckily no one came near us or looked in our direction. We waited anxiously for Joachim to come out and could not imagine what took him so long. We were afraid of being discovered in the meantime. When Joachim finally came out he slipped and it looked as if he would break his neck.

"What happened? What have you been doing all this time?" we asked.

"I cleaned up the mess inside! What do you think it will look like when they unload the wagon?"

We tried to take our bearings but there was no way we could see anything while we were still standing between trains. So we started to walk, not too slowly, not too fast, at first unsteadily but soon getting used to it again, trying to give the impression that we knew where we were going. Each of us carried something which made us look as busy as the railway people. We had the bag, the violin and the guitar. When we came to a wooden shed we remained standing very close to its wall. A door was opened right next to us. Fortunately we were behind the door. We heard voices and laughter from inside. As soon as the door closed and the man who had come out had gone away, we walked on and with luck found the exit from the station area. There was no one about and we wanted to leave quickly. But Kurt had left his violin somewhere while we were all trying to find our way. He told us to go on and went to get it. We walked out without incident. A few moments later a soldier was back on guard duty and a little later Kurt returned with his violin. This time I waited with Joachim for Kurt. It took some time till the soldier was looking away and he could come out without being seen. We all breathed more easily.

Then we walked towards the town. It was all lit up with shining lights and the bells were ringing. It was the most wonderful sight we had seen in years and the bells made the most beautiful sounds we could have imagined. New Year's Eve!

We reached the proper railway station which was not far away and phoned Mr Bergström who lived in Malmö and was handling the veneer in Sweden telling him that it had arrived in Trelleborg. Mr Bergström had been reading a thriller and found our phone call most suspicious. He told us to come the next morning around ten to his office even though it was the New Year. He then asked his partner to come and bring his gun along, just in case.

It is a long way from Trelleborg to Malmö without funds. Kurt, with the Danish he had learned from Danish workers in Berlin, succeeded in persuading the station master to lend us some money. He told him that we belonged to an English band, had lost our colleagues and that they had all our money. We left my wedding ring and another ring as security with him. The violin and the guitar had come in handy after all. Only later did we learn that at that time no Englishmen were travelling in Sweden.

We took the next train to Malmö. Joachim went and shaved. Kurt refused because it might attract attention. By now our euphoria had evaporated. We were tired, hungry and irritable with each other. We were also extremely apprehensive about our future. Knowing that the Swiss kept sending refugees back to Germany to certain death, we were not sure what the Swedes would do. We did not talk much, but kept our thoughts to ourselves.

Arrived in Malmö we found that the railway station was about to be closed. Some kind soul told us that if we had nowhere to go the police would be sure to give us a bed for the night. That was the custom in Sweden. He also pointed out a policeman near the station. We walked straight up to him in case the kind soul was watching, went on without asking for shelter, not even looking at the policeman, not wanting to have anything to do with him before we had talked to Mr Bergström. We went on and on and walked through the ice cold and windy night. Once in front of a bank, where we had put the instruments, walking up and down, we were told by a guard to beat it which we did immediately. I can't remember ever having felt as cold as that in my whole life.

As soon as the station opened again around five thirty or six we were there. It was then that Kurt decided to shave in the middle of the big station. Although Joachim and I found this very conspicuous nobody seemed to look at him twice.

At the appointed time we went to Mr Bergström's office and told him about our escape. He assured us that Sweden would not send us back, that many refugees from Norway were in the country. The refugees from Denmark arrived only later that year.

"The only thing to do is to go to the police. I'll come and vouch for you."

We told him that we had bought Danish passports from Danes who had wanted to help and needed the money. They did not have our pictures nor could we sign the names.

Mr Bergström considered this:

"Give the passports to me, I'll get rid of them," he said. "You'll make a bad impression if you take them to the police station."

We took Mr Bergström's advice and he went with us to the police and, as promised, explained how we came to be in Malmö and where we had come from. Then bureaucracy took over. Every single item we had was written down. I had the big handbag with all those odds and ends and the list of my belongings seemed endless.

At one point Joachim and I saw Kurt chewing. I was not curious and probably too tired to care, and said nothing. But Joachim asked:

"What are you eating?"

He got no answer from Kurt who was busy swallowing, and from his facial expression one could see that he did not wish to enter into a discussion. Joachim, who was apparently hungry, got a slight kick from me. One does not ask unnecessary questions in front of the police. It turned out later that Kurt had forgotten that he had a Danish birth certificate matching his Danish passport and had forgotten to give it to Mr Bergström, so he ate it.

I suppose at some time we got food but I can't remember that. I do remember that everybody laughed when I stated that I was married.

At last we were put in different cells, with an empty one between each of us. Later these were occupied by two Poles who had hidden on a ship from Gdansk underneath a load of coal.

Once in my cell I walked over to the nice clean bed and the minute I heard the door close behind me, I fell on to it and started to cry. The policeman who had shut the door came back in, put his hand on my shoulder and said:

"It's all over now! It'll be all right."

During all this time Mr Larsen was in Berlin. He got up every morning between four and five o'clock, got dressed and waited to hear if the Gestapo had caught us, holding himself ready for his arrest.

When everything was over and Mr Larsen came to visit us in Sweden, he told me that he had frequently thought he might have acted faster if his own daughter had had to be rescued from Germany. But there I think he was overly conscientious.

He was immensely gratified that I could send a postcard from Sweden to my parents in Theresienstadt and that they and especially my father lived long enough to know that we had escaped. He would say often and sometimes write in a letter:

"And so your father learned that you had arrived safely in Sweden."

Mr Bergström was also glad about the part he had played in our rescue and would later declare that it had been the best New Year's Day of his life.

Fifty years later when Joachim, Kurt and I were celebrating the anniversary of our successful escape, Joachim and Kurt reminded me of the lavish meal that Mr Bergström had ordered when he took us to the restaurant at the station before going to the police. Even then I could not remember anything about it. At this point Joachim laughed:

"I heard from Larsen's son, that Mr Bergström had sent the bill for this meal to his father."

At the Police Station

We were confined at the police station in Malmö for almost two weeks. The first three days Joachim and Kurt were cross-examined simultaneously. Kurt was taken to Trelleborg to show the authorities how we had managed to get out of the station compound under the eye of the Swedish army. He was afraid they were sending him back which would be worse than having remained in Germany and going underground. Only when it became clear that by evening he would be in his cell in Malmö did he relax and start to entertain the police force in Trelleborg telling stories and playing on a borrowed instrument.

We had decided how much to say to the authorities or anybody else before we arrived in Sweden. Under no circumstances would we mention Mr Larsen's name. He was still in Berlin, his family in Nazi-occupied Denmark. Nobody asked me anything. After two days, Joachim refused to answer questions unless he could see his wife. I was brought in and we were both given coffee and cake. The inquiries that day were about the food situation in Germany; to which Joachim replied that he was not a spy and only after some argument did he consent to tell the officer how much food the Germans were getting. To our surprise in 1943 the Germans got more meat than the Swedes who were also partially on rations.

After three days when the questioning stopped, we were put into a big cell together during the day. Kurt got his violin and started to practice. We shuddered and so did the policemen. They listened for a little while, then gave him an ultimatum:

"You can play – no practising. What a noise!"

Joachim and I were relieved.

Since we were always hungry, any food left over in the pots, was brought to our cell. We kept cold potatoes for the long evenings and peeled them with a nail file. The healthy and/or poisonous qualities of the potato peel had not yet been discovered.

The Chief Police Inspector visited each of us in his cell and introduced himself. He was a tall Swede, big in all directions, with a stiff collar that seemed to hold up his head. We were a sensation and people wanted to meet us. One newspaper even printed a few lines about our escape.

I had taken three books with me, *Faust*, *Trost bei Goethe*, and *Die Duineser Elegien* by Rilke and each of us had one in his cell. The Chief Inspector, who spoke excellent German, picked up the Faust in Joachim's cell and asked him:

"What have you got here?"

Joachim's answer was prompt:

"We took the most important things with us."

The Inspector then wanted to know if we had any special wishes. We had, we wanted to shower and get out into the fresh air. Our wishes were granted. We were taken to a bathhouse and for a walk. Anybody else who asked about my needs got only one short answer:

"Chocolate, please!"

One day one of the policemen took the three of us to his parents' house where we were invited for coffee and cake at a splendidly appointed table. Two cakes and seven different kinds of cookies. One eats only one of each kind even when offered a plate twice, as we learned later. Our hosts plied us with food, drink and questions and afterwards our personal policeman took us back to the station and our cells. There was no fear that we would run away from him.

For years I hated talking about our escape because I would start to shiver uncontrollably and, being ashamed that I did, would clasp my knees to keep them from shaking. If possible, I left the explanations to Joachim and Kurt.

Alingsås

The days at the Malmö police station gave us time to grasp the fact that we had succeeded in escaping the clutches of the Nazis. From there we were taken to a refugee home in Alingsås near Göteborg. Joachim tried to travel on the train with the yellow badge, but the accompanying officer would not allow him to do so.

In Alingsås we were taken to a big villa full of Norwegian Jewish refugees. Most were extremely suspicious of us and were full of tales about the Fifth Column that had operated in every country the Germans had occupied. I was the only dark one; the men and especially Joachim did not look Jewish. We had jackboots; we talked like Germans, naturally; and in spite of declaring that we had done forced labour in Germany, I could not even iron. I did not think it necessary to explain that I hadn't had an iron. It had been confiscated like every other electrical appliance. But suspicions once aroused are not easily overcome. I was not immune either, and had doubts about some of the people I met.

We had never seriously expected that we would not be believed. Rumours about us floated around. Gert Löllbach, secretary of the Hechaluz in Sweden, was asked to look us up and find out if we were who we said we were. He trusted us and we were grateful.

My feelings at that time were hard to define. The earth was white with snow and everything looked beautifully clean and bright and innocent. I heard Swedes sing hymns and looking at them I could not understand why they should worship God with sincerity, whereas the Germans whose appearance was so similar persecuted people with hatred and violence and murdered them systematically.

We had food, a roof over our heads and would not be deported. We saw our first movie in colour – a Carmen Miranda film with song and dance – we were overwhelmed. Kurt even sold one of his shirts so we could all see it a second time.

We walked the streets without fear.

But my parents were in Theresienstadt, we were afraid for Joachim's father and Jenny and our relatives and friends. The war was not over and I lived suspended in time, from day to day, from week to week, waiting for the end and the final news.

The Next Refugee Camp

The authorities distrusted us too, and we were sent to Tostarp, another refugee camp in the south. Tostarp was primitive, but Joachim and I got a room to ourselves. There was a laundry room where one could bathe once a week. The refugees did some agricultural work and the chores around the camp. A Swedish girl cooked and a Swedish handyman kept things going.

It was a camp for baptised Austrian Jews whom the mission had brought to Sweden. There were three missionaries, one a Swede who managed the camp. He and his family had lived in China and returned because of the war. The other two were baptised Jews with Christian wives. One couple had a thirteen year old son but never talked about him because they had only married a few years before.

The Swedish government had added several doubtful characters to this lot whom they refused to let loose in Sweden. We too belonged to that category.

Apart from us there were four who did not get residence and work permits immediately. A middle aged man who had befriended a fifteen year old boy, both from Norway. Neither had a family. The third man would have come under suspicion anywhere in the world. Just listening to him one automatically disbelieved every other word.

The fourth was Fritz Neufeld, a communist from Berlin who believed in Trotsky, and who had fled to Norway. At the time of the German invasion he had had a broken leg from skiing and, unable to escape, had hidden for two years in a small room, only going out occasionally in the evening. The

Germans who knew that he was in Norway had kept looking for him and when the Norwegians brought their Jewish nationals to Sweden, they took him along. We became very good friends and he helped us whenever he could.

When Joachim was told to clean out the latrines together with the Swedish handyman, he had a hysterical crying fit and Fritz did the work for him. Joachim only slowly calmed down.

The only grown man I had ever seen cry was my father when my mother became ill. That had been five years before. I had not known what to do then, I didn't know what to do now. I looked at Joachim in disbelief. We had promised ourselves and each other that if we reached Sweden, we would do any work. It would not matter what kind as long as we came out of the war alive.

Fritz, who had read Freud and took a great interest in the human psyche, tried to explain to me the pressure that had been building up in Joachim and that his reaction had been perfectly normal. That is why he immediately volunteered to go in his stead. I could not see it that way. I had been taught that you do any work if you have to.

Pessach came around and we asked to be allowed to go to a synagogue. We were given leave of absence, and a Jewish family in Malmö invited us to the Seder. Kurt sitting next to me, kept me from eating my soup. Every time I lifted the soup to my mouth he started slurping without eating and, embarrassed that our hosts might think I was doing it, I hastily put down my spoon.

Being starved of the lighter side of life we took in a movie the next evening instead of going to the synagogue.

Since the camp belonged to the mission, prayers were said at every meal. Short sermons were delivered by the three missionaries in turn before dinner. We did not especially mind that till one evening one of the Austrians said in his prayer:

"...and I hope that all amongst us will soon acknowledge the true faith."

Kurt and I were incensed. We asked for an interview with Mr Moen, the Swedish missionary, and told him that we had been sent there by the State.

"We have", we said, "been persecuted in Germany for being Jews and will not consent to listen to one more word against our faith."

No one ever mentioned missionary ideas again in our hearing. Joachim had not come with us.

Mr Larsen arrived from Denmark for a visit. It was a joyful reunion and we were all happy that our plans had worked out and nobody had been caught. He brought the little money we had left with him and we bought bikes and started visiting Gert Löllbach and the other chaverim in the Hechaluz head office in Hässleholm near Tostarp. We talked, played Mikado often and sometimes, when in funds, went to play mini golf. At twenty-five öre a game each it was the cheapest entertainment available. Riding the bike back late in the evening, we would eat strawberries in the fields.

Eventually we were given our papers. Kurt was engaged as a violinist in the Norrköping symphony orchestra, and we were told to make lathe casings in Tyringe. There were two factories producing the same ware. One exported to England and the other to Germany. We were sent to the factory that exported to Germany, as Mr Moen smilingly said:

"This is neutrality!" I had not smiled back.

We rented a small room. Joachim worked three shifts. Women were not allowed to, and I worked two; we did not see too much of each other. We were still near enough to Hässleholm to visit our friends. I roamed the countryside, picking berries or apples on abandoned farms. I learned to make jelly and jam. I sometimes cut wood for the stove I cooked on, and I started to sew.

Starved of books as of everything else, I read any that I could lay my hands on. When I read *The Forty days of the Musa Dagh* by Werfel, about the murder of the Armenians during WWI, I got nightmares. Joachim wanted to take the book away from me, but I would not let him stop me and finished reading it. I had to.

One of my worst nightmares was about my father. I dreamed that the Nazis had taken out his brain, that he was helplessly wandering around and did not recognise me any more. It took a long time to recover from that dream and I never forgot it.

Norrköping

In autumn Kurt arranged for us to come to Norrköping, where we were accepted at the Norwegian refugee home and started to look around for work that would not benefit the Germans. There we were not as isolated as in the small town of Tyringe. We met other refugees, some from Germany who had come before the war, some from Norway.

Apart from my parents I had written postcards to Uncle Adolf and Aunt Jenny, Uncle Ferdinand and Aunt Irma, who had also been deported to Theresienstadt. The written part remained with the addressee, the second half with the sender's name and address had to be signed by the receiver and came back. Sometimes it was stamped: "Verzogen!" – moved on – which was not a good omen.

When the first card with my mother's signature arrived, Joachim performed an Indian war dance in our room which I thought childish. Although I was very glad that we had received the card I was far from overjoyed. The war was going on, my parents were still there. It was again one of those moments of complete misunderstanding between us.

Joachim soon found work in a textile factory. We had little money but, as we paid no rent, we managed. We started to learn Swedish and tried to fit in. Kurt gave us the two free tickets that were his due as a member of the orchestra and we went to concerts every week.

We became friendly with Heinz and Elsbeth Freudenthal and their small sons, Otto and Peter. He was the conductor of the Norrköping orchestra, she played the piano and the cello and gave music lessons. They had come to Sweden from Germany before the war and now helped many refugees. One day Elsbeth offered us the maid's room in their apartment which was next to the kitchen and completely apart, if we were willing to use a toilet in the cellar. Elsbeth thought the refugee home unsuitable for a young couple. The maid slept at her home.

We accepted, bought two beds and linen and moved. I was allowed to use the kitchen where I learned from Elsbeth how to bake bread and make yoghurt, how to use garlic and where to buy it which then was at the pharmacy. At times I helped in the house and with the children. When the Freudenthals moved for the summer to a farm in Vallingdal, I helped Elsbeth to get the house ready. Together with Kurt we were invited for a vacation.

We also visited a Hachscharah group outside of Norrköping, riding there on our bikes together with the Freudenthals and Kurt, and they would play music for the youngsters.

One of the girls from the group would be sent by their madrich regularly to help Elsbeth with the laundry every week. She would, of course, eat with the family and if she was pretty, Heinz deplored that she had to work so hard. Elsbeth, who together with the maid worked quite as hard, resented this. All the girls, pretty or otherwise, resented being sent to do the laundry without pay for the Freudenthals.

II

My health had suffered during the last year in Germany and I was hospitalised and had to wait a while before I was well enough to get a job again. As soon as I was able I started to work in the Dutch-owned Philips radio company, and became a welder for the small parts inside the wireless tubes. We were metal workers and our pay was good. The engineer, who at first had refused to let me do piecework, saw that I was used to factory work and after a few days I got his permission. This bettered my wages even more.

It was not a bad life. We worked and talked freely, we rode our bikes through the beautiful countryside, but at the back of our minds there were always the thoughts about the deportations which we knew would go on relentlessly. At the factory I became friendly with one of the office girls, a pretty redhead, and spent my lunch breaks with her. We went together to Swedish gym lessons which were taught by an Austrian refugee and participated in a gym performance. I did not talk about the years in Germany and had no wish to confide in anyone. Life in Sweden was so far removed from our experiences in Germany, it would have been like talking to a blind person about a sunset.

Elsbeth and Heinz used to invite us with others for a cup of tea on Sunday evenings after Heinz had conducted the concert. The talk would be about music and musicians. Occasionally Joachim would prod me in company to say something, telling me also in company that I was not stupid. I was shy and the youngest and had certainly nothing to say about music, especially in that company. I loved going to concerts but those evenings left me bored and longing for other topics of conversation.

During that autumn we finally received a real postcard from my mother.

On June 24th 1943 she wrote:

> Dear children,
> Today I am glad to be able to write you how pleased we were with your news. My health is good. We were so glad to hear about your trip, it was Papi's last joy. Have you heard from Willi? Letters and packages are distributed here quite regularly. The Post Office is functioning very well. Do write again often. In the meantime regards and kisses.
> With love,
> your Mutti

The card was stamped by a post office in Berlin on October 2nd and arrived in Tostarp on October 13th. It had been forwarded to Norrköping.

My father had died in Theresienstadt and my mother had not dared write us in so many words or how he had died. She had been afraid that if she were too explicit the card would not reach us.

It was good to have had the postcard from my mother, to know that she was still alive, and that my father had heard that we had reached safety. I grieved for him. The pain was like a dull ache inside me; my father who had never passed a German beggar in his life without giving him money and had quietly helped many people, who for several years had read the newspaper to an old blind lady every day, had died without comfort or peace of mind.

I did not expect to see my mother again, too many people had vanished from my life for me to have any hope left. The war dragged on and I started to wonder whether my father had died the night I had dreamed about him.

We wrote immediately, but got no more answers. We did not send a package. We did not know how to go about it and the World Jewish Congress parcels were only organised a year later in Stockholm. Neither did I believe that my mother would get the parcel if I sent one. Right or wrong I should have tried harder. I could not stop worrying about it for years. Long after the war was over, I learned from Bill that our mother had died on January 30th, 1944 in Theresienstadt at the age of fifty-two.

III

Joachim decided to take a course in forestry and sawmill engineering to get a better job. He borrowed money from Mr Larsen and went to Härnösand up north. I remained with the Freudenthals, worked as usual, went to concerts, sometimes with Otto, and sat through Sunday evenings when invited, as best I could. Kurt also played in a small band in a hotel and I would sit at a table there occasionally and listen, once clapping my hands at the wrong moment and earning a furious look from him.

The management of the factory gave a dance for all the personnel which I attended by myself. Dancing with the Dutch engineers was preferable, they knew German and did not have hip flasks like the Swedes who used them during intermissions.

IV

Since I had married Joachim three years before at the age of eighteen, I had been very much his wife. Having complied with my parents' wishes, I had usually complied with his too. I had remained silent when I had disagreed with him when he thought too much about what would be good only for the two of us, disregarding other people. I had accepted his opinions and decisions, felt hemmed in by him and not supported, and actually found it difficult now that he was away to cross a street on my own.

We had both been young and inexperienced, under constant pressure, and had never led a normal life together.

Härnösand, where Joachim studied, was nearer the frontier and foreigners needed a special permit to go there. With Elsbeth's help I decided to visit Joachim and applied for one for a weekend visit.

We went for walks, and although we talked there was no dialogue. I remember telling him that I loved him, but it was more to reassure myself than him. When I came back to Norrköping I realised that I had fallen out of love with Joachim and there was nothing else in our life to hold us together. Unhappy and confused, I wrote him that I wanted to end our marriage.

It was a hard and sad time for both of us. I felt homesick and started to write poetry. The Freudenthals took Joachim's side and asked me to leave. For a while I lived in a hotel in

Norrköping, but then the metal workers went on strike. Strike money was not immediately available and I had to find other employment as soon as possible. I got a residence permit for Stockholm where I hoped that jobs were easier to find.

Stockholm

I arrived in Stockholm in the evening, armed with Gert Löllbach's address and the last of my money. He had married and Marianne and Gert shared a two room apartment with another couple. The front door of the house was locked. I could clearly see people inside on the ground floor where they lived but could not make myself heard. I had no choice, apart from breaking a window, but to take the train back to town where I booked a room for the night at the YWCA. I returned the next day and Marianne and Gert invited me to stay with them while I looked for work. The other couple had no objections and I slept in the dining corner.

I went to Jewish-owned stores and businesses and asked for a job. One Jewish businessman told me to go back to where I had come from. It was not clear if he meant Germany or Norrköping, nor did I inquire. I persevered. After two or three negative replies I needed some encouragement, and ate a cream cake which was cheaper than a real meal and better for my morale if not my health.

Among the businessmen I saw was Mr Masur. He phoned the offices of the World Jewish Congress asking if they had work for a pretty young woman about whose capabilities he knew nothing. They needed someone and I got the job.

Thanks to the many things I had learned in Berlin, I was well equipped for office work. At first all I had to do was send cables like "Mr X is looking for Mrs Y and her two children". I would spend hours on the phone spelling out names. Finally I was allowed to write these cables out and take them to the Post Office which, contrary to the opinion of my employers, was much quicker. I did other office work too, sometimes becoming the office 'boy' carrying parcels and finally I worked as a real secretary. When the war came to an end, work at the office doubled and trebled and more people were employed.

II

In my history book I can read that Lodz was liberated in January and according to the Red Cross, less than a thousand survivors remained in the biggest ghetto in Poland. From Auschwitz a death march left in January and then the camp was freed by the Russians. In April there were death marches from the camps of Buchenwald and Flossenburg. A death march is a march in which you walk till you fall by the wayside and are shot, or till you just die of hunger, thirst, cold, heat or sickness. Bergen Belsen was rescued by the British but tens of thousands of prisoners still died in the first few months after their release. The Americans freed Dachau and Mauthausen. On May 7th the Russians reached Theresienstadt.

On May the 8th, 1945 Germany capitulated!

We were relieved that the war was over, we were not jubilant. We knew that our losses had been too great to feel elated. But no matter how pessimistic any of us had been, we were all stunned by the immensity of the murder machine the Third Reich had called into being and operated.

It is said that the death of one child is a tragedy, the death of a thousand is a statistic. The murder of millions of people is not even a statistic. To imagine it, I think, defies the normal human brain.

Long after the war was over I talked with a German woman on one of my visits to my cousins. She had been a child during the war and fled from the Russians with her mother and brother or sister from East to West, enduring hardship and fear. I too talked about losing my parents who had starved and died in a concentration camp, while I escaped to Sweden to evade the

Nazis and death. She looked at me thoughtfully and said with a kind of surprise in her voice:

"Well, I guess you too have had your share of grief!"

I was speechless.

Later I came to understand that the death of millions of people killed in action or murdered in or out of concentration camps was history and had no meaning for her. She could commiserate with my personal fate but the only suffering that was truly real to her was her own.

III

Our boss at the office was Mr Rabl from Czechoslovakia who had come to Sweden from Norway. There was also a committee of three who were his superiors. One of them we never saw, the second, Mr Spivak, a distinguished looking gentleman, was responsible for the money management of the WJC in Sweden. Several times I had to go to his business offices and was given instructions and cheques. Whenever he gave me a cheque he looked at me piercingly as if to inquire how honest I was. I don't know if he thought that I would run away with it.

The third was Mr Storch, who was constantly underfoot, meddled in everything and seemed to have the feeling that the WJC was his private enterprise. He had other things to do and was a very successful businessman. Seeing him in our office this was hard to believe.

Mr Storch liked to touch people but nobody was crazy about coming into too close contact with him. Space was limited and running away impossible. Opposite me sat a young man whose cheeks Storch would pat occasionally. Seev then turned an unbecoming beet red not knowing what to do or where to look. Sometimes when Rabl came out of his private domain, seeing one of us in a corner with Storch cutting off a way out, he would remove his cigar from his lips and shout: "Storch! Come here!" and Storch would turn around and go.

Mr Storch had angina pectoris and was not allowed to smoke. His wife, he told us, went through his pockets to see if there were any signs of tobacco. He used to cadge cigarettes from the employees. One day Fredl, our phone operator, asked Mr Storch for some money and went out to buy cigarettes. He put them in his drawer and said:

"Storch, these are for you. Please, stop smoking ours, because you really don't pay us enough to keep you in cigarettes."

It was typical of Storch that he had given Fredl the money without even asking what it was for.

We had two ladies in their fifties in our office. One, the first employee at the World Jewish Congress, a fact of which she was very proud, was Mrs Obernbreit. Her name did not fit her, as she was so obviously 'unten breit'. She was also very proud of her son-in-law who had just completed his exams as an engineer and she mentioned him at least once every hour.

When he could not find any work she brought him with her to help around the office and he was also put on the payroll although he did not have any visible qualifications.

The other was Miss Fischer from Czechoslovakia and Norway, a highly intelligent and cultured lady, who was responsible for the card index of people looking for relatives. She was extremely conscientious and asked for the names of everybody who walked into the office. Making out the card she would then inquire:

"How do you write that?" The usual answer by people who were used to writing their names in Hebrew letters: "Es ist nicht asoi wichtig!" made her tear her hair in desperation.

Miss Fischer too would complain about Mr Storch's penchant for patting people and say: "Nothing embarrasses him, he even fumbles around with me!"

Vera and Eva, Hungarian survivors from Belsen, and two Czechoslovakian girls who had come alive out of the Ghetto in Riga, worked in the office. A Hungarian man who had survived the minefields worked in the Hungarian department.

A group of Jews were sent through a minefield, most of them were blown up and only afterwards did the German Army march through. The Jews had sacks over their shoulders to pick up the pieces of their comrades.

A Jewish girl born in Sweden whose grandmother had come from Hungary and who knew Hungarian, a Pole who had been in the resistance, and some Germans who had come before the war completed the ensemble. Apart from their native languages they all knew either English or German or both.

When visitors came, Storch guided them through the office, as if it were a zoo or a gallery, and explained where everybody came from and what he had done for them. When it was my turn he would say that he had picked me up from the street. Maybe he believed it. I hoped that nobody else did.

Storch signed some of the letters we wrote and he loved copies in all colours. We obliged him. His English was poor and he would sometimes yell at us: "What is 'kindly'?" pronouncing it the German or Swedish way.

"Why are you writing in English? [The letter was addressed to an office in London.] They don't understand it anyway!"

We didn't care and wrote the next letter in German. This did not please him either and he would then shout: "Why do you write in German? What am I paying you good money for?"

It was not a boring place and when the commotion became too much, Rabl appeared at his door and pronounced, overpowering any other voice: "Nobody shouts here but me!"

Some people thought deeply for half an hour before they answered any letter. They usually worked overtime. It was a good way to earn more money.

IV

As soon as I had a job I started looking for a room of my own. Marianne and Gert told me not to hurry and look for something really suitable. I found a cheap room in Lidingö with a refugee family from Denmark. Their daughter and I often took the train together to work. Sometimes I went by bike but it was a long way.

When Seev married I rented his so-called room nearer the centre of town. It was really only a little cubicle off the kitchen, with room for a bed, a very small table, one chair, and a tiny chest of drawers with a glass door, no privacy and no place to turn around. I was not allowed to bathe or cook. My landlady spent all her afternoons with her married daughter so occasionally I would make lecho which I had learned to cook from Vera and clean up so thoroughly afterwards that she would not notice that I had eaten. I took showers at the railway station for a reasonable sum.

Joachim had divided our things equally although he kept my mother's mink collar which Mr Larsen had brought, and sent my belongings to Stockholm. I had three teaspoons, a butter knife; he had kept the cheese cutter, the other three teaspoons and whatever he thought was his. I had three changes of bedclothes. For five kronor a month I got my bed linen from my landlady and gave my own to Fritz Neufeld who had also come to Stockholm and had no such arrangement.

Fritz had found work as a printer on a newspaper and we spent much time together. He called himself my uncle and cheered me up when I felt blue and I listened to his 'Weltschmerz' as a disappointed Trotskyist and European. He painted a portrait of my father from a very small photograph and bought the first drawing block and paints I had. He gave me cautiously good advice which I usually took to heart but did not always follow. During the divorce proceedings he helped me to get through this very difficult period, when I had no one else to turn to.

With Vera I became good friends, a friendship that lasted. She invited me to her room and I was dismayed to see that she had no bed linen. She laughed at me and told me how glad she was to have a bed of her own and a room with a door after Bergen Belsen. I gave her a set of my bedclothes. Now one set was always at Vera's, one at Fritz's and one in the laundry. They made the rounds with me as go between.

Naturally I went out a lot, movies, coffee houses, restaurants, now and then dancing, excursions on my bike on Sunday. A Danish friend, who was a count, took me out to decent restaurants although he had no more money, at least in Sweden, than the rest of us. His hobby was collecting inscribed cutlery. Once he dropped the knife, fork, and spoon which he had hidden in his sleeve. As he could not very well take them, he put everything on the table saying: "Oh, damn! Now we have to come here again!"

When the war was over he also took me with him to the stadshuset for a big feast where Danes and Norwegians were invited by the city of Stockholm. There was plenty of food and drink.

Having fortified himself with his and my drinks he secreted the cutlery on his person, but being full of alcohol he later stood in the street, pulling out his trophies and showing them to all and sundry. I left him to it and took the next bus home.

I became a member of the local library, went to museums and galleries, painted, sketched and took sculpture lessons. I also took a correspondence course in Swedish, took up Spanish again, and learned a few words of Russian. I bought the smallest radio available on the instalment plan and put it on the windowsill.

The office of the WJC had originally been a private apartment and the owner, a very amiable and very Swedish Swede, Mr Varenius, for a while retained one of the rooms. He kept the cellar too and let me put my stuff in it. There was quite a big kitchen, we got permission to use it and I donated my household items. Miss Fischer was an excellent cook and the younger people did the dishes. I was exempted as I usually had evening classes to rush to. Old habits die hard.

Sometimes we all went out together, guiding Miss Fisher across the street. She had travelled extensively and been to

New York and other big cities but as soon as she saw a car a mile away she cried hysterically: "A car! A car!"

Fredl Kalter, too, belonged to our group. I had met him first in the Hechaluz office in Hässleholm. He now studied mathematics and earned his living at the WJC. When I started sketching I sat opposite him, trying to draw his head while he was immersed in his studies.

We went out and had dinner together occasionally but he really preferred other girls, because I was the only one he knew who ate her own potatoes. All the others would let him have at least some of theirs. We went to concerts together. Money being in short supply, everybody paid for his own ticket and the tram to the concert hall but Fredl, as a gentleman, would pay the ten öre for me should I wish to leave my coat in the wardrobe.

Marianne

Marianne worked for the Jewish community and we used to meet in our lunch hour. We would go for a walk, sit on a bench if the weather was fine and sometimes shop, especially for bread that was not made with molasses. To Marianne's horror, I would eat in the street when I was hungry, a thing one did not do in Sweden. One could only eat hot dogs outside after a movie when it was dark.

Having left Joachim I had left most of the guidelines I had had from home behind me. With Marianne this was especially noticeable. She was conventional and literal, telling me that I should not call myself Mrs as I had no husband. I refused to become Miss Marcuse.

I mentioned my friend Vera to Marianne and she was dismayed: "But I thought I am your friend!" She found it hard to believe that one might have more than one.

When I was sick once and had to stay in bed for a week, Marianne let me come and stay with her and Gert so that I would not have to be alone in my rented room. I remember taking a taxi, getting my bed from the WJC cellar and a taxi out to Riksby with it.

In later years, when I was living in Israel, Marianne sent me postcards from all over the world with kind regards, and nothing more. She visited me with her daughter, Monica, I met her in Stockholm when she was no longer living with Gert. She never mentioned this with one word, pretending that everything was all right. She was always pleasant, I owed her much but could not reach her. There was no trust and nothing of our friendship remained.

An Odd Invitation

There was a pretty young married woman who sometimes did volunteer work at the WJC. She did not do much but talked a lot, especially about the man she idolised at the time and who was not her husband. She also used our phone quite freely. One evening she invited me to dinner. There seemed no reason not to go, she was a bit harebrained but agreeable enough.

Her modern apartment was unexpectedly messy with dirty underwear lying around. The food was good, but when she had put the main course on the table, she suddenly remembered an urgent appointment and left. Her husband did not seem put out by this and I could hardly get up and leave. I finished eating, made a few polite remarks and asked for my coat, which he refused to give me. I had difficulties making it clear to him that his advances were unwelcome, and it took a very uncomfortable ten minutes to get out of there.

Next morning the lady arrived at our office and accused me of husband stealing. I had never had such a clean conscience in my life and did not even answer her. I never accepted a casual invitation like that again.

Erich

I did, however, go with Vera to visit a friend of hers whom she said I had to meet. Erich Kohn was living almost next door to our office in a nursing home. He had emigrated as a young man from Hamburg to Denmark and then gone on to Norway. He had contracted a crippling disease and when the Germans came he had been hospitalised and the Norwegians had taken him with other Jews out of the hospital and brought him to Sweden. At the time I met him, he could on good days get to the bathroom on crutches. Later he was unable to move from his bed without help. Fredl took him out in a wheelchair whenever it was possible and as soon as he earned enough money, he paid for a phone for Erich which helped him to stay in touch with people.

Erich was over thirty-five, spent his days in bed, and Vera had said that it was the custom for visiting young women to give him a kiss. Although I had my doubts about wanting to kiss anybody who was bedridden and old, I went. I liked Erich from the first few minutes and he got his kiss. He always got his kiss and I came to love and admire him. I visited him regularly and usually stayed till late, sometimes, being tired, lying half asleep at the end of his bed. No need to be afraid that I would not know what to talk about. Erich always had plenty to say; sometimes we would just be quiet; I felt at home.

He had good friends who came to see him as often as they could. They would read books together and many heated discussions took place in his room. He also had a Swedish girlfriend but he could not often be at her house.

Erich did not complain, but one could see his suffering etched in his face. I thought of him and his compelling personality often in later years, especially when times were rough.

The Aftermath

When Joachim and I were still together, I had written to a cousin in the States whose address I had learned by heart. My cousin was in the Army and my aunt answered sending my brother's address. After two years in Cuba Bill had immigrated to the US and was also in the Army. When he got my letter he wrote immediately and sent us money. Then for a long and painful period I heard nothing from him. He had had an accident which had injured one eye.

More and more lists of survivors from the German death camps arrived at our office with the end of the fighting in Europe. All of us scanned them eagerly in the hope of finding relatives or friends. It was a rare occurrence.

Lutz, Herbert and his girlfriend had escaped in the spring of 1943 to Switzerland where Herbert's girlfriend had an uncle who had guaranteed their support and we wrote long letters to each other.

Sitting in the WJC office and getting all the lists at first hand, I thought it unnecessary to put my own name on a list, so that my relatives in Germany, Uncle Max's children, when they too searched for the family did not find me. They did not belong to the Jewish community any more and their names did not figure on the lists either. It took more than twenty years till we found each other again. I got my cousin Walter's address in Palestine and we started to correspond. He let me know that our relatives in Hungary were still alive and I wrote to them too.

Slowly I pieced together what had happened to the family:

Julius and Esther Berlowitz, my parents, were deported to Theresienstadt and died there.

Uncle Paul died in Berlin.

Aunt Martha, by then a widow, her son and his wife emigrated to the US.

Aunt Irma and her husband, Ferdinand Schaal, were deported to Theresienstadt; their three children, Walter, Gerhard and Hilde, emigrated to Israel.

Aunt Trude with husband, Hermann Berlowitz and daughters, Cuni and Lisi, survived the war in Hungary. My aunt and uncle were in the Ghetto. Their daughters did forced labour. When Cuni and Lisi were to be deported, a soldier with a gun pointed at Cuni's head ordered them to get up. Cuni, thinking quickly, decided that if she had to die, she might just as well die where she was. She courageously refused to budge, holding Lisi, who was about to get up, back. The soldier moved on. Maybe he had orders not to shoot then and there, or he did not relish killing two young girls. They joined their parents in the Ghetto and Cuni took care of children there. They were liberated by the Russians.

Uncle Adolf Kupferberg and his wife, Jenny, were deported to Theresienstadt. Their son, Kurt, emigrated to France and was deported from there with his wife to an unknown destination.

Uncle Max Kupferberg was killed in Poland, and Aunt Selma, his wife, had the smaller children baptised. They moved from place to place, being bombed out several times. The bombing explained their lack of suitable papers and food coupons. By the time the papers did arrive they would already be somewhere else.

When things got dangerous, Edith's boss sent her to Austria to stay for a while with one of his friends who was a Nazi but did not know that Edith was Jewish. Edith's boss hid several Jews in his apartment and saved them.

Horst, the youngest at sixteen, was called up for 'Leibstandarte Adolf Hitler' a last ditch defence unit. He was given his papers at the police station, when he heard his brother's name called out.

"Ferry Kupferberg has to be arrested for deportation today too!" someone called out loud.

Horst had to present himself in another building but gave the papers to the guard, who was busy with a girl, and told him that he had been instructed to hand them over at the gate. He then raced home to tell his brother to escape. Ferry, a few years older, refused. He was picked up every morning for two or three days but sent back every time; there were no more trains at the Gestapo's disposal for deporting Jews to the East. Before he was released, he had to swear never to tell anybody what went on in those transit camps and he never did.

After the war ended and Berlin fell, two of their sisters were raped by the Russians. The boys succeeded in saving Senta, who had just had a baby.

All of them survived and remained in Germany.

Aunt Bertha Blau was deported from Berlin when the Hungarian Jews were deported. Her eldest son, Josef, had emigrated to France and was deported from there. His gentile wife and their son remained in Germany. Her second son, Johnny, emigrated first to Italy and then to Uruguay with his family. They later came to live in Israel. The youngest son, Rudi (Micha), emigrated with his wife to Israel.

Aunt Selma Stransky, my mother's second sister, was deported with her husband and son. Sally, the son, returned from the camps and remained in Germany.

Uncle Jacques Kupferberg emigrated with his wife Eva, his children Heinz, who had been my playmate when we were kids, and Ruth with her husband, Eugen Israel, to Chile. They returned to Germany.

Aunt Hertha Basch, her husband and her son Heinz perished in the Holocaust. Their daughter, Hilde, emigrated to England.

Aunt Hertha's sister, Lotte, married to Georg Cohn, came to live in Berlin quite late. They had two children, a son who emigrated to England, became a major in the British Army and moved to the US after the war, and a daughter my age, Steffi, with whom I became friends. The parents were deported from Berlin. Steffi was deported with a group of youngsters from a Hachscharah centre near Hamburg. They did not survive.

Aunt Emmy Heyman was deported, her son came to live in France.

Joachim's father and his wife, Jenny, were also killed.

Youth Aliyah

Towards the end of 1945 I heard that Youth Aliyah had opened an office in Stockholm and needed an English secretary. I applied for the job and was accepted by Mr Melitz. I had met several people with whom I talked English and when Mr Melitz talked to me I had no difficulty answering him intelligently. The salary was somewhat better, there would be no overtime and the days promised to be less hectic, and smokeless.

I gave notice at the WJC and whereas Mr Rabl was quite sympathetic, as the WJC's work would not go on forever, Mr Storch was enraged at my disloyalty. He went out of his way to tell Mr Melitz that I did not know much, that he had picked me up, not from the street but from the gutter, and anyhow I knew no English. This was a mistake, Melitz had just come from London, where he had spent the war years. His English was excellent and he approved of mine. Melitz asked me what this was all about. I had no idea, but was not overly surprised by anything Storch said or did. Having known him for a year, I remained calm and quiet and got the job.

Melitz had adopted a stiff English manner during the war years along with his first-rate English. His included putting commas where they belonged which mine did not. He would read out the offending passages and inform me in no uncertain terms where they should be. This was sometimes quite frustrating and in the end I put in no commas at all and left it to him to provide them. It was a compromise which he accepted.

He was a bachelor and lived in a guest house not far from the office. When he had a cold and did not feel well I had to bring him the mail, so he could sign it. He would lie in bed unshaven and without moving, impressing on me the severity of his illness, occasionally asking a small favour for a bedridden invalid. What with visiting Erich and having seen sicker people I was callously untouched.

I did as I was told without fluttering an eyelid when he asked me to put an unpeeled banana on the heating element for him. But then unable to keep my mouth shut, I said:

"I can't imagine that a hot banana is going to be very tasty!"

"I don't want the banana to get hot," was his answer, "I just want the outside to be warm to the touch when I peel it."

I said no more.

At first Youth Aliyah had a very small room in the Palästinabyrå which was in a cellar on Strandvägen. Then Melitz rented a bigger room not far from there with light and air. I often visited my former colleagues and ate with them after work. We did not have a lot of people coming to our office but now and then chaverim from Palestine would come in to see what went on. Nothing much happened and when Melitz went to Switzerland or other places I had the office to myself. I was not used to such a quiet life and got a second job with a recently immigrated businessman who traded in skins for sausages. His name was Fleischmann, his cable address was Fleischdarm. I asked Melitz for two hours off for lunch instead of one and worked during my lunch time and Saturdays, when our office was closed, for Mr Fleischmann. It almost doubled my salary.

Hillel Storch

After I had finished writing about the WJC and the people I met in Stockholm, I felt that there had to be more to Hillel Storch than was visible at our office. There were many rumours about other funny things that Storch had done or said. His language was Yiddish and his Swedish was not good. But it was unbelievable that he should have been such an important member of the WJC if he had been only a figure of fun, not to be taken seriously. I wrote to Gert Löllbach, explaining my problem and asking for help. I knew that Gert had had dealings with Storch at the time and long after I had left Sweden.

Gert's answer was surprising. He had had contact with Storch till shortly before his death in 1982. He had been present when Storch talked several times on the phone with Olaf Palme and Palme had written an obituary for Storch, which must have been a rare occurrence as Gert could not remember any other instance. I think that Gert was quite glad to be able to write to me about Storch as he had always thought that Storch never got the credit for the things he did. His behaviour had been unconventional, sometimes irrational, and he had probably had enemies and admirers but no friends. Still, he had had contact with high Swedish government officials and earned their respect. He had been full of the most outrageous ideas, some workable and some not. He had had a burning desire to save Jews and had succeeded in many cases. He had been generous with his money (also later when Gert had been in need of large sums of money for the Mossad), first giving and only later inquiring if he would get it back, which he sometimes didn't.

There is no doubt that he had established contact with Himmler's personal physician; the Finn, Dr Felix Kersten, influenced him and convinced him to influence Himmler to revise some of his decisions, which saved the lives of Jews and other prisoners. He had had contact with Schellenberg, the number two man of the Gestapo, and caused him to retract the order to annihilate survivors in the camps during the last weeks of the war and to put a stop to the death marches. For these and other orders, Schellenberg was kept under house arrest in Sweden through the offices of Storch till the Allies demanded his extradition and the Swedes delivered.

His ideas shook up other people who had not his initiative and will to fight to help save human lives. Storch managed to get a hearing with Folke Bernadotte under whose name about 10,000 people, mostly women, few men, but also French, Spanish and Polish people were saved. Storch had started the whole immense operation and prodded others to carry out his will.

He was supposed to travel to Germany in the spring of 1945 and meet with Himmler, but the Swedish government refused to give him a Swedish passport as they were unable to guarantee his safe return. Gert was present at the meeting at which Norbert Masur, a Swedish citizen, volunteered to go in his stead. It was a very courageous deed, as nobody could guarantee his safe return from Germany either. Masur got the credit which was his due, and much that should have gone to Storch.

On the other hand Storch could come late to meetings with high government officials, tiptoe around behind them, reach into the breast pocket of one of them, take a cigarette case, extract a cigarette, put the case back and then go to the next in line and ask for a match. I have no difficulty picturing this scene. The only thing I find hard to do is imagine the faces of the high government officials.

In Gert's opinion Storch should have had a monument or a foundation in his name. That he did not get one was not because he had not earned it.

The other day I visited the museum of the Kibbutz Lochmei Haghettaot, the Ghetto fighters, and I saw there a picture of a small girl and underneath it said:

Eleonora Schwab File, centre for Holocaust studies, Yaffa Eliach College.

"Eleonora Storch, taken on her second birthday November 25, 1940, Riga, Latvia, just prior to the family's departure to a safe haven in Sweden.

"Her father, Hillel Storch, was instrumental in arranging the rescue of Jews from German concentration camps in the spring of 1945 and in sending Red Cross packages to the camps through Count Folke Bernadotte."

So it really was no wonder that Mr Storch's Swedish was weak!

Looking For Greener Pastures

In 1947 Youth Aliyah was closing down its office in Stockholm; most of the kids had either emigrated or had grown out of YA. Mr Fleischmann, my other employer, wanted a male person full time. I thought travelling a good idea before settling down to another job. I had earned good money and had salvaged my mother's mink collar from my messy divorce with the help of Mr Larsen, who had talked Joachim out of it. If I sold it I might just have enough money to go to Switzerland for a month and visit Lutz. The first long distance trains went to the continent from Denmark and the train trip was much cheaper than flying.

Herbert had married his girlfriend who was expecting a baby and they were on their way to the US. He had gone to England first to tell his fiancée, who had waited for him throughout the war.

I started to make preparations.

Years ago, in another life, when Bill and I were still in Rome, my mother had taken us to Zürich for a two week winter holiday. My father had a cousin living there, the owner of the prestigious Bahnhofs Apotheke. Bill and I had stood next to my mother in the pharmacy as she left some jewellery with the cousin's son. We were not invited to their home for a cup of coffee, something my mother would certainly have done had it been the other way around. We were very much the refugees although there was no question that Bill and I would go back to Rome and my mother to Berlin.

I still remembered the cousin's name and the name of the pharmacy and wrote him. I mentioned that I had escaped from

Germany and lived in Sweden. I would soon come for a visit to Switzerland and would like to collect my mother's jewellery. Since my name was now different I wrote that I was divorced. I did not keep the letter I got in reply, but I remember it well.

There was not a word of regret that my parents had perished in the Holocaust. No rejoicing that I had survived. Naturally there was no word of his looking forward to seeing me in Switzerland. There was 'good advice'.

We had had, he wrote, a female relative in the family who had been alone, not of course divorced, who had learned how to sew brassieres and corsets, and had supported herself honourably, without help from anyone. Needless to say, the cousin himself was rich. He advised me to learn the very same profession and support myself, preferably without coming anywhere near him. I answered, that I had worked since I was seventeen years old, was supporting myself, thank you, in the profession I had learned: namely as a secretary.

I refrained from writing that I was sure that my chances of supporting myself honourably making bras and corsets were pretty slim.

Lutz, who now lived in Basel, had ascertained that I needed a guarantor, giving a guarantee of one thousand Swiss francs that I would leave Switzerland again. He also knew a couple where the wife had converted to Judaism and whom he had instructed. They were complete strangers to me but gave that guarantee without hesitation.

Since Germany had lost the war it was now occupied by the four victorious nations: the Americans, the English, the Russians, and the French. Travelling through Germany I needed visas from all of them. I also needed an extra visa to travel through France. It meant a lot of running around but there were no real difficulties. I had an unpleasant shock at the Russian consulate. When I was let in, the automatic door closed behind me and the one in front was still locked. Today we are accustomed to this, every bank in Spain seems to have an entrance like that, and so has El Al in Zürich. Then it surprised me completely and, not being overly fond of Russian communists together with my memories of the Nazis, the experience was frightening.

When all arrangements had been made, I set out one morning to catch the train to Copenhagen and the train from there to Switzerland. Fredl accompanied me to the station. As I waxed slightly sentimental, setting out on a long journey through Germany to visit a friend from my younger days, Fredl soberly remarked: "Well, you'll be back in four weeks!"

"Yes, of course!"

We saw each other again, when Fredl and his wife, Lies, came to visit us in Israel about twenty years later.

Fredl had also taken Vera to the airport, when she had insisted on going back to Hungary as a communist and a Hungarian, telling us that her country needed her. Then he and other friends had tried hard to convince her not to go. And Vera had come back to Sweden with nothing more than a rucksack on her back, having walked away from her native country and communism in 1956. She stayed for some time with Fredl and Lies in Stockholm and then went to London, starting life once more from scratch.

Travel

Nobody had told me that one had to take one's own food on the journey as there would be nothing available on the train. A Dane, supplied with appetising sandwiches, who sat opposite took pity on me and gave me some of his. Unfortunately it was a long train ride and two sandwiches were not enough. By the time I reached Basel my stomach was seriously upset.

At the German frontier I showed my Swedish passport for aliens and when asked questions answered in English. The official looked again:

"Aber Sie sind doch in Berlin geboren!" he said brusquely.

"I don't speak German!"

He shrugged and left.

In Hamburg many children stood near the train begging and the Scandinavians threw chocolate to them, murmuring words of pity and compassion. Remembering what had happened to our Jewish children in Germany, and although I knew that these children were victims of the war too, my sympathy was limited.

Hamburg was in ruins and not a pleasant sight with burnt out buildings, single walls still standing and ragged brickwork visible from the train. I was glad when we left it behind us.

Basel

Lutz picked me up at the station. I was tired, hungry and dirty, but we were both happy to see each other again and he took me to the small hotel where he had reserved a room for me. We talked about the past in Berlin, and exchanged memories. We told each other about the intervening years and what had happened to us, our friends and our relatives. We talked about our plans for the future. Lutz was still studying and had lectures to attend, but we saw a lot of each other and on Sundays rode bikes through the Swiss countryside, visiting the Goetheanum in Dornach. We took up our old discussions about anything and everything, went to the opera and had a great time.

I wrote again to my father's cousin who was now retired and lived in his house in Ascona. His son was living in Basel but, of course, the cousin never mentioned that, probably for fear I might ring his son's doorbell. I gave him my address in Basel and asked him politely to send my mother's jewels. The cousin maintained that he had received them with the express instruction to give them to my brother. The war had been over for about two years, and he had made no move to send them. I let him know that I had my brother's permission to take the jewellery and he and I would arrange matters between ourselves. I got no answer. My time was limited and a lawyer I consulted wrote an expensive letter, telling me at the same time that there was nothing he or I could do if the cousin refused my request. The lawyer's letter was successful and I got a small parcel with the jewels together with some money which my mother had apparently also left. I had hinted in my first letter that I might sell some of the things, thinking nothing about it. Now I wrote him a 'thank you' note and mentioned that one of the rings was mine given me by my mother and that naturally I would not sell it. The only thing I eventually sold was a golden powder box which had been made especially for that purpose. Not that I really thought it was any of his business.

Lutz and I were invited to the home of my guarantors in the afternoon for coffee and cake. They were very friendly and pleasant people, completely unafraid of me. Quite different from my relatives.

When alone I walked through the city enjoying my vacation, seeing the sights and visiting the bookshops. I bought German books and sent some to Bill. It did not worry me that I had no job to come back to.

The time came to leave and I decided that I might as well make use of the French visa and see Paris, the famous city, before going back to Sweden. The visa was good for travelling through France, not for staying overnight. Knowing that my Hebrew teacher from the Herzl School was head of the French Youth Aliyah office, I wrote him a letter introducing myself as a former pupil and former secretary of Youth Aliyah in Sweden, asking if he could possibly arrange a cheap hotel room for a few days for me and pick me up at the station so I could see Paris. His answer was affirmative and I wrote the exact date and time, asking him to wear a red carnation in his jacket as I might not recognise him and he would certainly have no idea who I was.

France

I said goodbye to Lutz, we promised to stay in touch and write regularly and the train took me to France where a very correct Hans Gärtner awaited me with the carnation in his buttonhole. He threw it away immediately after I introduced myself. We went to the hotel, which he said was sometimes raided by the police to see if everybody had a visa. This was the bad news. Then he showed me Paris and I was delighted. It was spring and we were looking down on the city from the Arc de Triomphe. I decided I'd had enough of Sweden, I had no job to go back to, the war was over, I would remain if I could.

Gärtner said he would help and asked an acquaintance from the OSE, a French Jewish organisation, to accompany me to the proper authorities to get a student's residence permit. The lady from OSE tried giving money to the official which he refused with indignation. I got the permit but was not allowed to work. For three weeks I participated in two courses for instructors for children's summer camps, organised by OSE. My French was half forgotten but I managed.

The only thing I remember from these courses was that we were giving a performance on the last day having eaten spoilt white beans for dinner. Everybody got diarrhoea and when not on stage, was standing in line for the toilets, shifting from one foot to the other or doubled up groaning. It was terrible. So probably was the performance, but we felt too awful to care.

After the course I was sent to work in a vacation camp in Montluçon. I received bed and board but no pay. We were four instructors, one of the male instructors and I were over twenty, the other two a girl of seventeen and a boy of nineteen.

Some of the kids were eighteen. There were about sixty children, a married couple who only cooked, and M. Singer, pronounced the French way, which confused me as it sounded so un-Jewish, the manager.

We divided the kids among us, with me, because of my insufficient knowledge of French, getting the youngest. It was an unfortunate mixture with many boys and only a few girls, so I exchanged my three girls for five boys from the next age group and had now fourteen boys. Some were so young that they had to be bathed. Not being afraid to delegate responsibility, I asked the bigger girls to help me, which they did with pleasure.

Our day started early, getting the kids ready for breakfast, supervising them and then going for walks or arranging games for them. After dinner at midday we put the kids to bed and then proceeded to do the dishes as the couple who cooked refused and there was no one else. By the time we finished, it was time for the youngsters to get up. We cut bread, gave them something to drink, and were busy till the kids finally went to bed after a light supper which the cook and her husband prepared.

Reading stories to the boys in the afternoon or evening was no problem, I could read French fluently, although I did not always understand what I was reading. Apparently the boys did.

When all the kids were asleep, the four of us would sit down, trying to figure out what to do with the children next day. It was important to know which group would be where so that we would not trip over each other. Since we were all dead tired this took some time. Being young and healthy we were also hungry. It was Suzanne's and my unenviable female duty to flirt with M. Singer and convince him to give us the key to the larder. If we did not succeed we would try to steal food, and in this case too, M. Singer's mind and eyes had to be diverted.

We worked like slaves day in, day out, never getting any time off. Only once did we have a free evening. On the 14th of July we went dancing in the streets of Montluçon. A unique and memorable experience for me.

After about three weeks I got a cable from Youth Aliyah: "Secretary leaving for London come immediately!"

I boarded the next train to Paris.

Living it up in a Hotel

I went to the same hotel where I had stayed before. They had no vacancy but were willing to give me a bathroom. The bathroom had a bed and I was not supposed to sleep in the tub. On the whole the bathroom was a bit bigger than the room I had had in Stockholm and my possessions were few.

The hotel was full of Palestinians, mostly from kibbutzim. I did not know what they were doing there, some were on hush-hush business and I never asked. They were all complaining about the heat in Paris even if they came from Tirat Zwi, one of the hotter places in Palestine. I spent quite a bit of my time with the girls in their room on the third floor. The hotel had a typical French hydraulic lift. When three persons were in it the lift would get stuck between floors. Luckily the shlichim from Palestine were young and supple and one of the men would climb out, make his way up and press a button so that the lift moved on.

I left for work in the morning and came home in the late afternoon. One day I was early, and trying to open my door I found myself locked out. I banged on the door, but got only an indistinct reply. Complaining to the owner of the hotel, I was told that there was an American lady whose room key fitted the bathroom and she took a bath whenever she wanted to, they were quite helpless in the matter. I did not believe a word of this, and was sure that she paid for the privilege of having a bath. I went back, banged some more on the door and shouted, this time in English: "Open up, immediately!"

The lady came naked to the door. She was middle aged, with a body that ran to fat and it was not a pretty sight.

"Please, get dressed and out of my room, now!"

She was flustered but complied. I averted my face and waited outside.

I needed another hotel where no one had a key to my room but the chambermaid, and the police were not occasional visitors. Although I had a permit to stay, I was working illegally. I found one not far from the Étoile. It was cheap and my room was a normal sized hotel room on the first floor, so that I was not dependent on the lift. The night porter looked as if he was permanently under the influence.

There was a connecting door to the next room but a big wardrobe stood in front of the door and I had nothing to worry about. My neighbour was a good looking Egyptian who was having a stormy affair with a French girl and I was occasionally disturbed by their violent arguments. When the affair ended he sometimes serenaded me through the open windows, singing and playing his guitar till he found someone else.

As soon as the summer vacation was over M. Singer returned to Paris. He phoned that he, a Hungarian, wanted to show me his city. He started with the famous cemetery, Père Lachaise, which I did not appreciate so short a time after WW II, and without the key to the larder he was less attractive than before.

I had run out of money by now and was loath to ask for an advance on my salary. I had occasionally worked for Aliyah Beth in my spare time in Stockholm. When Abi, who had dictated long lists to me, heard that I might go to Paris he had given me a recommendation to a colleague there. I received a loan from Aliyah Beth and was allowed to pay it back in monthly instalments. I also received a dinner invitation, being a young woman on one's own sometimes has advantages. Of course, young women get paid less for their work than young men. Melitz too, when he came to Paris, took me out to dine with him a few times.

Youth Aliyah in Paris

Work at the YA was interesting and many sided, and working for the European department, I had two bosses. One was Akiba Lewinsky, head of YA for the whole of Europe, from Ma'ayan Zwi. Akiba had had his doubts about taking me on as his secretary, only when Gärtner told him that I had been a pupil at the Herzl School in Berlin, did he consent. The other was Meta Flanter from Jerusalem, who was managing the financial side. I had a colleague who was beautiful – tall, blonde and also very nice. Marlitt spoke German and Spanish. She and her mother had survived the war in Spain. When they came back to Paris, Marlitt's mother married again, gave birth to twin daughters and went with her Hungarian husband to his country.

Marlitt remained alone in Paris studying music. She was nineteen and I was told to keep an eye on her at work. I did not need to; even though I sat with my back to her, I knew exactly when she was typing private letters and when she was working for the office. The tempo and the noise level changed whenever I got up from my chair. I also knew the sound a piece of paper makes when it is hurriedly drawn over something you want to hide. After a week when I knew her better, I told her that I could hear what she was doing and if she had enough time she could write the occasional letter. If she wrote too many, other people might notice. The atmosphere in the office eased up and we became friends.

Marlitt was responsible for filing and for anything French that was going on. I did the English and German correspondence. We sat in a big room together with Mrs Flanter who was very proud of 'her girls', one blonde, one dark. Mrs Flanter liked cakes and cookies and when we drank tea in the morning she would offer us something sweet from her drawer, choosing it very carefully.

Working with Akiba

Akiba had a small adjoining room. He and Meta were of course supposed to work closely together. Sometimes they did the exact opposite. Still, communication channels had to be kept open. When they were not on speaking terms I was called in. "Please, tell Akiba that..." I would walk into Akiba's office, who was ready with his answer: "Tell Meta that..." If this went on too long I stood in the doorway tilting my head once to this side and once to the other, while they conferred in the third person. Even when talking they were not overly fond of each other. Especially Meta deplored often and audibly that someone as intelligent as Akiba read nothing but detective stories. I wondered how she knew and didn't tell her that I read a fair number of those books myself.

Meta was against my working overtime for Akiba. This had nothing to do with money as extra hours were not paid. Maybe she only wanted a just division of my time. But Akiba travelled a lot and when he came back he was busy seeing people. When I asked him to answer urgent letters, he would send me away, offering a cigarette as a consolation. I seldom smoked, as I found it an expensive habit and did not enjoy it much. On these occasions, when things began to calm down around four o'clock, and everybody went home, Akiba started to dictate. Mr Pelcman, the Hebrew secretary, would also vie for Akiba's attention; glad when it was finally my turn, I did not object.

Working late, one had to eat dinner at some time, and we occasionally went to a restaurant. There was nothing in our immediate neighbourhood, and as far as I know Akiba never walked anywhere, nor did I ever see him take the Métro. So we took a taxi. Taxis at that time in Paris went more or less where their drivers wanted to go, which was quite often either home or for a meal somewhere.

Riding with the OSE lady in a taxi to a government office, the cabbie had driven to a bistro, eaten his lunch, leaving us all the while in his cab, and only after he had finished, did he take us to our destination.

We rarely had difficulties getting a taxi to a restaurant. Getting back to work was harder as the office was in a residential area where the cab driver did not easily find another fare. So it happened a few times that Akiba decided that we would not go back to work but round the evening off with a visit to his favourite nightclub, with a belly dancer who was a grandmother and a soulful Russian balalaika player who confided in us but whose confidences I have forgotten. Since I was very fond of dancing, I got Akiba one night to dance with me there. Possibly the only time he ever did a thing like that.

After one of these occasions I was extremely tired the next morning and looked it. Mrs Flanter immediately jumped to the conclusion that I had been working all evening. She was incensed and went on and on about Akiba and how inconsiderate he was. I did not contradict her. She did not get on with Akiba too well anyhow, why spoil her fun? She would not have approved of the nightclub either.

It also happened once that Mrs Flanter stayed till late and the three of us worked till ten, in this case overtime was all right, and we went for a late dinner to a good restaurant but it was much too late and I was too tired to enjoy it.

My Boss, Meta

Meta was really very nice to Marlitt and me. She would invite us now and then to a movie or a play, but this could be quite embarrassing. Once at the movies she refused to give a tip to the usherette, because in Jerusalem one did not do so. The French girls, on the other hand, got no salary and were dependent on the tip. I had no money ready or none with me, as I had been invited. The usherette shone her light at us for some time and then gave up.

The movie was about a torrid love affair with most lights extinguished. Meta's French was not good, though mine had come back by that time, and her eyesight was not good enough for that kind of movie and she kept asking me: "What are they doing, what are they doing there?" Since sex had not been one of my educational subjects I was at a loss to explain and just mumbled something.

Meta, too, took trips, usually only to Switzerland. When she came back she would give me a list of her expenses which I had to type out, meticulously mentioning everything a body could spend money on. From tram fare to hotels and restaurants, from postage to coffee and cake, nothing was missing, and at the end there was always a small entry "and sundry". Sundry could only mean that either the sums never added up or that she had been to a public toilet and was too shy to mention it. As a lowly secretary, I did not question her.

Once she travelled to Switzerland together with Gärtner. She did some shopping for food and instant coffee which one could not get in France. Hans Gärtner, on the other hand, was high-minded and refused to buy anything, declaring haughtily that he would eat what the French people were eating. But he visited Meta quite regularly in her room after the trip and was not above eating the goodies she had brought.

Meta's hotel was naturally better than mine and she had a bath. I was persona grata there, the employees knew me and she let me use her room and bathe when she was away and also sometimes when she was in Paris.

She would phone regularly from abroad and when I answered, I asked politely: "How are you?"

This was a mistake because she told me exactly how she was. She told me how she had slept, awakened and what she had felt at the time. When she finally got down to business, I would be feeling slightly hysterical. On one occasion the reason she phoned was to ask me to send her some papers.

"You will have to go to the hotel", she said slowly, "but that is no problem as the porter knows you. When you are in my room go to the cupboard on the left side and open the door on the right. Now in the third drawer on the left at the back, underneath my underwear, you will find a green file. The papers I need are underneath that."

By that time I had difficulty keeping my composure. I looked around, saw one of the shlichim and told Meta that Chanan wanted to speak to her and, pressing the receiver into his hand, told him that Meta was on the line. Then I ran away to burst into unseemly laughter.

Life in Paris, Winter 1947/8

I had written to Marianne and Gert to dissolve my so-called household, to return the radio and get back the money already paid and send my personal things to Paris. They could keep my bed, my down duvet from Germany and the bed linen. I did not need my pots and pans but would like to retain my three teaspoons, the butter knife and my books as well as a few knick-knacks that had accumulated over the years in Sweden, and my drawings. I hoped that the money I still had there would be enough to cover costs and if anything was left over to send me *Alice in Wonderland* illustrated by Hoegfeldt.

Marianne and Gert faithfully did what I had asked, settled with my landlady, sent my things and in due time the box arrived. I received a chit of paper telling me where to go to collect it.

I set forth in a good mood, full of anticipation, and was astonished when the official told me I could not get the box.

"But it arrived!" I said pointing at the paper.

"Certainly!"

"So will you please release it?"

"Not just yet."

"Where is the box? It isn't here!"

"Yes it is. But the paper still needs to be stamped!"

"Can't you do that?"

"Yes, but not at the moment."

"Why?"

He finally realised what a fool he had in front of him and hissed at me, "You have to pay me!"

"Okay!" I said, taking out my purse. "How much?"

"Not here," he hissed again. "Go downstairs over there and wait for me next to the men's toilet!"

I did as I was told, feeling silly in front of the toilet door. When he came I gave him the amount he stipulated without bargaining. He counted the money hastily and finally I got my box.

II

Paris, so short a time after the war, was not a comfortable place but probably a lot better than some of the other countries in Europe. There was one strike after another. Sometimes it was the Métro which had two unions and whose strikes were not always synchronised. If only one union had called for a strike, police would be on the platform and push people into the trains that were still running so that the doors could be shut. The second union would usually join the first a few hours later.

Sometimes the buses were on strike, sometimes everything together. If the buses were on strike 'camions' (trucks) went around collecting people and taking them to work. Luckily I lived only half an hour's walk from the office and went on foot anyway.

When the dustmen were on strike, the streets were full of refuse. When the Post Office was on strike it made our life at the YA difficult. The trains might not be running. Even the museums were occasionally closed because the attendants were out on strike. It was like a crash course, a preparation for my later life in Israel.

Some food was rationed. Marlitt had coupons for milk left over from her little sisters and she let me have a few. Nothing was nice and orderly as it had been in Sweden.

I ate breakfast in my hotel room and made a cup of instant coffee, if I had any, from the hot water tap. We had lunch at the YA for a small sum, and I mostly went out for a meal after work. One could eat quite cheaply and I did, unless invited to dinner. At the end of the month I ate bread and cheese.

My salary at the YA was not bad, as the powers that were responsible took into account that most of us were living in hotels and eating in restaurants. I earned about as much as a worker with a family. No wonder they went on strike every few weeks.

That winter heating, too, was a problem and my hotel room was cold. But I had a fireplace and when Mrs Flanter gave me brochures about Palestine and Zionism I burnt them to warm my hands after perusing them fleetingly. Once I burnt a thriller that belonged to Akiba and told him so. He was standing up at the time and sat down abruptly, much surprised at my cheek. When in my room, I spent most of my time in bed. Quite often it was not only cold but dark too when there was a 'coupure' which meant that the electricity had been cut off. I went to the cinema, seeing some movies twice just to sit in a heated hall.

The office too was cold and I started to wear my long pants which were usually reserved for hiking and biking. Rousseau, one of our French colleagues, made a big fuss and promised that he would soon come to work in a skirt. Other people looked askance at me.

Pelcman's and my work sometimes overlapped. Once when we were working together he brought his very lovely lamb-fur vest for me to wear, probably because my clattering teeth were disturbing him.

Another time, not being bothered by the cold or a 'coupure', we were looking for sixty million French francs. As we could not find them, we went to the cinema. I don't remember if we ever found them, if somebody else did or they never really went missing.

Pelcman taught me Hebrew in our limited spare time. Marlitt quite often at the same time would sit with Meta and give her free French lessons. The difference between us being that I had to learn all the new words and Meta, being the boss, did not. Democracy – and how it works!

III

Paris that winter was sometimes bleak, but even with little money it was exciting. I walked for miles, I went to museums, I fell in love with the Ste. Chapelle. When I got half a month's salary as a bonus I bought a stylish Parisian winter coat. I went to see *Les Compagnons de la Chanson* and Edith Piaf; I saw and heard them a second time. I saw the Dutch ballet *The Round Table* which impressed me greatly. Diplomats dancing around the green round table negotiating and disagreeing. A war with men dying and women mourning, and at the end the same diplomats again dancing around the same table negotiating once more. I went to the theatre and saw Barrault in Kafka's *Process* and in a pantomime. I saw *Oedipe Roi* with Pierre Blanchard. I saw Louis Jouvet and other famous actors. I listened to concerts and took private sculpture lessons working from sketches I had made in Sweden. It was a whole new thrilling life.

The sculptress who taught me was a lady who lived in a big studio. The first time I rang the bell I was bidden to enter by an unembodied voice. I took one careful step after the other in a studio full of finished and unfinished sculptures and, looking here and there, saw no one. Suddenly something jumped on to my shoulder, I turned my head cautiously and there to my consternation sat a cat. I persuaded it to get down and a little later found my teacher. She had a bedroom one flight up and came down to greet me. Her grown daughter lived with her most of the time. The daughter died tragically a year later saving a child from drowning.

Falling in Love Again

Lea, who had been Akiba's and Meta's secretary before I came, had introduced me to my various duties prior to leaving for London to join her fiancé. Among other things she had given me some letters for Ernst Weil, sent to him by his mother in Chicago.

"Keep them and give them to him when he comes again. He is a very nice guy. If I were not engaged, I might fancy him myself."

I met Ernst Weil, gave him the letters and learned that his name was now Josef, at least in Palestine; that he was a friend of Akiba's and lived on the same kibbutz. He was a little taller than I, had blue eyes, dark hair, and a light complexion. He had lived in France for a while before the war and before he emigrated to Palestine. He could speak French, order a meal in a restaurant, loved French chansons, the theatre and paintings.

Josef was also one of the few Palestinian shlichim who didn't need a clothes brush, he always looked and was spruce and clean. He had been sent to France to raise money for the budding car repair shop of the kibbutz and do a few other things while he was in Europe. Josef was over thirty and divorced. I gave him his letters, he invited me to dinner and we got better acquainted.

I tried to persuade him to come and see my love, the Ste. Chapelle, but nothing came of it, because we had lunch first, drank a bottle of wine and went to the movies where we held hands. Somewhere along the line we fell in love.

Josef travelled around Europe doing odd jobs for the Yishuv and when in Paris and not busy raising funds for a lathe for the kibbutz, or buying spores for mushrooms, he hung around the office, waiting for me to finish work so we could go out together. Going out with him often took a lot of walking as he usually remembered a small restaurant with really good food which he wanted to take me to but could not always find immediately.

We went to 'Les Oubliettes', a former dungeon underground, where prisoners had been put without charge or trial and forgotten. There we would listen to old French and Canadian songs over a drink of wine or lemonade; no food was served. It was a family business and the whole family, dressed in folk costumes, sang, the father explaining where and when the songs had originated. Quite often everybody would join in the refrain. People were asked which region they came from and when the answer was: "From the South of France!" it meant that they were Arabs from North Africa.

While Josef was waiting for me in the office we sometimes asked for his help. Marlitt had to file the Hebrew correspondence, and it was difficult for her to know who had written and what the letters contained. We would both try and guess where to put them. Pelcman, sitting in another room, was very busy and not readily available.

We would give Josef a pile of those letters since he knew Hebrew and ask him to make notes as to what they were about. Josef would perform this task in an exemplary fashion with short and succinct remarks. When it came to some very long letters from Holland, he would consider them for a moment and then classify them as: "Nonsense!" and they would be filed as such.

When Josef went back to Eastern Europe I waited anxiously for his return. In Prague he came down with a bout of malaria and other Palestinians took care of him as the doctors there had no idea how to handle his fever attack.

Going through Austria the Russians took him off the train with his luggage. Lighting a cigarette while waiting he saw the Russian sitting at the desk eye his cigarettes hungrily and offered him one. The Russian took the whole package, whereupon Josef took his passport from the table, grabbed his suitcase and ran back to the train. Luckily it was not me because I would still be standing there.

When Josef had accomplished his missions he went back to Ma'ayan Zwi, and we wrote long letters to each other. I asked for a picture of him and received the smallest snapshot of a big Leyland truck with a miniature Josef standing next to it. With all the strikes going on I received some letters that started: I have not written, because your Post Office is on strike anyhow...

We eventually decided via letters that it would be a good idea if I came to the kibbutz to find out if I could live there, and if I couldn't but we decided to stay together, we would leave. I was no idealist, life on a kibbutz had no appeal for me and I made no secret of it. We were both divorced and were convinced that we had learned to be tolerant and understanding.

I gave notice at the office and immediately met with difficulties. Mrs Flanter was loath to let me go. An appropriate substitute had to be found. She rejected several applicants and told me she had to think of herself too, not feeling at all well. She appealed to my conscience as a Jew and a Zionist. I had not been sent from Palestine and supposed that if I had been found wanting, I would have been dismissed without much ado. Meta and Akiba travelled a lot, so quite often there was no one to even talk to.

It took months for Meta to find a suitable secretary, and when she finally did, I talked to Akiba who gave his blessing and wrote a letter to get me an early crossing to Palestine couching it in such terms that it sounded as if I was momentarily expecting a baby and had to be married immediately. I introduced the new secretary who had succeeded in getting Meta's approval, to the mysteries of the office and was free to go.

At the last minute I tried to give my travel iron, good for any kind of electricity, to Pelcman for his wife but he refused it, telling me that I would probably need it in Ma'ayan Zwi. I was nervous when Akiba brought me to the train, and when he offered me a cigarette I accepted.

I got on the train and duly arrived in Marseilles.

Part II
ALIYAH

Aliyah, February 1948

My big suitcase was on board ship. It was too heavy and no one man could lift it. Half of it was full of books which I could not bear to leave behind. This was against regulations. But Moshe, with whom I had become friendly, had, as promised, given a sign to let it go through to the guy who weighed the luggage at the camp.

Some of my clothes I had left for Marlitt, it was still difficult and expensive to buy them in France. But there was a new nightgown among my things, sewn and given to me by the dressmaker who worked for Youth Aliyah, as an early wedding present. There were no plans for a wedding yet. First I had to find out how kibbutz life would agree with me.

Now I was standing in line with the other passengers on the small Greek steamer that would bring us to Palestine. I had spent two weeks near Marseilles in a refugee camp. It was the beginning of February 1948. Palestine was not a healthy place, and war a certainty.

A lot had changed in the country since autumn. On the 29th of November the partition of Palestine had been decided upon by a majority of more than two thirds in the UN. Arab raids had become more frequent. In January, Kfar Szold and Yehiam in the Upper Galil had been under attack. The raids were repulsed. The situation was serious, but with youthful optimism I had decided to go.

More and more people boarded the ship, they were all emigrating with forged papers. Aliyah Daled – illegal Aliyah First Class.

The two weeks in the camp had not been arduous. I had arrived at the same time as a French girl, Tamar, who had been in the Maquis, the French underground. We were put in the same room and understood each other, not only because we could talk the same language but because we had survived the war without having fallen into the clutches of the Gestapo or having been in a concentration camp. Neither of us could conceive the anguish and fears or imagine the memories of those who had.

Tamar introduced me to camp life, showing me how to make sure my bed had no other inmates by brushing the mattress thoroughly. Men and women slept in the same rooms. In our room one couple occupied a big double bed; I never saw them get up and perform any of the daily tasks of ordinary living. They too had been in a concentration camp and on board the *Exodus* like many of the other people in the camp.

Much has been written about the *Exodus*, it was a ship carrying 4500 concentration camp survivors from France to Palestine. The ship was stopped and after a short battle boarded by the British. There were some casualties and the survivors were sent back to Sete, France, by the British and a month later returned to Germany by the French. Suddenly the world was shocked and perhaps the enormous impact of this caused the UN to vote for a Jewish state.

The refugees in the camp had usually arrived in groups and didn't know any French. They worked shifts in the kitchen. I sat in the office and answered the phone.

We were not allowed to visit Marseilles. Nobody wanted Jewish Displaced Persons to attract the attention of the British. The French knew that we were there and, for political reasons of their own, approved. The camp was run by English-speaking Jewish ex-soldiers; English, Scots, South Africans. They were the ones who could give us permission to leave the camp.

My English came in handy and a few times I was taken out by one or other of them for a walk or a dinner. We also played chess in the evening. When I had to have my picture taken I was allowed to go out on my own. It rained heavily that day, I got completely drenched, looked like a wet cat on the photograph and hurried gladly back to the camp without taking a second glance at the city.

Forty-three years later, in 1991, I visited Marseilles with my granddaughter, Maya, who was excited and moved to see the port from which her grandmother had set out on her own personal odyssey on the way to marry and start life anew. We had dinner together in a restaurant on the first floor overlooking what by then was just the old harbour. I barely recognised it, but nothing else.

Two families from Norrköping came to our camp with a small child each. They had been on the train continuously from Sweden and were exhausted. Especially the mothers. Knowing my way around I could help them a bit.

There had been some difficulty with my Swedish passport for aliens. I had sold my foreign valuta on the black market in France and had nothing to show the authorities. This did not faze Shula Arlosorov whose department this was. Another trip to Sweden and back to France was falsely stamped in my passport and there was no need to account for the missing money.

I got my passport back about half an hour before boarding the ship and at the same time became the mother of two Polish children, a girl named Besiah aged four and a boy aged five. They were not related to each other, had been hidden by Polish families and, having lost their parents, were on the way to Palestine where they might have relatives. On the whole they were quiet children. One of them had a small rucksack with a change of clothing and the other a very small suitcase. My practical experience with children this age was inadequate, in spite of my stint in a French vacation camp. There I had had helpful colleagues and my French had at least been sufficient.

I asked Shula Arlosorov how she expected me to take care of two small children who spoke only Polish when I did not know a word of the language. She turned on me and almost bit my head off.

"Everybody is doing their best, only you are being difficult. There are enough Polish passengers on board who will help you!"

Actually none of them did, but Shula had effectively stopped any further objections.

II

The queue moved slowly on and the kids became impatient and started to run around the office. They climbed on chairs trying to look out of a hatch. They could hardly fall into the water and seeing that they could come to no harm and did not yell, I left them to it. But the voice of officialdom cut into my thoughts:

"Whose children are these?"

I admitted parenthood and was told to call them and make them remain at my side. This presented my first problem. I had two oranges in the big bag that had been my mother's, and had taken the precaution to ask what an orange was called in Polish. The answer had been 'pomeranz'. Having seen the book *Roite Pomeranzen* when still at home, I had no trouble remembering that word. I now bent down and whispered into their ears: "Pomeranz, pomeranz!"

It worked like magic, both kids came and stood patiently next to me till our papers had been examined and approved, and each got an orange for their good behaviour. We found our narrow and stuffy cabin which we shared with a lady who was less than enthusiastic about her fellow travellers.

There was a young Dutch couple who had been given a little Polish girl to take with them. She was too young to talk or walk much. They used to sit on a blanket on deck and play with her, while I was rushing around after my charges, throwing envious glances at this picture of a happy, unhurried little family.

On the first day I asked one of the younger officers whether the boy could be shown around the ship. He asked who the boy was.

I firmly said: "He is my son!"

After some loud and hearty laughter he agreed to conduct a guided tour.

Besiah wet her bed every night and there were no fresh sheets. I had to dry the ones we had been given. She was also seasick in choppy weather, poor kid. That was the only time that an elderly man, probably in his fifties, one of the Polish emigrants, was willing to watch the boy as long as he would sit next to him without moving, while I rushed downstairs to clean up and comfort Besiah in our cabin.

Maybe the other refugees found me slightly ridiculous, worrying all the time about two small children who were not in any real danger after all the terrible suffering they had seen.

Among the passengers was an ex-navigator of the RAF who gave me a helping hand with the kids. Though neither of us could talk to them, they recognised superior force whenever Leon was around. Besiah never gave any trouble but the boy sometimes did. Not that I blamed him, he could not tell me what he wanted; I could not explain. He disliked the food we got, stamping his feet in protest. I too disliked the food but there was nothing else.

One morning the boy woke up with one side of his face all swollen. I took him to the ship's doctor who was French and not Greek. At least I could talk to him if not to the boy. Having met with stony stares before, I did not ask for help from the Polish emigrants. The doctor asked what was wrong with the child.

"The swelling hurts," I said.

What else could it be? He told me to keep him in bed and put hot compresses on his face. So I did, I rushed to the kitchen, where the crew, who were a friendly lot, obligingly saw to it that I always got sufficient hot water immediately. I kept running around, I could not tell the kids where I was going or when I would be back. Luckily, by the time we reached Haifa the boy was well again. I don't think he had the mumps, that would have taken longer. But who knows?

After I had tucked the kids in in the evening Leon and I would be in no hurry to go back to our small cabins. There was nothing to do, nothing to drink, nothing to eat in the evening. No lounge to sit in.

We were on a ship with concentration camp survivors and refugees numbed by the awfulness of their experiences and their apprehension about the future, a Greek crew and the dark and choppy sea all around us.

The second or third evening the purser, who was also bored, invited Leon and me for a cup of coffee to his cabin. We accepted with alacrity and sat with him sipping the strong, hot brew from small cups, trying to make conversation. We had no Greek, he knew nothing else. He knew, of course, that we were bound for Haifa, and probably also that all our visas were forgeries, but that was not what interested him. He tried to warn us by gesticulating wildly with his arms to convey to us the danger we were sailing into. We smiled and nodded our heads to indicate that we knew.

Looking back on those tense days, I doubt if we did.

When the purser saw that he could not convince us with Greek words or sign language he would yell loudly: "Haifa! Boom! Boom! Boom!"... and shake his head sadly at our stubbornness and stupidity.

He invited us again and again and the same conversation was repeated with similar words and gestures ending with a resounding "BOOM!"

Weather permitting, we would sit on deck for a while in the evening and talk about the war years, how we had escaped getting killed, why we were going to Palestine and of our private hopes and expectations. I spoke about my anxieties about coming to a strange country, a strange life to be with a man I had only known a short while. He told me about the girl he had left behind and his hopes of her soon coming to join him on the kibbutz.

When we duly arrived in Haifa, the ship lay at anchor outside the harbour and we remained on board, there had been shooting in the area and it was not safe to land. Next day we were taken ashore in small boats. We went through Customs. The inspection was very perfunctory, but I was deeply ashamed of having with me two small children who had nothing but a small rucksack and a small case, both almost empty; no toys, whereas I had that big fat suitcase with heavy books and some clothing. These were all my earthly possessions, but compared with the meagreness of theirs I was very rich indeed.

Leon and I said goodbye, I saw him only once more when he came to visit me in Ma'ayan.

During the Independence War some months later, his plane exploded and he was killed. He had been a warm-hearted human being who, having come unscathed through WWII, had decided to try and build a new world. He had planned to live quietly on a kibbutz, and like so many of our generation had had no wish to fight, but had been ready to do so for a better future.

A New Beginning

We had been forbidden to write to friends to let them know when we would arrive or the name of the ship. I was among the very few who followed this order, so Josef did not know that I was in Haifa. Some people were collected in the harbour by relatives. The others were driven in buses to Har Ha-Carmel and given lodgings. People were asked their destination and after a day or two sent on their way.

The kids, knowing that now they could do so, pronounced their surnames. I had been sure that they did not know them. They had been asked several times on board ship what their names were and never said more than their first name. They had been instructed very carefully.

When I was called to the office for the second time, I was given my bus ticket to Ma'ayan Zwi and told to leave at once.

"What about the children?" I asked.

"What children?"

I explained and said that I couldn't leave two small children on their own. The guy looked at me nonplussed. Finally he said: "Well, put them here in my office!" as if they were two parcels.

I did not have much choice and brought them to him. Later I heard that they were sent to Ra'anana and taken care of by Youth Aliyah.

I was taken with my luggage to the main Egged station downtown. There I was shown the bus to Ma'ayan. My suitcase was being loaded on to it at the rear, but as I tried to board I was told it was the wrong bus. I refused to be separated from my suitcase and said so to the guy who was loading the luggage.

There ensued a probably interesting, lengthy shouting match between the two men at either end of the bus. I did not understand a word and awaited the outcome anxiously.

The man in front won, and my suitcase was unloaded. I was grateful, but not for long, because when I turned around to take my bearings the bustling station that had been milling with all kinds of people minutes before had become as empty as a desert. All the buses had left and the people and their luggage with them.

There I stood, undecided what to do with a suitcase I could not move and with no idea when my bus, or for that matter any bus, would be coming. I went to make inquiries and was told to wait. I felt very lonely.

Eventually more buses arrived and I found mine. It was not a regular bus but an armoured one. And when it stopped twenty minutes later in the middle of what seemed to me to be nowhere, people jumped up from their seats, shouted, got all excited and tried to look out through the small slits that an armoured vehicle has.

Nothing happened, everyone calmed down and we drove on. The man sitting next to me, seeing that I was new and unused to people jumping about in a bus, asked me where I was going.

"Ma'ayan Zwi," I answered. "How long till we get there?"

"Oh!" he said, "not very long, there is a chaver from Ma'ayan sitting right in front. He will take you."

He called out to him in Hebrew and I was helped off the bus at the right station. My suitcase was deposited at my feet and Heini, the chaver from Ma'ayan, took one look at it and said:

"No one is going to take THAT. Leave it here!"

He told me to go to the dining hall, as there was a good chance that Josef would be having his tea at this hour and showed me the way. When I entered I saw him sitting at the very last table near the kitchen with his back to me. I walked through the whole dining hall steadily enough, thinking all the time: "I hope it's not his brother!" I had been told that he and his younger brother, Walter, looked almost alike. It wasn't. Josef got smartly to his feet when I addressed him. I had arrived.

Life on a Kibbutz

Ma'ayan Zwi is a beautiful place on the spur of Carmel Mountain. The air is good, the view beautiful, and that spring, outside the fence between the rocks and the grass, cyclamen and anemones grew in profusion.

There were few houses in Ma'ayan, most were for the children and all had gardens. The majority of the chaverim lived in cabins, built-up tents called mushrooms, concrete buildings, regular tents, and in summer in 'suckoth' made of leaves and reeds.

The wooden dining hall had a big lawn in front, and opposite the door stood a large tree and a bench where on summer evenings people who liked their comfort, or pregnant women, sat.

It had rained, everything was green and colourful, only the footpaths were muddy and one left one's shoes or rubber boots at the door. In the dining hall this often led to confusion. The rooms were cold, which I was used to, but most had a miniature kerosene cooker for boiling water and heating or, if one didn't mind pinching, baking a cake. It took some time for me to get used to the idea of taking margarine, eggs and flour from the kitchen for private consumption, and I was never very successful. Josef was quite reproachful:

"All the other women are baking cakes. Why don't you?"

People who wanted both warmth and company congregated in the kitchen in the evening where the big stove burnt till late. They quite often kidded each other and some horseplay took place. One evening, so the story goes, Yankel threw up one of his legs and the slipper he wore flew into the air and vanished from sight, to be found again two weeks later when they cleaned out the big kettle where the tea was brewed every day. Nobody had noticed any difference in its taste.

The cow shed and hen houses lay somewhat apart. The farmland, the fishponds, and the garage that belonged to Ma'ayan were on the plain on the opposite side of the highway.

Josef was rooming with two other members in a small concrete building at the edge of the kibbutz where, at night, one could hear the jackals howling. It could be used as a strong point for defence in times of need. From its window I could see the Mediterranean Sea behind the fishponds and the fields, the land down there belonged to farmers living in Zichron Yaakov, one of the older settlements in the country lying even higher than Ma'ayan on the mountain.

When I asked where I would stay he was astonished:
"Here, of course!"

Shloimele and Avraham moved out the same day. The room was only meant for two. Avraham had knocked at the door one night asking for asylum when his tent had collapsed during a heavy rainfall. They collected their belongings, a few from under the beds, and left. I don't know where they both went or how they felt about being dumped so unceremoniously. At that time it was the custom to put singles in married couples' rooms when no alternative could be found. They were called 'Primus'.

Next morning I woke up late and was reluctant to go to the dining hall for breakfast. This was noted in the kitchen and Minna, who had lived in France, been there during the war and had belonged to the Maquis, brought me breakfast. We talked a bit in French and German and then she went back to work.

When I unpacked and put my things away I discovered a silver handgun and two grenades in the cupboard which I left strictly alone. Having finished, I thought it might be a good idea to wash the floor. There was a water tap outside but I could find no pail or rag. I went to my next door neighbour's, Mrs Jakob, who lived in a wooden cabin about thirty metres distant to borrow suitable tools. She was the mother of one of the chaverim and at that time, in her sixties, still darned all the socks for the members of the kibbutz. She also knitted a pair of boots for every newborn baby and on Shabbath afternoons made coffee for all comers with an extra ration from the kitchen. After a few polite words, everyone silently read the papers at her house.

When I stated my errand she was amazed: "But it's not Friday!"

II

My future sister-in-law, Walter's wife, paid me a visit and asked my name.

"Gerda?! You can't keep that name here. There are already two on the kibbutz. One is stupid, the other is chutzpedick. What is your Jewish name?"

"Ruth!"

"Oh my God!" she said, "There are seven Ruths here and I am one of them. We can't have two in the same family. You better pick another name for yourself!"

I chose Dina and never regretted it. I had not liked Gerda much and nobody had ever called me Ruth.

It did not take me long to find out that everybody on the kibbutz called Josef 'Pampf'. He was not the only Josef in Ma'ayan and I got used to his nickname which he had earned for himself one way or another when still in Germany. I, too, proceeded to call him so.

I had come to the kibbutz in the firm belief that now my somewhat slapdash existence had come to an end and I would settle down to a serious life of labour, and love, of course. Soon I would be twenty-five. I was unsure how I would stand up to the work, the climate, the social life that went with a kibbutz, and having to speak yet another language, but was prepared to do my best.

Much to my surprise I was told that I would not have to work the first week. In retrospect it is obvious that the people who assigned the work didn't quite know what to do with me; they didn't want to send me to the kitchen to wash dishes for hours and there was not much else they thought me fit for. Josef was popular and nobody wanted me to leave right away and possibly take him with me.

During those first days Chava, a young mother, with her newborn baby had to be brought home from the Hadera hospital. This was a good opportunity to ferry rifles from one place to another. Mr Paster from Zichron with his taxi was recruited.

"Come along for the ride," Pampf said. "Just remember in case the British check us on the road, you are only hitch-hiking and don't know any of us."

That was almost true.

I had been given an identity card for Palestine together with my ticket in Haifa. At the same time, my Swedish passport had been taken away for further trips by other people. My identity card was stamped with the notice:

> Possession of this card in no way constitutes
> evidence of legal residence in Palestine.

It was just as well that no one stopped us.

III

The War of Independence had begun as soon as the UN Assembly decided in favour of a Jewish state. The British refused to collaborate and implement the UN resolution. There was chaos. I don't wish to give an account of the war, many people better informed have written about it and conditions in the country. With my feeble knowledge of Hebrew, I seldom knew what was really going on unless it happened in my immediate neighbourhood.

In 1948 it was not deemed necessary, and probably there were no funds, for new immigrants to have foreign language newspapers. Working for Youth Aliyah in Sweden and in France, I had known much more about Palestine than now living in the country. One was supposed to learn Hebrew quickly, although this was, to say the least, difficult on a kibbutz, where everyone spoke German and very few had the patience to talk slowly in Hebrew and wait for an answer. Neither Swedish nor French had been a real problem for me but I found learning a literate Hebrew difficult and time consuming. Then too, I discovered that some of the Hebrew spoken in Ma'ayan was very bad indeed and not fit for imitation. Lessons were sparse and given by untutored teachers who sometimes read the papers to the class more for their own information than ours.

In Sweden I had already decided that the cheapest way to read was in English, in France it was the same and so it proved in Palestine; pocketbooks were inexpensive and affordable. For better or worse, I adopted the English language.

That year it was decided that we could order one book a year but it had to be in Hebrew. Needless to say, neither the quantity nor the language appealed to me. Many others were not pleased with this arrangement and wherever I went I was asked if I had German books. I had, and lent them out. It never occurred to me that living in a community of earnest socialist idealists I would not get them back. I remained with Rilke's *Duineser Elegien*, *Faust* and *Trost bei Goethe*, which I had brought from home as consolation. All my other German books but one by Giono vanished.

I wrote to my cousin Walter in Haifa. He came and visited me at once in spite of the insecure roads and having to board an armoured bus. He brought the Hebrew dictionary I had asked for and some cash. There was still some of my parents' money left over. Walter had sent money to Bill in Cuba during the two years that Bill had been waiting there for his entrance visa to the States. With the rest of the money Walter had bought shares and Bill had written that the shares and anything else was mine.

We decided to leave the shares for an emergency and buy a radio with the cash. When Pampf had to go to Tel Aviv he took me with him. There was no question of going shopping from one store to another. One knew people who gave a discount to kibbutzniks and bargained on top of that. There were already a few radios in private possession in Ma'ayan and owning one was not against the rules of the kibbutz. The minute we came home it was bruited about that again Pampf had proved what a wonderful fellow he was. I had hardly arrived and right away he bought a radio for me. What pampering!

As Pampf had to attend to other matters in Tel Aviv, he suggested that I look around by myself. This was a somewhat limited stroll because he told me at the same time:

"Don't walk down this street too far, because the Arabs are sitting on the other side and don't go to your left, that's where the shooting comes from. Be careful!"

On the way back Pampf overtook a stationary bus on a hill when another car came towards us. Being an excellent driver and able to assess a situation in seconds, he went over to the far left so that the oncoming car passed between us and the bus and an accident was averted. Luckily the other driver didn't have the same idea and there was still a piece of road and no tree on that side.

IV

Many of the new chaverim in Ma'ayan came from Germany, but had been in Britain during the war. Walter, Ruth and their older son, Mikey, had been among the first to come from England two years earlier. Those who came in 1948 had mostly been sent to Cyprus by the British to cool their heels, till the State of Israel came into being. With them I studied Hebrew, learned how to hold a rifle, fall down with it at the ready, and throw hand grenades. There were not enough arms, and once six of us had rifles, and one of the girls had picked a bunch of flowers and stood at attention with it.

One day Uri, our instructor, was about to open a harmless grenade to show us how it worked, when suddenly he exclaimed: "Holy Moses, it's a live one!" and hastily put it together again.

I did my share of guard duty, sometimes sitting at the intercom and occasionally reading amusing poems in German to the other sentries to make the night pass faster.

There was a guard in every bunker and a man and a woman walked around the kibbutz together from one bunker to the other to see if everything was all right. Both carried loaded German or Italian rifles. The women usually got the Italian ones because they were much lighter. The men one did duty with came in all varieties. Some were pleasant to talk to. Some tried to make the woman's lot easier by walking part of the rounds by themselves.

"You stay here!" said Wolfgang one night to me. "I'll go up the hill to the last bunker and see if everything is okay. I'll be back in about five minutes."

He was, but in the meantime I almost jumped out of my boots when a cow mooed just behind me. I had had no idea that I was standing right next to the cow shed.

Werner S. was so little concerned with any possible danger that he sat on top of the bunker with the searchlight trained on himself reading a book. A perfect target.

A few of the men were unexpectedly afraid. There is, of course, no reason why all men should be fearless, but it gets awkward when one has to follow the lead of one who isn't.

Uri had told us not to walk along the barbed wire fence because if there were enemies about they could easily grab your legs and render you helpless. When one of my comrades in arms made a beeline for the fence I found this alarming. I had no choice but to tag along, I hardly knew where I was during the day and I certainly didn't know my way around at night. I strode behind him over rocks and plants and stumbled. The only thing I could grab was the barbed wire which cut into my hand. I started to curse loudly, something I could do nicely in several languages owing to my extensive education.

My colleague never even turned his head; I could have dropped dead and he would not have noticed. I complained to Pampf, who answered:

"Oh, him, don't pay any attention to him, he's scared!"

V

On the 15th of May the British Mandate ended and the State of Israel came into being. We were now Israelis and the Arabs had become the Palestinians. A machine gun was mounted on our abode with a guard sitting on top, watching during the day. A few times when I was sick he would come down and sit with me instead of the machine gun. Levy had been sent to Holland from Germany as a child and had thus survived.

Pampf was in charge of the defence of the kibbutz and we had an intercom in our room. Several times he was called in the middle of the night. He was a very light sleeper and when once he heard a shot he was wide awake instantly and could answer the chaver who called up to say:

"I heard a funny noise in the bushes, should I shoot?"

"You already did!"

Another night he was called to come without delay as Max, a Berliner who had arrived from England via Cyprus, had disappeared. He had not called in from any of the bunkers, he was not answering from the one where he was supposed to be. Pampf got up and went to the office, but reluctant to wake people and send out a patrol at once, turned on the whole switchboard first. Listening carefully he could discern Max's Berlin accent quite clearly from one of the bunkers:

"Where in hell is the damned entrance?"

I was not the only one blundering about in the dark.

VI

I would have liked to go to Haifa and visit my cousin Walter. But Pampf, being responsible for the lives of the people in Ma'ayan had to give his permission and he refused to let me go. The road to Haifa was not safe. Not much was!

With independence of the State, members of the kibbutz were called up for military service and courses. Pampf was sent to Tel Litwinski to complete a course for defence and Haim Friedman was his deputy. Communication in the country hardly existed, and whenever Haim heard something he would come to me in the dining hall and whisper in my ear that Pampf was all right. He also gave me permission to go to Haifa.

I asked around if anybody was going into town next morning; there was a truck and sitting between Eli H. and Haim Massad, both with revolvers but neither impressing me as great fighters, we made our way through Wadi Milik. I saw my cousin in his law office and he invited me to lunch which was a nice change from the wooden benches, tin or plastic plates and one knife for six people of the kibbutz. I looked around town where it was quite safe and later found my way back to the truck at the appointed time. The way home, too, much to my relief, was without incident.

Tel Litwinski was bombed and the washroom hit while many men were taking a shower. While there had been disorder before, there was greater confusion after the bombing and Pampf used the muddle to come home, telling me:

"If they really want me they know where to find me!"

Regional and national interests at that time often clashed and Pampf was given a hint to stay put so he would remain on the kibbutz. Chances were that if he went back and finished the course he would then be sent to some other location.

VII

One Saturday morning Pampf and Avri had to take a compressor to a kibbutz in the Emek. I went along to see more of the country. When we got there a plane suddenly appeared overhead, the alarm sounded and we all jumped into an open trench. Remembering the German Stukkas exercising in the outskirts of Berlin during World War II, the noise they made while diving and the fear I had felt, I could not take this plane quite seriously. Illogically I had always been more afraid of the German Stukkas than during a real so-called enemy air raid. Even so, as soon as the plane left and our business was finished we drove away without further ado; we did not wish to be caught by the next plane and stuck in a ditch.

We were driving in an English Standard tender, freshly overhauled and painted in grey with the steering on the right side. On the way back Pampf took on a hitchhiker with a small barrel of black paint. I was sitting on the left side in front, Avri and the hitchhiker were sitting behind me, also on the left.

The road was almost empty. Suddenly, at a turning which had been hacked into the hill, we were confronted by an armoured truck which was cutting the corner. The driver did not see us. Pampf steered our car as far to the right as he could without crashing into the rock but the truck did not change its direction. It is an uncanny feeling to watch a heavy armoured truck with two too small windows rolling inexorably at you. There was no time to yell. The truck struck us on the side, taking off the handle of my door, bumping Avri slightly in the back and hitting the hitchhiker more severely. The barrel of paint overturned, leaving black pools on the floor of the newly renovated car.

By now the driver of the truck had realised that he was not alone on the road and had stopped. I got out and sat down with wobbly legs at the edge of the road trying to recover from the shock. Pampf first assured himself of my well-being and then convinced the truck driver to take the hitchhiker together with his paint to a hospital. It seemed to be a heated argument but then all discussions in Hebrew at that time sounded stormy to my ears. Avri came over to see how I was adjusting to life in the Holy Land.

Much as I wanted a quiet life I did not seem able to attract it.

VIII

When I had arrived, Pampf, never one to embellish a situation had told me:

"It looks very bad for us, but the main thing is that you are here now!"

However there was a host of other problems.

The difference between living in Europe and Palestine was extreme. Museums and bookstores, bright lights, theatres and concerts had been part of my daily life, especially in Paris. Culture shock was not talked about and was surely one of the lesser difficulties that beset a country at war where many people suffered from it, more or less.

I had started work in the garden around the dining hall but after a few days was sent down to the fields to do whatever needed to be done. One day I was told to help Moishe F. who was already out ploughing with a mule.

"You go down, then straight till you see the woods and turn left. There you will find Moishe and Egon, the mule."

This proved to be difficult as I saw no woods. There were some eucalyptus trees that neither in Sweden nor in France would have rated such a title.

When I finally found them Moishe gave me the reins and told me:

"Lead Egon along the furrow to the end of the field and walk back in the next furrow. I'll handle the plough."

Willing but inexperienced I walked on the wrong side of Egon and he stepped daintily on my foot when we turned. My heavy boot saved it from being crushed.

I planted bananas with Max and we saw that all the plants but one stood nicely in a row. He looked askance at it and commented in his thick Berlin accent:

"That one must have been run into by an earthworm!"

We had neglected blackberry plants that had to be separated runner by runner. I was sent to do this. It involved dragging and pulling the stems, and when the runner could not be dragged any further, one cut it off to wind it around the wires that had been put up for this purpose. The second day I received help, a boy from the Romanian Youth Aliyah group. I explained what we were supposed to do. We worked quietly for some time and then I went over to look at his work. He had advanced quickly, mainly because he had been merrily cutting off both ends.

"How do you think this stuff is going to grow?" I asked him.

He had no answer. It made no difference to the outcome, our work was not commercially profitable in any way. Some people made wine with the berries that eventually grew there and drank it.

Later in the year while four of us were harvesting cucumbers, an Egyptian plane flying very low surprised us and we threw ourselves into the prickly plants. The plane was on its way to the Zichron Yaakov Railway Station on the plain not far from our fields and the garage, and Friedl, who worked there, went out into the yard and shot at it with a rifle. The plane departed, although I don't think it was the shooting that frightened it off. The pilot may have felt that he was too far from home.

My years in Germany had left their mark in more ways than one. I was underweight and anaemic and agriculture did not agree with me. The doctor ordered additional food. I got a lumpy vanilla custard with my lunch every day, which I gave to Dolfi who was usually sitting at the same table in the dining hall in the yard near the garage. Dolfi was always hungry and even as a toddler had had such a good appetite that his grandmother and his mother had to feed him together, alternately putting a spoon into his mouth, or else he would yell between mouthfuls. Neither of us gained an ounce.

Then one day I struck it lucky. There was no work in the vegetable garden and Dvorah, my colleague, and I, loath to deliver ourselves up into the kitchen, went to the garage and the yard to ask for work. In the garage there were screws to sort and other labours to perform. I liked being out of the sun and handling metal again. Every evening I would ask Avri, who was the manager, if they had work for me. Slowly I made a place for myself in the workshop and in the seven years that I worked there I advanced from lowly diesel part cleaning to grinding valves, teaching apprentices and finally being in charge of the stock and the tools and at the end of my career doing the accounts and calculating the wages for those mechanics who were not members of the kibbutz.

By the time Avri resigned from his post as manager and Pampf took his place, I had already worked in the garage for some months and he, of course, knowing that I preferred work in the garage to anything else on offer and seeing that I did my work well, let me stay on.

IX

I had no trouble making friends and got on very well with the people who had just come from England and of course Minna. We had had common experiences. To make friends or be accepted among the older members was more difficult, they had been on the kibbutz all through the Second World War, and though rightfully proud of their achievements under difficult conditions, the more prejudiced among them didn't believe that other people might have worked as hard and experienced privations too.

They seemed to ask:

"When everybody slept in tents and people had malaria and typhoid and nothing to eat, where were you?"

X

In a small community people constantly talk about each other.

When one of the women went to Ra'anana I thoughtlessly remarked to her, "What a pity I didn't know, I could have sent some chocolate to my children," meaning the kids I had brought into the country.

I immediately became an awful mother, who had sent her kids to Ra'anana instead of having them with her.

Having committed the ultimate crime as a newcomer of taking away one of the best looking and most eligible bachelors in Ma'ayan, there were other more direct remarks:

"We were so curious about what kind of a girl Pampf had brought home this time!" And: "You have probably never ever really worked before, right?"

What did they think I had done? Fallen out of a tree? Received a pension?

Chary of criticising the kibbutz openly so soon after my arrival, I was considered by some naive, and possibly stupid. I liked everything, or so it seemed. Unless directly addressed I was blissfully unaware of rumours and undercurrents at first. In time I learned to distinguish between those to be taken seriously and those to be disregarded.

I was in love, I was happy, and for the first time in my life I planted a garden. It gave me the greatest pleasure to see the flowers grow and bloom.

I was young and adaptable and Pampf helped me wherever he could.

XI

When the women were called up after work to clean chickens or fish which had been condemned to death just before they were about to give up life anyhow, Pampf always offered to go in my stead and naturally I did not object. I got so used to not cleaning dead fish, that years later after we left the kibbutz, when Motke, our friend, former neighbour and colleague, brought fish from Ma'ayan for the holidays, he too cleaned them for me.

Weddings

When it had been certain that I would go to Palestine I had written to Bill who had expected me to join him in the States. He had postponed his marriage so that his affidavit as my brother without a family to support would have more weight. Now, though disappointed, he and Shirley, his fiancée, set the date for their wedding.

Bill had asked me to send one piece of the jewellery which I had collected in Switzerland for his future wife, one that our mother had worn and which he might remember. There was a pearl necklace of intricate design and a beautiful pendant with a big aquamarine and small diamonds fashioned like a dew drop. My mother had worn these often together and I hoped that Bill might recognise them. I had liked the pendant too and had worn it occasionally in Paris on a gold chain.

When I heard that one of my acquaintances was on his way to New York, I asked him to take the jewels and give them to Herbert Strauss who now lived there. Herbert would send them on to Bill in Milwaukee.

"How do you know I'll deliver?" the man asked.

The question surprised me. All my friends thought well of him and although I had not known him long it had not occurred to me that he might not be honest and reliable, and keep an heirloom. Indeed I had picked the right man for the job and the jewels reached my brother fairly soon.

I may not have picked the right jewels though. Most of the time they have been in a safe and when the string of pearls broke Shirley and Bill had a hard time having it restrung and it was very expensive. Only rarely has Shirley's conscience, or my brother, allowed her to wear it.

II

Pampf and I decided to get married too. Our life together was working out. We had interests in common and on many important issues thought alike. Pampf had come to Palestine as a convinced Zionist who never doubted that the kibbutz was a just and socially useful unit, necessary to build up the land. He wholeheartedly believed that this country which he loved was rightfully ours, knowing that many of the Palestinian Arabs were latecomers to the country who had come because with the immigration of the Jews there was work to be had.

I was no idealist, had no natural leanings that way and there had been no suitable time to develop in that direction. But I could see other people's point of view and so could he.

Pampf's vision did not make him either starry eyed or narrow minded, and he never talked about good or bad 'human material' a term quite fashionable among the hardcore Zionists of that time which is still used even today. The idea behind this phrase gave me the creeps and I came to detest it together with the people who used these words. My tolerance of other people and their beliefs was not without exceptions.

Pampf had a sense of humour and had over the years become more patient; he had also, I was told, given up the habit of saying: "You want to bet?" about almost any subject under the sun, for which he had been famous in Ma'ayan.

The kibbutz was interested in having several weddings together because it was cheaper. Minna and Kulle, our locksmith, also decided to get married and we all liked the idea of having the ceremony on the same day. We chose a day in June. There was another couple eager to marry but the bride-to-be was so visibly pregnant, that they did not wish to postpone their wedding even by two weeks and wait for us.

In the meantime I was in trouble with the rabbinical law. My marriage to Joachim in Berlin had been legally binding according to Jewish law because two Jewish males, our fathers, had been present. My divorce by a Swedish court was not according to Halachah. The rabbi wanted to consult with two colleagues. I was told to translate the Swedish divorce document which was eight pages long. Before we left the rabbi turned to Pampf and asked him:

"Do you believe her?"

Pampf answered with a firm "Yes!" but remarked later laughingly: "What else could I say? You were sitting next to me!"

I shortened the eight pages considerably. The three rabbis conferred and decided in our favour. I became a 'genitzte Kalle' worth only half the marriage price as written down in the Ketuba, the marriage contract. I was worth fifty pounds, Minna a hundred.

The great day dawned and I went to the Mikweh, the ritual bath. Minna, who could not go that day, sent a substitute and went to work in her stead in the kitchen. Leni was very nervous and kept telling me to be quicker in case the rabbi came and saw us. I did not think that this was one of his tasks and we had our bath complete with dunking and nail cutting under the supervision of a woman only.

In my room again, I took out my light beige dress, which when bought at a sale in Stockholm had had a lot of decorations. I had taken them off immediately. The dress looked suitable for my wedding. Minutes later Ruth appeared.

"What are you going to wear?" she cried.

I showed her the dress.

"Oh no! Give it to me, I'll wash and iron it and get you a suitable veil."

Minna had been promised an heirloom veil from a Dutch lady; I got married with plain mosquito net. Ruth arranged our dresses, hair and veils and told us not to move till we were called. Being nervous, the second she left we both lifted our veils and lit cigarettes.

As is the custom we walked around our newly acquired spouses several times. We should have been accompanied by two female relatives. I had only one, Ruth, who caught at my dress and muttered into my ear: "Don't run, I can't keep pace with you!"

The other young woman who walked with me had longer legs and did not complain.

After the ceremony we went home with a fried chicken, our wedding present from the kibbutz. It was said that a kibbutznik got to eat chicken if either he or the chicken was sick. Weddings were an exception. We proceeded to eat it without delay, eyed hungrily by Pampf's little nephew, Joshki, who had come with us and got to lick the bones.

Since there was more space around our house than at Minna's and Kulle's we had decided to have the reception, such as it was, at our house for the four of us. We invited some people for the afternoon. Minna, who had worked with the Romanian Youth Aliyah group, had invited the whole crowd. The real festivities would be later in the dining hall for everybody.

Conditions in the country were unfavourable for making trips and no guests from other places were expected. While we were pouring out juice and offering cookies, a swarm of Minna's relatives suddenly arrived and after a short conversation Minna took them to her room and vanished for the afternoon leaving me stranded with all the guests she had invited.

I don't remember much about the evening's entertainment, probably because I didn't understand it. On a kibbutz one married on a Friday and got Saturday off. My second honeymoon was even shorter than the first.

III

Pampf had been a bachelor for some years now, I too had been on my own and done as I pleased. Saturday mornings we would breakfast early together although I would have preferred to sleep longer. In the afternoon and now and then in the evening our paths diverged. I sat in the tents of the English chaverim where people talked and Pampf read the papers at Mrs Jakob's where silence reigned.

During the week Pampf would spend evenings in discussions about the next day's work, which cars and trucks had to be repaired and which cars would be available. I would read plays in English with a group or go with some chaverim to Zichron to take drawing lessons with an English painter.

Miss Violet Zitron was a nice lady but not a teacher. Her own paintings were lively and colourful and although we did not learn much we were at least sketching, a change from the humdrum life on the kibbutz. We would bring cookies and tea which Miss Violet would prepare for us and once, as an extra, she made us a Sandtorte that really tasted like sand. If we found a victim we would bring a model. Since Kulle was among the painters, Minna would occasionally come with us. Sometimes when we had no model, Miss Violet would sit on a chair put her right hand over her left and say: "What would you like to sketch? Perhaps my hands?" Or do the same with her feet and say: "Perhaps my feet?"

IV

Neither Pampf nor I had any great ambitions: we wanted to live our life together decently, if possible in peace, and have a family. I was not disturbed by the fact that our house was exceedingly small, that it was sparsely furnished, or that we had no money.

All the same I resented suddenly having to ask for things I needed, like a pair of socks, with every chance of getting a

"No" for an answer because it was not "my turn"; or if they were available some other woman would get them to prevent an asthma attack.

A small item like that had never been a problem before. I had bought what I needed within reason, juggling my money around or as in Sweden working at two jobs. The kibbutz didn't give one either of these opportunities and I found the constant reminder that others made decisions about my life stifling and not very reassuring.

When I was given two odd sandals for work in the vegetable garden and remarked that my feet happened to be the same size I was told:

"You act as if you were paying for them. Have you seen the dentist yet?"

This question had nothing to do with my well-being. The dentist himself was not sure how to act when a filling fell out and it had to be replaced. He did it the cheapest way, to the detriment of my teeth. But when he found out that I was Pampf's wife, he changed his tune as well as the treatment.

"Do you need something for the summer?" I was asked.

"No, thank you!"

"Well, you haven't been here long enough to get anything."

Ille, my friend from Berlin, invited me to her home in Rehovot, where she now lived. Her mother had died and I visited her and her father with his second wife. Ille gave me material for a new summer skirt as a present. I also bought a cheap dress with the money I had left over from the radio. In Sweden I had not needed many summer dresses and most of my time in France had been spent during the colder season. It didn't occur to me to try and get what I could from the kibbutz.

V

Every woman had to do night duty for a week, watching over all the children, including about eighteen babies. I refused. I was not going to be responsible with no one else around, feeding babies at night when I had never even held one in my arms.

During the day the baby house was off limits to all, mothers being an exception, but even they were eyed warily as a disturbance. At night any female could take care of all the kids. My refusal did not make me popular but there was nothing anybody could do.

Several of the young women who did guard duty at night without having children of their own ran into trouble. One of them heard a baby cry at the end of a week's watching and found to her astonishment that there was one more room in the baby house than had been shown her and for the whole week she had never gone near it.

When finally Nava was born after long and exhausting treatments I had one more thing to gripe about. I was less than enthusiastic about kibbutz childcare.

VI

Nava was a lively child, pretty and with a strong voice. Any new worker in the baby house would be given Nava, who smiled at people especially if they gave her food. If she cried, chances were that this new person would not be given another child to hold, bathe or feed. I did not like this arrangement.

When Nava was only a few months old I arrived one winter morning tired and cold at the baby house to nurse only to find her fast asleep. The chavera who had watched over the children had filled her up with sugar water instead of waking me. The young woman had had no experience with babies and nobody had told her the ins and outs of babycare. I suppressed my anger, I thought it unfair to reproach her, she had watched over the babies all night. Years later I met her in a concert and she recalled the incident, thanking me laughingly for not having bawled her out. She had seen on my face how difficult this had been for me and had appreciated it.

Then one of the mother's asked me not to turn the lights on when nursing in the evening, no one else was feeding their baby at the time and it disturbed her daughter. I was furious. I went to the dining hall to look for Pampf and told him that I would neither sit in the dark, nor start a quarrel in the baby house. He agreed with me immediately, called Walter and together they brought the cot to our humble abode the same night. We took our baby home, and I cared for her myself. I had to go to work, though, for a few hours every day; then Nava was alone and asleep till I raced home to her. It was not ideal but in the baby house too, the children were alone for several hours every day. An indignant nurse tried to convince me to bring Nava back. But only when I had stopped nursing, had to work longer hours, and a new wing was added to the baby house, did we return our daughter.

A great to-do was always made when personnel in the children's houses was changed and long discussions about the probable damage to the little psyches ensued. But when Nava and Arnon, who was a few days older, were moved to another children's group because of their age, their nurse took each under one arm and right away placed them in a different environment with strange playmates and left them there. Tirza, Arnon's mother, and I didn't really think it would hurt them and made no fuss. Both kids were quite tough characters and they got one of the nicest nurses on the kibbutz. But it was one more inconsistency in kibbutz life.

Lea and Benjamin Seelig's son, David, was in the new group too. Benjamin, whose name in Europe had been Klaus, had been together with Bill and me in the Florence Landschulheim. He had one day crossed my path in Ma'ayan and I had recognised him immediately. We had talked about old times and now, the difference of a few years no longer important, became friendly. When Benjamin married Lea and she came to live on the kibbutz we became good friends. Lea and I had much in common. We had married into the kibbutz, we had previously worked and earned our own money to do with as we liked. We both believed that children should be cared for by their mothers. Quite naturally we had gravitated towards each other. And when later both our firstborn belonged to the same children's group we spent even more time together. Benjamin often took David and Nava for a walk and gave them tea afterwards. Having finished two glasses of tea with sugar, Nava declared once when asked if she wanted a third glass:

"No, thank you, I don't like it!"

Occasionally Nava would call Benjamin 'abba' – daddy – much to our amusement.

Ilana too I had met for the first time by chance with a friend in the streets of Uppsala, in Sweden, where she worked at the time. She came to Ma'ayan because her sister lived there. Ilana was more of an idealist than either Lea or I and when she and Menahem, her husband, eventually left the kibbutz it was because he wanted to try his hand as an independent farmer.

Ilana and I tried to read a book in Hebrew which I at least never finished. Not only was it in Hebrew but it was also boring. Ilana and Menahem were sent to England as delegates for two years and I doubt if Ilana finished the book either.

A Journey to the United States

When Nava was two and a half, in the summer of 1954, Pampf's youngest brother, Jack, invited us to Chicago where he lived with his wife and his mother in the same house but in different apartments. We travelled on the old SS *Jerusalem* which creaked a lot, as originally it had not been built for passengers: twenty-one days to New York and nineteen days back. The ship went to Greece, and stopped at Ceuta, Africa, where we were permitted to visit the town and look around. Since everything was closed there was not much to see. We found a small coffee house and ordered some coffee. A few of the Israelis insisted on milk with theirs and after a long argument got goat's milk, which made it undrinkable.

When we landed in Canada, Israelis were not allowed to go on land which we would have liked to do after the ocean crossing. Finally, we arrived in New York where it took hours to get off the boat as all the Israelis on board were screened very carefully.

We stayed at a cousin's house on Long Island before going on to Chicago. I was just bathing Nava when a strange man with a familiar face entered. My brother, longed for and worried about for sixteen years, suddenly stood before me in the flesh. I got up hurriedly and we hugged and kissed. My feelings were not easy to describe. First of all I was happy but then I was also anxious, the last time we had been together we had been children. In the meantime our lives had been so different and still were. Now that we were married and our loyalties had changed would we go on understanding each other? Would the four of us get along? And I heard my father admonishing me as he had done time and again:

"When you and Bill are married and together again, see to it that there will be no quarrel in the family!"

I needn't have worried, there has never been any difficulty.

Jack and Bill had arrived by car and we drove all together back to Chicago. Bill then went on to Milwaukee. They confided separately that although Jack was really a nice guy he was always in a hurry, and that Bill, though nice too, wanted to stop for coffee every half hour.

Jack and his wife Paula had adopted a little girl, Nina, and now Paula was pregnant with Brian, who was born while we were there.

Nava took well to private life. She enjoyed the special attention and being together with us. She stopped wetting her bed, refused to wear her old-fashioned and too short dresses from the kibbutz and explained, luckily in Hebrew, that she would not play with the neighbour's child as she was too dirty. Nava spurned most of the many sweets that friends brought. The cupboard was soon glutted with these treats and I had to go out and buy carrots, spinach and olives for my daughter's delectation.

In Milwaukee we stayed with Shirley and Bill who then had two children, Bruce, aged two, and baby Elliot. Nava played with Bruce or quarrelled with him as the mood would strike them without any language difficulties.

We went dancing one night and Shirley left her good dress in the bathroom when we returned. She did not want to disturb the children by putting it in the closet in their room. Next morning she woke just in time to prevent the children, totally united at the time, from dunking her evening gown in the toilet.

II

On hot days Shirley put a plastic pool in the backyard for the kids. Nava, who had never possessed a bathing suit, took off her panties before stepping into the water. Bruce imitated her with pleasure.

Shirley got excited:

"They can't do that here! It's forbidden to bathe naked outside! What are the neighbours going to say?"

We all laughed at her, the kids were not yet three years old. But she was right. A policeman called within the hour and it fell to Shirley's lot to talk to him.

"You see, Mrs Berton," he said, "the neighbours can see into your yard and have filed a complaint. And, of course, we have to follow that up. I'm sorry but the kids have to get dressed. It's against the law to run around naked at any age."

Shirley was quite contrite:

"It won't happen again, officer!"

Bill, Pampf and I sat in the kitchen grinning, not believing what we heard through the open door.

"I told you so!" Shirley cried. "I told you so! I've never been so embarrassed in my whole life!"

III

We remained in the States for three months. Jack may have hoped that his brother would stay, but neither Pampf nor I had any wish to live there.

Life was too different. We were Israelis. I had a hard time coming to grips with people throwing out perfectly good food because it had been bought a week earlier. I had been very hungry during WWII and had met many people who had starved during that time; my parents had starved in Theresienstadt. Even now food was not plentiful in Israel. And food cost money.

Neither could I comprehend that a woman would buy eight pairs of black shoes in one afternoon, and all her friends would exclaim understandingly:

"Oh, well, she has always been a bit like that and she is pregnant after all."

I was pregnant myself by then and trying to keep it from my mother-in-law, who would have fussed. But even had I told the world and had had the money to boot, I doubt if buying a row of black shoes would have occurred to me or would have been one of my most urgent desires.

Listening to the young women around me I felt not only an outsider but from another planet. I had felt an outsider in the kibbutz too, but at least with a chance of making understanding friends.

Before moving into our cabin on the ever-groaning *Jerusalem*, with the walls this time decorated by our fellow travellers with long fat sausages, I got a three-day vacation from my family. I spent it in New York all on my own and Pampf and Nava remained with my mother-in-law in Chicago. I went to see the Modern Museum, the UN buildings and walked the streets in places that looked safe to me. My hotel was near Times Square and I hadn't lost my feeling for big cities and crummy neighbourhoods.

IV

I met Benno in New York. He had lived in Ma'ayan, where his brother was a member, with his Polish wife and son for two years. She had hidden him during the war and saved his life. We had a great evening talking over old times and news from Ma'ayan where we had worked for half a year together with Yael in the kitchen, on the same fast wavelength.

Our understanding had been that we would never have to clean the huge pots and pans. He would never have to wash the floors, neither would he tell us any of the vulgar jokes from his abundant collection. I had over the years gotten used to people telling me mildly dirty ones but his were in an entirely different category.

He would pile up the big pots with water melons, oranges or other foods and then save us from lifting them by lying in wait for the men when they came home from work and asking them to carry the big containers with him into the kitchen.

"Come on," he would say, "help me bring these in. It'll only take a minute, we can't have the women carry these loads!"

Some made long faces but most lent a willing hand.

We had been working so fast that when the help that we got for three hours in the evening once did not arrive, we finished almost as usual. Then seeing this could be a good thing, we got no help for several evenings in a row. We were told that there was nobody. As far as I was concerned this was not sharing everything alike – the motto of kibbutz life.

I sought out the woman who was responsible for the women's work roster. "That's really not my affair, the men have to send someone," she said. I found the chaver whose job it was to prepare the next day's work list.

"Look," I said, "we need a fourth to do the dishes! We have been working overtime for some days now!"

"Sorry, everyone has finished working, there is no one."

"Okay!" I said. "We'll wait ten minutes, and if nobody comes I am closing the kitchen!"

The answer, I thought, was typical of kibbutz-induced thinking.

"Go ahead, I have already eaten."

This incensed me even more. We put the food in the dining hall, locked the hatches and waited. I apologised to Ruth who was serving at the tables. She took it in good spirits:

"You are quite right!" she said.

The three of us were anxious to see if anybody would come. It had probably never occurred to Yael that one could strike on a kibbutz. Benno was not even a member but a working guest on the way to the US and his mother. I was not a member either though I don't think anybody knew that. I was just uneasy that Pampf would not be pleased with me. As it turned out I had underestimated him, he not only thought that we were justified he was even proud of me.

When nobody appeared we went home. At four o'clock next morning there were two people, apart from the morning shift, washing all the remaining dishes and we were never left without help again.

Back in Ma'ayan

Rona was born in March 1955 and showed early signs of jealousy and determination. Every third Saturday I worked in the baby house as I had done when Nava was an infant, taking care of her and five others in the morning and from midday till the parents took them home in the afternoon. Rona cried as soon as I went near any other baby. I had to feed my daughter, change her diapers and put her on the porch so that she could not watch me. I asked to be relieved of my duty and get a different task. This was denied till the baby nurse in the next room declared to the woman who assigned the Shabbath chores:

"Look, I can't do my job listening to Rona's crying. How do you expect the mother to work?"

I did not see my children a lot. Rona at the most for two hours in the afternoon. She was not like Nava who liked her food and did not care who gave it to her. So now I usually looked to see if Rona's regular nurse was working or if it was somebody else, in which case I would go to the baby house early and feed her myself before going to work in the garage. Then I knew she had eaten at least one meal properly and would be less grumpy in the afternoon when I took her home.

When Rona became a toddler she continued to cry angrily when she wanted anything so that the new nurse gave her food and dry clothes before all the others. As soon as she could crawl, any time Nava came near me Rona would leave whatever she was doing to demand my care and attention, so that Nava sometimes proclaimed:

"I'll visit the neighbours till you've put HER to bed!"

We were good friends with our neighbours, Kurt and Friedchen, even after Nava picked some of their flowers. Kurt took Nava by the hand, pointed at the flower beds and asked;
"Who planted these?"
"You did!"
"Who is watering them?"
"You do!"
"And to whom do they belong?"
True to a socialist education perfectly understood, the answer was:
"To the whole kibbutz!"

II

Of course, not everything on the kibbutz was bad. If husband or wife were sick either one could stay in bed, get the food brought to the room by the sick service and let other people worry about where the money would come from or who would do the necessary work. In any case the family would be taken care of.

From spring to autumn the kibbutz management would take a house in Nahariah and three couples could stay there together for a week's vacation. One chose the friends one wanted to be with and a plan was made up for the season. A truck would bring us to Nahariah and, conveying the next shift, take us home again. We would get provisions from the kitchen, chickens from the hen house and fish from the ponds. We had to cook and do the dishes but the men helped with both and doing dishes for six people, after being accustomed to doing them for several hours, was not much of a job. And we had fun.

We usually sold the carp from our ponds at the nearest grocery and got other food that we preferred. The house was near the beach and we went swimming, in the evenings we went to the movies or ate ice cream and played table tennis in a nearby restaurant.

On one occasion we were given three live cocks who woke us up at four in the morning. This was not what we had come for, so in the evening Pampf gave them some beer to drink. We always had plenty of beer. Pampf had a relative who was manager of the Nesher brewery in Bat Yam and gave us a case of beer whenever we had a vacation. The cocks drank their beer joyfully, staggered and fell asleep. Next morning punctually at four o'clock they woke us up again. In the evening they were given sleeping pills which was not easy. Someone had to hold the poor things and another person would push the pill into the chicken's beak, to the accompaniment of much good counsel and hearty laughter. To no avail, they woke us up again in the morning. It was their last triumph. Thereafter they came to rest in the fridge.

The children remained at home in their accustomed environment and were taken care of in the afternoon by friends who had children the same age and with whom one very carefully did not spend the vacation.

III

Shortly after Rona was born I developed stomach trouble and after several unpleasant examinations the doctors determined that I had ulcers. At that time it was thought that one of the main causes of them was a stressful environment. Today it is said that stomach ulcers are an infection.

I received treatment in the form of Roter tablets from Holland and was put on a diet. Sometimes I went from the garage to the restaurant next door and bought half a pint of milk, which I was allowed, with garage money. This was not strictly adhering to the rules of communal life, but taking victuals home to bake a private cake wasn't either. I was called on the carpet by our nurse, although not for spending the money:

"It has come to my attention that you're drinking cold milk. That's not good for your ulcers!"

Being by now over thirty, a mother of two, my own childhood far behind me, I would have liked to ask: "Who is the busybody who told you?" But only said mildly but guiltily:

"I don't drink the milk cold, I wait for it to get to room temperature."

Incidents like this one didn't make me happier or more satisfied with kibbutz life. I complained a lot but drew the line at issuing an ultimatum about staying or leaving. Pampf loved Ma'ayan, he worked hard to make a go of the garage. The kibbutz was his life. It certainly wasn't mine. Not that Pampf did not see many things, especially about the education of the children, the same way as I did; but he would rather have tried to change matters from within.

There was a long and intense meeting about the smaller children sleeping in children's houses or not. The decision went against those of us who wanted their children at home, and one chavera told me after the session when we were still bitterly discussing the matter, throwing back her head in upright indignation:

"Well, if that is how you think, you shouldn't live on a kibbutz." I agreed with her but was not hopeful.

And then one day at the end of the summer in 1956 Pampf came home and said:

"I have a job in Haifa, we are leaving!"

He gave no reason for this change of heart. Whether my ulcers had something to do with it, or it was because he had spent some of his formative years in a school in Switzerland and was against children being away from their parents. Maybe he thought that I had done what I had promised, I had tried and now it was his turn. I was too happy to need explanations, too anxious how I would acquit myself on the 'outside' with two small children with my rudimentary knowledge of housekeeping and children in a country I knew only from the cushioned viewpoint of the kibbutz; where I had never shopped in a grocer's store, never been in a post office, registered my children for kindergarten, or paid taxes. I had never seen a doctor without the kibbutz nurse making the appointment, and it was her decision as to who needed the doctor most urgently. She could transfer my appointment to someone else. And she did.

Town Life

Pampf rented a house in Kiriath Haim. I had looked at it and declared myself satisfied. It was old and decrepit and the area around, although big, could hardly be called a garden. The earth was parched and bare and apart from some dusty trees there was nothing, not a flower nor a bit of grass, growing. I did not care, as long as it got me out of the kibbutz and into the privacy of our own home. Pampf did not ask me about anything else.

"If you are willing to live in that house, you'll be happy with whatever I decide," he said.

When we were ready to leave in the autumn another war broke out. The Sinai Campaign.

April 18th 1956, a ceasefire came into force between Egypt and Israel.

June 13th, the last British troops left Suez.

On the 24th Nasser was elected President of Egypt.

July 20th America and Britain withdrew their offer to help Egypt finance the Aswan dam.

On the 26th of July Nasser announced nationalisation of the Suez Canal Company.

30th of August, French troops arrived in Cyprus.

October 28th, Eisenhower called upon Israel not to "endanger the peace".

On the 29th Israeli forces invaded Egypt and after five days fighting controlled the Sinai peninsula.

October 30th, Britain and France issued a twelve-hour ultimatum for Egypt and Israel to stop fighting; Britain and

France vetoed the US resolution in the Security Council for Israel to withdraw behind armistice lines.

31st, Anglo-French offensive launched against military targets in Egypt.

24th of November, the General Assembly of the UN called for Britain, France, and Israel to withdraw troops from Egypt. They left. The campaign was over.

So far my history book.

II

The General Assembly of the Kibbutz decided that we should not quit but take an extended leave, so that we could come back to Ma'ayan after a year if we wanted to. Pampf had started work in Haifa and was not drafted but quite a few men from Ma'ayan were and I was asked to stay on for the time being. The man who was to take on my job in the garage would not be free to do so. And our friends and colleagues asked reasonably:

"Why leave now?"

"You don't know anybody there!"

"Stay here with the kids! What have you got to lose?"

"Wait till it's all over!"

I was not too pleased to remain, I wanted to get on with my life. But I listened to them and to Pampf who also wanted me to wait. He might still be drafted. We stayed a few weeks longer, partly because I felt a responsibility towards my job, partly for the children's sake.

The management of the kibbutz had been very generous with furniture, kitchen utensils and clothing that we could take with us. Few kibbutzim at the time gave leaving members as much as we received then. Today there are laws about the rights of people resigning from these communities and the decision is not left in the hands of the kibbutzim any more.

This had its ironic side. After living on the kibbutz for nine years without a raincoat I now asked for one and it was approved without a murmur. In town one had to dress! With my upbringing at the Herzl School I wouldn't have dreamed of asking for an umbrella. One woman from England who had married into the kibbutz had come provided with one and used it. She was the talk of the place.

We moved to Kiriath Haim, a suburb of Haifa, as soon as conditions had stabilised. Nava had a long walk to her kindergarten because we had not known that one had to register children in summer if one wanted them nearby. I put her on the bus for the two stations she had to ride and a very nice woman, the owner of the fish shop where I bought the fish fillet we lived on, saw to it that she got off at the right station. She would walk home on her own unless it rained. Then I would put Rona to bed in her cot, hurry to the kindergarten and rush back home with Nava, afraid that Rona might wake up in the meantime.

Nava was told not to speak to anyone in the street and one of my neighbours informed me that I had nothing to worry about because Nava, usually a friendly child, would not even answer her "Shalom" if met alone on her way home. There was something else to worry about though, but I didn't know it at the time. Nava, who was very curious and I suppose still is, did not have to cross a main road and it had not occurred to me that she might be inquisitive enough to go back and forth between both sides of the road when she saw something interesting. She confessed this only much later.

The obstacles of town life proved to be manageable. Some foods were rationed and we ate frozen meat and chicken once a week. The rest of the days it was fish fillet. We had a mulberry tree in front of the house that I climbed to pick the ripe, sweet fruit. I had cooked in Germany with little food and in Sweden with little money, I was not spoiled. I had nice neighbours and learned from them how to get along. We watched each other's children. Now and then we had a chat over one cup of coffee in the morning, coffee was rationed too.

So was electricity. If you used more than your share, it became more expensive. Pampf had relatives in Kiriath Bialik, a town outside Haifa not far from us, who were among our first visitors. Selma and Bernhard were some fifteen years older than we were and both very family minded. When they saw me use electricity with no thought to the rationing about which I knew nothing, they were extremely amused.

When I asked Selma for a few tips on life in the city, she told me that in winter she never ironed the backs of her husband's and sons' shirts because taking them out of the dresser they could not see them and wearing pullovers over their shirts nobody else could; Bernhard was not amused.

There were no more communal duties and we spent the evenings quietly together. Nava was happy to sit with us, after Rona was asleep, drink a glass of tea and listen to or tell us a story before she went to bed. The movies we went to singly, babysitters were costly. Only once did we take one in order to see *Guys and Dolls* in Haifa which was so long that we took a taxi home. An expensive evening.

III

Lea and Benjamin left Ma'ayan with their two children, David and Nurit, about a year later.

Benjamin had spent the war years in Switzerland. Lea had been taken from her home in 1944 with her parents, sisters and brothers. Her home, originally in Romania, belonged at that time to Hungary. Lea's mother, with a long tradition of hospitality, had cooked a meal for the German soldiers. The soldiers in their turn had watched over the family's possessions during the night before they were deported so that the neighbours would not steal them. The parents were sent to an extermination camp, and the youngsters to work in factories in Germany where they survived the war. All of them emigrated to Israel via Switzerland and Cyprus where a brother and two sisters were already living.

Lea had been cooking for the chaverim in Ma'ayan, heavy work and not always easy for a newcomer. Benjamin had worked in agriculture and had to learn a new profession. For a few years they lived with her brother in Ramat Gan, then they moved to Ashdod, a new harbour south of Tel Aviv, where Benjamin was employed by the electric company.

In spite of the difficulties, (neither of us had a phone or a car at the time) we stayed in touch. We visited each other, spent vacations and held the Seder together.

A few years later Ilana and Menahem too left the kibbutz with their two sons, Hanoch and Yishar. Menahem had emigrated with Youth Aliyah, but having a mind of his own he preferred to do his own thinking and not leave decisions to the majority.

Ilana had been sent to Denmark, also through Youth Aliyah, as a youngster to work on a farm as preparation for her future life in Palestine. She had escaped from the Nazis with the help of the Danes and had lived in Sweden till she could move on. Ilana and her group had been held up in Belgium for several months, and when they finally boarded a boat for Palestine the British had caught them, subdued them with tear gas and sent them to Cyprus where they remained till the end of the British mandate in Palestine.

IV

The second year in Kiriath Haim, Nava started school, a formidable event that almost moistened her father's eyes. With the many immigrants that had come to the country during the past years there were not enough schools or teachers. Nava, not yet six years old, started school in a class of over fifty children with seventeen kids who knew no Hebrew. The teacher was near pension age. It was not an auspicious beginning.

Rona in the meantime was busy visiting the neighbours. She would sneak out of the house, knock at the neighbours' back doors and ask for something to eat.

"My mom gave me no breakfast!" she would say. But when offered bread she refused it. She accepted pretzels and sweets. In later years and in another place she would push her younger sister Shlomit, by then old enough to walk and talk, in front of her towards our neighbours' door telling her:

"Ask for candy! Ask for candy!"

When I became pregnant again I sent Rona to a private kindergarten, so the two occasions, kindergarten and a new baby would not be connected in her mind. The kindergarten was in the same street. There were no sidewalks and almost no cars where we lived; one walked in the middle of the road and stepped aside when eventually a car came by. Not Rona! Once when she came home from visiting a neighbour (according to reports she had taken off most of her clothes), there was a taxi and she would not budge. The driver asked her nicely to step aside but made no impression. In the end it was the taxi that went around her and drove through the sand. I asked the neighbour who told me:

"Why didn't you take her off the road?"

"I had to laugh," she said, "it was so funny, like watching a play. I had to see who would quit first."

V

Shlomit was born in January 1958. We now had three daughters and I had a baby to bring up by myself for the first time. No more second-hand reports of how sweetly she had laughed during the hours I had been at the garage. Luckily I had worked in the baby house and knew a little more than the average kibbutz mother.

By then Pampf, as the manager of a big garage in Haifa, had the company jeep at his disposal. We could take the children to the beach in summer or go on short drives. The jeep was not trustworthy enough for longer outings.

Quite often it would not start and Nava and I would push it.

In the summer of 1958 with apartment prices down for a while we bought one in Kiriat Bialik and moved to the same town where Selma and Bernhard lived. Pampf bought an old bike for me and things became easier, although I still had a hard time making his salary last till the end of the month. Pampf did not want me to go to work:

"You wanted to be with the children," he said, "better stay home!"

Between the two of us we managed to paint and repair everything that needed it. We bought a sewing machine and I saved money mending and sewing. Pampf cut the children's hair, I cut my own. We managed nicely.

Reserve Duty

During the British Occupation Pampf had been a member of the Hagana and had been among those who were instructed by Orde Wingate in guerrilla warfare. Wingate had passionately believed in the Bible and the Jews' right to Palestine. On one occasion the company had lain in hiding and on the road below an old Arab had ridden by, Wingate gave the order to shoot him. Nobody obeyed and he was exasperated:

"You'll never win if you don't learn!"

Later Pampf had been responsible for Ma'ayan's security and when this was not necessary any more he was called up for reserve duty regularly as was everyone else. In 1959 he was a liaison officer between the UN and the Israeli Defence Forces. It was not a tough task but potentially dangerous. The Israeli and the UN officers could be shot at, but were not allowed to shoot back, they were observers and went about without weapons.

In November that year when Pampf was somewhere in the Galil, my neighbours got a phone call and were asked to tell me that I should not worry about him, he was all right. I had been busy with the children and the household, had known nothing and had had no time to worry. But now I started to.

It was only a little border incident worth no more than a few lines in the paper. Pampf and his colleague from the UN riding about in a jeep had been shot at but not hit. They had jumped into a ditch and later beaten it back to their post. A few days after Pampf came home he received the following document from the UN unit:

Number: 36

This is to certify that
Second Lieutenant Josef Weil of the I.D.F.
has been fired at by the Syrians whilst on duty on
November 15, 1959
at the Jordan River South of Khouri Farm
and is hereby admitted as
a member of

"THE ORDER OF THE SITTING DUCK"

Signed by the chamberlain and the grandmaster in
Tiberias, 17.11.1959.

II

After Pampf had had an operation to free his sciatic nerve from between the vertebrae, he was not called up for active duty again. The garage he worked for had a contract from the Army and his reserve duty became to remain at his job and see to the immediate repair of all Army vehicles that were sent there during a war.

The children slept in bunk beds and when Pampf came home from hospital and went into their room, Shlomit jumped from the upper bunk joyfully into his arms only a few hours after he had been told not to lift anything.

Moving Again

With the children growing, we moved to a slightly bigger apartment with two rooms for the girls. No more bunk beds. Nava as the eldest was to have the smaller room for herself, but preferred to share with Shlomit. The girls kept exchanging rooms, usually against my wishes, during my afternoon nap, the holy hour of the day, called 'Schlafstunde' in Israel in varying pronunciations.

Shlomit now went to the State kindergarten around the corner where she made friends quickly. When parents and teacher had a meeting one late afternoon, I was surprised to meet Noemi, a young woman who had belonged to the Hachsharah group in Norrköping.

"There is somebody else you know here," she said. "Look!"

She pointed at the porch of the next house.

"That's Gad over there! Remember him?"

Indeed I did. Whenever we had visited the Norrköping group I had seen Gad standing near the radio listening to music when the Freudenthals and Kurt were not playing. At that moment another young woman came over, and shaking hands with me, introduced herself as Sara, Ilan's mother:

"I hear that our children are great friends!" Then she too pointed at Gad, "That's my husband!"

We decided to meet and did so often. Gad had come to Israel with my friend Ilana's group via Belgium and Cyprus. He now worked at the polytechnic. Sara, a Sabra, was a teacher.

When the children moved from kindergarten to school Shlomit and Ilan went hand in hand towards this new experience. At one time Ilan decided to marry her. And when Sara asked him where they would live he said:
"Here in this house!"
"And where are we going to live?"
"Oh!" he said, "you can stay in a tent."
For Sara's and Gad's sake I am glad that nothing came of the match and they are still living in their house.

We bought a used car and made trips, visiting Ilana and Menahem, now on a farm in Nahariah, and often helped them pick fruit on Saturday mornings. We would finish around noon and then could all go on a picnic together. Yishar, their youngest son, and Shlomit, born in the same year, became good friends. They had much to talk about and stayed at each other's houses during vacations. When Shlomit spent a week or so in Nahariah Yishar would tell his friends that she was his cousin, forestalling any ugly gossip.

II

When in third grade, Rona came home one day angry and crying:
"If you want me to study you'll have to get me a private teacher. I'm not going back to school!"
There had been too much noise in the classroom and Rona hadn't liked that. I persuaded her to come with me next day, without her books naturally, and tell her troubles to the headmaster.
Mr Tamir looked earnestly at the child and told her to come to his office. Preparing to accompany her, I was stopped by him at the door and told to wait outside. Mothers are always such a disturbing influence. When they returned, looking serious, neither was upset.
I dared ask Mr Tamir what had been decided upon.
"It's going to be all right!" he said.

"What exactly does that mean?"
"She'll come to school tomorrow."
"What about today?"
"She can stay home. Goodbye!"

I couldn't quite believe it but Mr Tamir brought his wife, an excellent teacher, to take over the class the next day and the other teacher, who had not been able to keep the children in order, was relieved of her duties.

III

One of my wishes in Ma'ayan had been to possess a good typewriter. My handwriting was nothing to brag about and quite often I could not read it myself. I wrote many letters, especially as Pampf had handed over the responsibility of writing to his family to me. I, loath to use the phone now that we finally had one, presented him with all my cousins in Israel to stay in touch with. It was an admirable arrangement and we were both eminently satisfied.

Pampf, seeing the justice of my appeal, gave me a typewriter for one of my birthdays. Soon I started to translate assessments for an insurance company from Hebrew to English, at first with his help and then on my own. I did not earn much, but it was nice to earn at least some money and I could do the work at home when the children were at school.

The typewriter came in handy for entries for a column called 'Keeping Posted' in the Jerusalem Post, the English language newspaper of the country.

Shlomit came home one day asking me if I knew what an opera was. Curious to know what she had been taught, I asked her to explain. She called Nava, and then stamping forcefully on one of her feet, she pointed at her yelling sister and said:

"That's opera!"

I wrote this up for the paper and theoretically got five Israeli pounds for my endeavour. In fact, for reasons unknown to the simple populace, the paper's accountant deducted income tax from this enormous sum, and subtracting the stamp, just enough was left, as one woman pointed out, to take the bus to visit her children and invite her only granddaughter for a very small ice cream cone.

Still, when my mother-in-law was in Israel on one of her frequent visits to see her sons and their families, we had an adventure that I decided to share. She had gone to have her hair done. Knowing neither Hebrew nor the hairdresser she had nodded several times when addressed and in consequence had received an excessive bill for unwanted lotions sprayed on to her hair. She had paid but came home complaining about this kind of exploitation. I went to see the woman to get a receipt to send to a consumers' organisation and to find out what exactly had been done. I also told her what I thought of her behaviour. The hairdresser refused to write a receipt, I refused to leave. She phoned the police. Being now enraged I waited for them to make an appearance. When they came I was asked my name, address, father's name, (you couldn't and still can't move without giving it) and when I was born.

"June, 29th, 23!" I said shortly and inwardly boiling.

The policeman looked up from his pad, glanced thoughtfully at me for a moment and then asked:

"Nineteen hundred?"

I turned around and raced home to the nearest mirror to see if I really looked like something left over from the beginning of the last century.

The paper sent another cheque for 1.75 IP. I was not earning enough to pay income tax at all, but getting back what was rightfully mine would have cost me even more.

June 1967: the Six Day War

The weeks before the Six Day War wore down our nerves. Jordanians, Syrians, Egyptians and Iraqis assembled their armies. Many of our reservists were called up, but it remained quiet. Too quiet! What would happen? Would our government wait till it was too late? The Arabs had time and again promised to drive us into the sea. Would they win this time? A decision had to be made soon! When would this be done? The tension was almost unbearable.

Were we Jews, now that we were Israelis and had weapons, going to sit still, waiting too long? Pampf came home after work so worried he could hardly talk.

One of my friends had been told that she had ulcers and to stay calm and not worry. This was difficult, as her husband had been recruited and for three weeks she had not heard from him.

The shelter, our bathroom, had to be readied. It was really too small for the whole family to sit in, with a wooden cupboard at one end and a wooden door at the other. It was not safe even if only splinters were flying about. Pampf and Nava went to the opposite lot where a house was being built and filled sacks with sand that Pampf brought up to the first floor where we lived and stacked them in piles against the cupboard and in front of the door, leaving space for us to use it. For the blackout only the two little windows in the toilet and bathroom doors were taped with dark paper. It would be too hot to close any windows in June and we would just have to sit in the dark or go to bed.

In a country where so many people had been in Europe during the Second World War people's thoughts went at once to the food situation and other necessities one might need. People bought what they could but there was no actual lack of anything and no panic ensued. My grocer confided to me that in Europe people would buy and stock alcohol, here they bought Jahrzeit candles.

When the war started on June 5th we were relieved. Action was taken and we could hope again.

There were only a few air raid alarms and one of my neighbours, whose husband had made no provision for his family thinking it unnecessary, came over to our bathroom with her two daughters. The girls sitting in the tub made so much noise that we did not even hear the 'All clear' signal.

Our Army was successful and Nava with her father's help noted down the victories on a map. She was quite astonished when they did not advance every day. What had they done during the past hours? she wondered. At her school, with too few shelters for the children, the older pupils were told to lie on the grass in front of the school in case of a raid. The kids in Nava's class had stopped studying and distributed mail.

The whole country was mobilised.

East Jerusalem was taken on June 7th, the Golan Heights on the 9th and 10th...

The war ended as abruptly as it had begun. Lights went on all over the towns and villages and people were jubilant and relieved, having escaped a great danger.

The people from both sides of Jerusalem started walking towards each other as soon as the shooting had stopped, and friends visited friends.

Ilana, Menahem and their kids came from Nahariah in the evening to celebrate and many children congregated at our house. Among them was Erez, my son-in-law to be, whose joyful smile made a great impression on me. We went out and talked to the neighbours and one of them confessed that she had thought that we were hoarding sugar in big sacks when she saw

Pampf carrying the sand upstairs. She had also heard a conversation between him and his mother in Chicago in the night. He had repeated a phone number in German and this in the middle of a war had sounded ominous to her and she had thought that we were spies.

My mother-in-law had objected to her youngest son's fighting with us in our latest war. She had asked my husband to call and tell Jack that his coming was unnecessary.

The war was over and when the summer vacation had started we decided to go to Jerusalem with Ilana and Menahem Iron and their children to see the old city. The town was filled with people. Glad faces and sad faces, strange people, monks and nuns, bearded and bekaftaned Jews, hundreds of street hawkers. Little boys yelling:

"It's only one pound, everything for one pound, no more!"

There were pencils and shawls from China. Ilana and I both wanted a shawl and Pampf bargained. Four times all of us moved on and four times the vendor called us back:

"Havadja! Come back! I'll give you a better price! Let's say 2.50!" We moved again, we came back again. In the end we bought them for one pound each. You have to bargain, Pampf explained, otherwise you disappoint the shopkeeper and he thinks that his first price was not high enough.

There were baskets and copper work in profusion. Nargilehs and keffiahs could be had. After sightseeing we walked up and down the streets and I became tired from watching as well as from feeling how futile war was. In one of the quieter corners I looked wistfully around for somewhere to sit, looking also by chance into one of the windows of a flat. A young Arab woman opened her door. She asked us in, and offered us chairs. Ilana and I accepted. We sat down for a few minutes and smiled at each other. We could not talk to her but she saw how grateful we were for this moment's respite. Any joy I had felt at the beginning of the day seemed to have evaporated and only sadness remained.

Today an incident like this is unthinkable. Hatred has been piled upon hatred.

A Last Visit

My mother-in-law came for a visit shortly after the ceasefire, it was her last. She died on November 29th 1968 of cancer. She had been generous and good humoured, although she never stopped worrying about her sons and their families. We had been very fond of each other.

My greatest difficulty had been how to address her. I had called my own mother 'Mutti' and I was loath to call anybody else by that name. But the whole family and quite a few people who did not belong to it called her that: and one cannot have a close relationship with anyone for twenty years without addressing him or her directly. I had finally convinced myself that 'Mutti' was just another name that I would use and that it would take nothing away from my feelings about my own mother. The regrets and might-have-beens that I felt so often when I saw my girls with her, knowing how much my own mother had loved babies and small children, would remain the same. My mother and father had been left to die in a concentration camp like millions of others, what did one little word matter?

Now, since her death, when my children and I talk about her and we quite often do, we talk about her as Oma, grandmother.

A Wedding in Kabul

Pampf knew an immense number of people, wherever we went he was hailed and sometimes long conversations with lots of reminiscences ensued. He could also usually tell us what make of car they owned. He knew them from the garage in Ma'ayan, his present place of work, his Army service and from the time when he had been a truck driver travelling up and down the country, driving to the Lebanon in the north and Gaza in the south during the Second World War.

He was well liked and got a great many invitations, mainly to weddings. He seldom went. Now that the children were old enough to be left alone in the evening I asked him to accept an interesting invitation occasionally and we would be able to go together. It turned out that he had just been asked to wedding festivities, not the actual wedding, in a nearby Arab village. Two of the villagers worked at the garage. He promised that we would go if he could persuade a colleague who had also been invited to come too and bring his wife. Otherwise, I would probably be the only woman on the scene.

Michelini and his wife were both Italian. Michelini had been in the Italian Army during the Great War. He had ended up in Palestine and, having no wish to return to war torn Italy, had remained, finding work as a mechanic and learning Hebrew. He and his wife were both from Florence, both very tall and not dark at all.

The four of us set out in our car to Kabul in the Galil. The village had no electricity owing to the fact that the villagers had refused to participate in the cost of laying cables to the village.

We arrived, parked our car near the main square which was almost dark and packed with people in a circle with clearance in the middle for the dancers who also sang. All were male: the dancers and the spectators. The minute we were recognised four young men jumped up and offered us their chairs in the front row. We sat down and strong sweet coffee in four tiny cups on a tray was brought. The cups were only half full and I thanked God for that, as the coffee was so strong that it was almost like poison.

Mrs Michelini refused hers and asked for a cold drink. This presented some difficulty. The nearest cold juice was at the grocer's who had locked his store for the day. First he had to be found in the semi-darkness. Then he had to get his key and send someone to open the shop and finally Mrs Michelini received a bottle of orange juice and a glass.

In the meantime the performance went on, there were about ten or twelve men holding on to each other, rapidly moving all around the square with every sign of high enjoyment. After our eyes grew accustomed to the meagre light we saw that the women of the village were there too. They were standing on the roofs around the square, clapping their hands and now and then joining in the singing and ululating.

When it was over the village elders sat down at a table and were offered a festive meal. We were invited to see the bride and meet her mother who was standing in the kitchen busily cooking and could barely spare a glance for us. The bride was dancing on a little porch with several other girls around her, holding her hands above her head. Her fingernails had been painted with henna and she was pressing her nails hard into the soft flesh of her hands so that the henna would make little moons of colour. As long as the colour lasted it would be her 'henna' or honeymoon.

Then we were asked to sit down in one of the rooms and told that we, as the second most important guests, would have to wait till the elders had finished eating. This turned out to be unnecessary as a neighbour invited us to his house for a meal together with a couple from Nazareth. This man, possibly a Christian, had brought his wife too. There were two more men at the table and the host served the food which his wife handed him from the kitchen. We never saw her. We had lebeniah, some kind of sour milk, over boiled mutton and other assorted delicacies, with which we drank beer.

Our host excused himself, talking to Michelini: "I am sorry, but our food is not kosher."

Michelini, a Catholic, accepted the apology with a straight face: "It does not really matter to us!"

It was pretty late by now. I had eaten and drunk sparingly, but still I needed to go to a bathroom. It was no use asking the lady from Nazareth. She was a stranger there herself. Our host, who was of an imposing size, seemed to me unapproachable for a mere woman. I longed to go home soon. A forlorn hope.

The second young man who worked in the garage insisted that we come to his house to see it and honour his mother. Pampf and Michelini decided that we had to go. Mrs Michelini and I should wait where we were, in the middle of an Arab village in the dark, and they would bring the car and drive us there. We stood and waited and not for the first time I envied the men for being able to go into the bushes without further ado whilst women have to stand around and suffer till opportunity presents itself.

Five minutes or an eternity later a small van drove up with three or four young Arab men, none of whom we knew. They stopped, and all but the driver hopped into the back of the van:

"Come on in, we'll take you!"

"Oh really, we shouldn't, we're waiting for our husbands, they'll be here any minute now," we demurred.

"Well they won't be able to drive up to the house in their little car. Come on!"

This didn't sound reassuring.

"Now what?" I asked Mrs Michelini in an undertone.

"I don't see that we have much of a choice," she murmured back.

We stepped into the car and for the next eight minutes or another eternity we bounced up and down on what could hardly have been a road, which made my prayer for a bathroom even more imperative. Any fear I might have had was submerged by my most urgent need.

When we got out of the car I knew I had had it. No matter whom I asked I had to relieve myself. I asked the young man who bade us enter and was apparently our host to show me to a bathroom first. He did at once. Taking a kerosene lamp and guiding me to the other side of the house to a wooden door which he opened, brought me to what seemed to be a big laundry room underneath the living and bedrooms. There in a corner was the toilet, not the kind you sit on but the kind you squat over. He brought a small stool, set the lamp down, showed me where the hose was for flushing and left, closing the door behind him, all in such a gentlemanly manner that I really admired him. He might have been showing me a bathroom at the Ritz.

When I joined the others the men had arrived, our host had woken his mother to greet us and his little sister to translate for her.

We were sitting on the porch and were being offered fruit when suddenly Mrs Michelini smelled basilicum:

"My God," she said, "you have basil. How I love it! There is no fresh basil to be had in Haifa anywhere, and no Italian food is worth anything without!"

It was decided right away that Mrs Michelini could not be allowed to go home without fresh basil. Someone from the household was dispatched to don other shoes and go into the field to get several basil plants for her. That took another fifteen minutes. Shortly thereafter we said our goodbyes and drove home, arriving about two o'clock at night.

In our street there stood three young girls, our daughters, yelling:

"Where have you been? We were ready to call the police!"

Occasionally I have since reminded my daughters of this night when I have been worried about them, that they too once feared for our safety.

Our Trip Abroad

In the autumn of 1971 we took our first trip abroad in years. We flew to Paris, and then on to London where we went sightseeing and where every second street sounded familiar from the many detective stories I had read.

We took a plane to Stockholm where we stayed with Lies and Fredl Kalter who had visited us in Israel a few years earlier. We met Gert Löllbach and his second wife again, whom we had also seen in Israel.

Kurt came from Uppsala, where he now lived, to spend time with us. I had not been in touch with him since the Forties. It did not matter, he was the same old Kurt and talking to him was as easy as ever.

We took a car and visited Esther and Erich Künstlicher in Helsingborg, Erich was an old friend of Pampf's from way back in Frankfurt, and there too we were received with open arms.

We drove back to Paris in a rented car, and visited the places we had seen together ages ago. The 'Oubliettes' was still open and the same family operated it. This time, with more funds available, we also went up the Eiffel Tower and took a trip to Versailles.

Paris was still as beautiful as we remembered, London had been as interesting as we had expected and going to the theatre there was a marvellous event for both of us.

Sweden that fall made me ask myself why I had ever left. Not that I regretted it, at the time it had seemed cold and boring compared with Paris, now after more than twenty years in a hot and unquiet country with excitable people, its quiet beauty enchanted me.

We returned to our own little provincial town with many new impressions and certainly with a newly widened horizon.

1973

1973 was an eventful year. Nava had finished her Army service and had started to study art. She met Seev Efroni through a friend. They fell in love and at the beginning of that year decided to get married. The marriage took place in a small circle at the rabbinate in Bialik with a hot lunch for the immediate family afterwards. Nava refused to go to a restaurant:

"Please, Mom, let's eat at home!"

There was a very good Hungarian restaurant inside Acco's old fortified walls which we reserved for the reception of relatives and friends in the evening. Instead of a band we had a record player which added to the friendly and intimate atmosphere, as we could move around and talk to people. The food, I was told, was excellent but I was too nervous to eat. Pampf, being a splendid host by nature, made the rounds to see that everybody had a place to sit and enough food and felt welcome. I am unfortunately not very good on these occasions and behave as if I were a guest myself.

II

After many doubts and second thoughts, I decided to learn to drive a car and get my licence. I had translated too many assessments of accidents to do so with a quiet heart. When Pampf had been on one of his trips to the US, I had to use the bus during the week and had to stay home with Shlomit on Saturdays as the buses didn't and still don't run on the Shabbat. I enrolled at a driving school and got my licence many months later. I have thanked my lucky stars and Pampf for his patient encouragement that got me through the test although by then I was already a grandmother.

Pampf had always tried to induce me to learn to drive, as in his opinion all women should. In our circle he was the authority about cars and anything to do with them and many a friend came to ask him what he thought about their wives getting their licences. He told them all that women drivers quite often turned out to be as good or better than the men. I think some of our friends hoped for a different opinion so that they could go home and say: "See, even Pampf disapproves!" and keep the car their very own domain.

It helped both of us enormously that I had my driver's licence, especially when in later years Pampf became ill and I could take him to and from the hospital and did not have to trouble our children.

III

Maya, Nava's daughter and my first grandchild, was born in September, the newest addition to our family, a lively and noisy baby and a joy to us all. Rona was in the United States visiting my brother and his family having finished her studies and before doing her Army service. Shlomit was the only one at home now although for a time Nava, Seev and the baby lived with us too.

So that Shlomit wouldn't be too lonely, we asked for and got a puppy from our butcher who was looking for good homes for some of the puppies he had. The dog was named Speedy Gonzalez by Nava, Speedy for short. His mother was a ratter, his father a poodle and he was quick, clever, very loyal and smiled crookedly whenever Pampf came home from work.

IV

On the 6th of October, Yom Kippur, The Day of Atonement, when half the population was praying in the synagogues and the others were at home, Pampf and Shlomit were busy gluing a model truck together. Slowly we became aware that here and there some cars were starting. Other cars could be heard driving along the Acco–Haifa highway. We could not understand what had happened; unless there was an emergency people just did not drive on Yom Kippur in those years.

Then, shortly after two o'clock, the sirens howled and everybody turned on the radio. Israel had been attacked by the Egyptians and the Syrians. Their armies had crossed into Sinai and had overrun the Golan Heights.

In a way it was fortunate that it was Yom Kippur. The men and women who were called up were either at home or at the nearest synagogue and could be found quickly. It was a short and bloody war with many sacrifices.

Some of the young men from Ma'ayan who fell in this war I had known as babies or very small children. They were about Nava's age and I had changed their diapers or fed them. These were heartrending thoughts.

The government and the military leaders could and should have had an inkling of what might happen. The nation as a whole had had no way of knowing.

Part III

THE CHILDREN GREW UP AND BECAME PEOPLE

Letters from Israel to Friends in Sweden

D.M. D.G. Bialik 17.5.74

The Post Office has been on strike, and I could not send any letters. Now that the strike is over, I can write but not receive mail regularly, because, so we have been informed, the Post Office has so much undelivered mail that it keeps them from distributing letters every day. I know it sounds odd, but that is what they say.

Our library is going on strike too. Long live the workers! It is for three days only and is in favour of the low income bracket, which means me too. Inflation, of course, goes up with every strike so I don't really approve of it. On the other hand I did not go to the meeting and can't complain. Not that I regret that.

All the municipal workers were on the verge of striking all over the country and, when it came to the vote here, the library contingent demanded an explanation as to whether the vote was for or against the strike, but this was not made clear to them. Many people who voted were not counted; probably on the principle that if the first fifty were okay the second fifty would be too. So the library employees left and I did not miss anything.

My children had promised me heaven and earth if I wrote a book about myself and I had actually started. But then I found that I had nothing to wear, and since heaven and earth do not include a wardrobe or a lot of help either, I put the two pages that I wrote aside and started sewing.

How would you like a family of three visiting you a week before Pessach without prior announcement? Well, that's what happened to me. The fridge was full of good things for the Seder for four to fourteen people, two vegetarians included. Nobody had yet decided if they were or were not coming and I hate to go shopping at the last moment. Naturally I could not cook any of the stuff I had and went out and shopped anew for Pampf's cousin, Martin, his wife and teenage daughter, cleaned and cooked and went to work at the library.

Pampf picked them up in Ma'ayan where they had visited Walter and the whole carload stood in front of the library at the right time to take me home. I refused, and it took some time to convince my relatives, including Shlomit, to let me walk and breathe some air. I don't know why people are so insistent on ferrying me from one place of work to another at maximum speed and in minimum comfort. The guests were quite helpful and left the day before the Seder which gave me time to clean and cook again. All fourteen persons arrived and the Seder was a great success.

Pampf has been sitting on an imaginary suitcase since January. He and the boss were supposed to go on a business trip to Bruxelles and Chicago. Imaginary, as he actually bought the suitcase only at the last moment. I went with him four times but then refused to look at any more luggage, much to his regret. I took him to the airport and went on to Ashdod to visit the Seeligs.

Not knowing exactly how to get there I stopped at one traffic light between lanes prior to deciding which way to go. A bus driver asked me pointedly if I had already made up my mind as he would like to use the road too. So I asked him if he could tell me from his greater height where the road to Ashdod was. He did and that is how I arrived contrary to all expectations at 7.30 in the morning for breakfast.

D.M. D.G.   Bialik 18.8.75

   We had an invasion of cockroaches and Pampf sprayed the kitchen with a poisonous substance in an effort to get rid of them. Most of them died a cruel death, the survivors moved south to the living room. We have tried vainly to interest Speedy in cockroaches as a food supplement. He prefers chicken – cooked or fried.
   Cockroaches are a taboo subject here although there is an abundant supply in this country. They are seen, heard, but not talked about. Some people have given up the unequal struggle and I wished to join their ranks but Pampf would not let me. It is said that we have had the cockroaches in hordes ever since we got central canalisation. When it is cooler they hide, coming out again when we start heating. We now heat less partly because of the roaches and partly because of the fuel prices. But nobody can cut down on the sun where it shines.

*

D.M. D.G.   Bialik sometime same year

   Tried to convey your regards to the cockroaches but they are not here any more. Maybe they went even further south to the neighbours. There are a few very small ones left, a kind I have not met with before. They are black instead of brown. I have an idea which I dare not quite mention in case they put me away. The mass poisoning, that awful massacre that Pampf staged might have affected the eggs or genes and through some kind of mutation these small ones are really them in plainclothes outfit.

*

D.M. D.G. Bialik 10.2.76

I hope that you will come soon for at least a weekend in Bialik. All our beds are suitable for bad backs. Also, although I like talking to either of you, I wouldn't mind having a conversation with both of you together which is palpably impossible in Nataniah's main square.

We have been hunting for mushrooms and Weinbergschnecken. We found lots of mushrooms and fifteen snails which are not enough for a decent meal.

We kept the poor things in captivity and there developed a minor war between Pampf and me. I wanted to give them their well-earned freedom, he, usually more pessimistic than I, was sure that we would find the missing forty-five. Weeks passed and I found myself busy feeding them; they prefer Chinese cabbage to almost anything else, which gets pretty expensive. I cleaned out their messy box, and occasionally hunted them down as they escaped and moved freely around the kitchen porch.

One bright and sunny Saturday I put the box together with the picnic things expecting someone to take it to the car. When I asked Rona if the snails had left for their destination she said:

"Sure, they are not on the table!"

Being less trusting I told her to go and look, and there they were on the porch again. Rona smuggled the snails into the car and Pampf's smug grin was wiped off his face when he saw them at the picnic. We found no more snails that day, the captured ones were given a ceremonial release and rushed off as fast as they could.

Nava and Maya hitchhiked on a plane that seeds rain clouds from Tel Aviv to Haifa. When Maya was told that she could look down she covered her eyes with both hands and said, "Ugh!" Apparently both mother and daughter were glad to get off the plane.

Rona is working in an office in Haifa and hating every minute of it. Both Erez, her boyfriend, and I have been counselling her to look for another job so we won't be exposed to her bad temper when she comes home from a boring day.

We still have two musk oxen hanging over the phone which remind us of you when you were in Norway and apparently looked like them, or that is what we picture. How about sending a new postcard to change your image?

*

D.M. D.G.   Bialik 19.10.76

One of the things that does not go well with gracious old age is getting into the middle of a dogfight. I was sitting on a mattress at Nava's on the floor, so far there is nothing else, when a big Schäferhund that Seev had adopted displayed signs of wanting to do away with Speedy. Speedy, showing more heroism than accuracy, closed his teeth on my arm as I was trying to protect him. Shlomit, quick-witted as ever, grabbed hold of the Shepherd. Otherwise I might have been bitten by both dogs, and would now be making a list of people to bite as I might have rabies. The Shepherd left Seev a few days later much to everybody's relief.

We took a week's holiday, the first in four years, so don't brag about how hard you work. We went to Zfat where I intended to have a complete rest. Unfortunately my husband is constitutionally unable to rest for more than a few hours. We toured the countryside every day.

Our first day was easy. We found a motel and had a picnic in the woods, tried to read and sleep, but were ousted by millions of flies. Next day Hazor and Tel Dan. The Hazor water system has, so they say, one hundred and fifty steps down. I think I counted nine more. We put the food and our feet into the Dan river to cool off, as there was a nice Hamssin going.

On the third day a young friend of Pampf's, named Zwicka, picked us up to take us to Mt Hermon. He came in a Ford Transit, a big van, on rough roads good for getting concussion. We saw the inside of the bunker on Mt Hermon which was seemingly built by the Druse who live nearby, and looked very forbidding.

For lunch we were invited by one of Zwicka's Druse friends to the village of Migdal Shams on the Golan Heights. At first coffee was served while we were sitting on a sofa. Lunch was served on big trays while we were sitting on mattresses on the floor. This was nothing new to me. See Nava's apartment above. I forgot to take my shoes off but nobody complained. Otherwise I acquitted myself quite well, eating chicken with my hands, no real hardship, and everything else with Druse pittot, thin as paper, big as tabletops and folded like napkins. Extremely tasty.

The lady of the house did not appear but passed the flavourful dishes through an opening in the door to her husband who served and ate with us. We got wet towels to wipe our hands and cushions to make ourselves comfortable. There were a dresser, many mattresses, rugs and plastic mats, two small sofas and curtains. A small coffee table, no pictures but knick-knacks on the dresser, no lampshade but lots of glasses, some in their original packing. Everything looked clean and new. On our way out, we were allowed to look into the bedroom. There were more mattresses and more glasses. Maybe glasses are a status symbol. The ones we drank tea from came from the kitchen. Lunch took two hours.

Before we went back we visited some outposts of the State of Israel and of the UN on the Golan Heights. As far as I know we had no business being there and I personally had no wish to be. The UN observers were Austrians and they observed us going by into no-man's land. Pampf sat next to Zwicka, I sat on the bench behind. There are a lot of curves up and down the mountain and we got a guided tour through two wars. Zwicka explained everything with one or both hands off the steering wheel, turning around to see if I was following his every word.

It was sad and frightening driving through an empty, dead landscape with faded colours, bare and unused, no people, no animals, dotted with burnt out tanks and bunkers.

We visited the new cold storage plant in Migdal Shams for the apples that grow on the mountain and received a whole box of apples as a present.

It was a memorable day and I must have kept my cool because Zwicka was quite willing to take us again on another trip.

Next day we drove to Nimrod's Castle, one of the biggest crusader fortresses in the country, and we left no stone untrodden. At least Pampf explored every nook and cranny. I found a quiet place to sketch the thing. Visiting parties came and went and we were still there looking around and enjoying the magnificent view. The crusaders certainly knew where to put their castles.

It was a very hot week but every day we found a cool place with some running water although once I had to wade ankle deep through cowshit to get there. One day after visiting some galleries we even rested.

Shlomit is quite happy in the Army, Rona has started work in a bank, Seev is still holding down the same job and Nava is studying. Maya for some time now has refrained from asking for chewing gum all day long.

I wish you a happy New Year, Shana Tovah.

*

D.M. D.G.   Bialik 23.3.77

While Lies and Fredl were here Pampf, with a nice sense of timing, went down with a temperature of 40°. He was then ill for three weeks, went back to work still sick and after another three weeks was miraculously cured.

I have to write this letter with interruptions as Speedy threw up in the living room next to the carpet, not on it. The dog is still not feeling well and has to be pampered, and he really knows how to make the most of a little sickness.

Just now we own quite a lot of bare floor. Rona took two carpets when she moved out a week ago. Yes, Rona has become quite modern and taken an apartment with Erez. They are now busy touring the country in search of furniture and anything else that might come in handy. We bought them a fridge and gave them one of our heaters. Nizza, Erez' mother, contributed a cooking stove. They went to Jerusalem, where Motke, Erez' father lives with his second family, to bring home a cupboard and took along a rusty table and a small dresser. I phoned Selma, a cousin, nearby and she donated an old suitcase that has been in the attic since 1934. It will be used as a coffee table in the living room. Some kind soul lent them a bed.

Rona comes here every day after work for a hot meal, and they both come for Friday night dinner. I haven't had time to see their apartment yet and await a formal invitation. We were expecting to feel a bit lonely without Rona and Erez who has been a steady guest in our house, but the first evening after they moved out they came to watch a baseball game on TV and brought a friend. Shlomit was also home from the Army and there was hardly any room left for me.

Shlomit has been sent to Tel Aviv by above mentioned Army to study typing. She has one lesson a day and since this is a pretty strenuous schedule, they have no lessons on Fridays. She now comes home on Thursdays. This week it was very lucky for me because the dog came home on Friday black from one end to the other and had to be washed for half an hour and I could not spare the time. Washing the dog at odd hours is a smelly business and I find it difficult to get accustomed to this.

The other day I was on my way to the Haifa shouk and on one of the hilly streets a car behind me started hooting in what I deemed to be an unpleasant manner. As I was driving on my side of the road fairly fast leaving plenty of room for anyone wishing to overtake me I could not make out what the complaint was about. The complainer, an Arab, passed me making a lot of, to me, meaningless signs, and as I was just about to pass the little bridge that gets you into Haifa proper, I was too busy watching buses and taxis and what the Dutch call fietsers, who tended to get in my way.

I did my shopping and, coming back to the car, I saw it leaning to one side. I had a puncture, that's what I had been signalled about without paying attention. A puncture in Israeli language is a panscher. Pampf had explained to me the rudiments of changing the wheel but to take out the spare wheel I would have had to open the front of the car, and I had no idea how to do that. I said my prayers and drove to Pampf's garage. He brought me to a panschermacher, German pronunciation, in Israeli language the guy who fixes your punctures, and got home late but not too late to fix dinner for the expected guests over the weekend.

I have started a hydroponic garden in my kitchen with great success. One is supposed to make salads with the produce of sundry containers, but the kids eat everything as it grows, so whenever I want to make a salad I still have to buy vegetables.

*

D.M. D.G.   Bialik 15.6.77

Congratulations on Monica's independence! People often take it for granted that mothers wish their children to stay at home indefinitely. They do not consider that it is a whole lot less work when the kids move out. Although in Rona's case this is not exactly so. She still comes regularly for her midday dinner, usually breakfast, and a little snack after work, apart from bringing me all her laundry, including towels and sheets.

Shlomit complains less about the Army, Nava is getting on with her studies and we have already two of her drawings on our wall. In the near future we will get a sculpted head which I will then have to dust. We have had the kitchen and the bedroom wallpapered so we won't see the cracks in the walls. The cockroaches enjoy the wallpaper, apparently I hit on just the right colours. Pampf sprayed again. As was expected some died, some moved, some stayed. The dog was sick again in the bedroom. Luckily it was before Pampf left for work, so he cleaned it up. Maybe some insecticide got into his drinking water. He looks wan but ate a few simple cookies to do me a favour.

The political situation is lousy and Pampf sits in front of the TV occasionally laughing out loud, wondering at my melancholy face, as he thinks there is nothing else to do but laugh. The only person that I know who was elated by Begin's victory is my brother, who, living in the US, has been a staunch revisionist since 1935. In his last letter he offered that in case Begin proved too much for Israel he would be willing to give us Peanuts instead. Pampf is quite agreeable, he says Peanuts changes his ideas very often whereas Begin has not done so even once in the past thirty years.

Coffee and tea have gone up again. A woman in a shop the other day almost fainted when she saw the prices. We now drink mostly tea from leaves that we pick in the woods nearby. It is quite good, and cheap if you discount the gas you need to get you there.

Last week I was a bridesmaid or maybe I should say a coachman at a corgi wedding. Those are the dogs that Queen Elizabeth II of England keeps. They are very, very expensive and one little corgi is worth between two and three thousand pounds. Having assisted at the wedding night procedures I can tell you why.

Selma and Bernhard, our relatives, by now an elderly couple, own the only male corgi in the country. The female of the species lives in Nataniah and is the only one in Israel. The owner of the female desires corgi progeny. They have tried twice without success. So this time the two ladies, the owner and her dog, made an appointment at the vet's at six o'clock in the afternoon for the ceremony. Selma phoned for help. Bernhard, who is partly paralysed, has to be wheeled, and bringing him and the dog to the vet's is too difficult for her, so I took them in our car. With maidenly reserve the females did not show up and around seven I drove all three, Selma, Bernhard and the dog, home with the promise that I would bring Pampf the next time to stay with Bernhard and only take Pim, the dog, and Selma to the wedding. A little later I got a phone call that the appointment would now be at eight o'clock, the females having finally arrived; they were late because the dog had not been allowed to get on the bus.

At eight o'clock both dogs and owners were present but the vet had gone out. As it was impossible to keep Pim from getting overexcited too early, I drove him and Selma home again and waited for a call from the vet. Around nine the call came, we went back to the vet's and the fun started.

Have you ever seen a corgi? It looks quite normal when it sits or lies down. But it has exceedingly short legs and is not really built for procreating. Pim did his best quite a few times, but kept falling off as his legs were always in the air. So the vet and his helper tried to keep him up once he had got there by himself. He even fell on his back – Pim not the vet. The lady who owns the female, (we were never formally introduced) suggested putting bricks alongside her dog but the vet rejected the idea. By eleven o'clock everybody, even Pim, had had enough. The vet was not sure whether the coupling had been successful and told the females to come back in two days. The human female thanked us and said: "See you again soon!" It was my turn to fall on my back.

*

D.M. D.G. Bialik 22.1.78

Shlomit is in the Army somewhere north of here and very happy now. She has told her superiors that she has to be transferred as she does not get on with her mother, and even when she comes home she visits with her sister. She forgot to mention that said sister is living at the moment at her mother's together with boyfriend and a big Belgian Schäferhund called Lady who immigrated here from Italy, and when she takes a drink, apart from stopping all traffic from and to the kitchen, makes such a mess and awful slurping noises that any self-respecting pig would be ashamed of.

Lady and Speedy get on quite well, although Speedy would prefer to be sole master of a house that he has become accustomed to considering his own with plenty of food and servants.

Nava is happy and, it seems, successfully teaching difficult children to paint. Maya is a pleasure in small doses. Rona is learning bookkeeping and has speculated well enough to buy a car that she is afraid to drive.

*

D.M. D.G.　　　　Bialik, sometime after Pessach 1978

Here things are as exciting as ever. Speedy bit Erez' little brother. The dog sits on a leash in front of the house because the mailman has complained about him. Not satisfied with this arrangement, the mailman comes upstairs and kicks it. Since then Speedy has tried to bite everybody who comes near him. Erez gave the mailman a serious talking to and he stopped coming and kicking.

Speedy also bit the man who repaired the boiler. This was partly the man's fault because he put his hand into the dog's muzzle, and Speedy showed quite good judgement because the boiler broke down immediately after the boilerman left and I had to wait quietly but with mental hand-wringing for Pampf to come home and repair it. In the meantime I had the Niagara Falls at home and had to shut off the main tap. The repair took more than two hours. Only then could I wash the salads for the Seder.

Sundry people arrived at my home. Among them Shlomit who wanted a vegetarian meal, two young men who took tables, chairs, candleholders, knives and forks and also gefillte fisch for the Seder they had planned with Rona and Erez.

By five o'clock everything was finished including my nerves, and we awaited the arrival of the Efroni family. The Seder was held in Nahariah at the Iron's home, and salads, the fish and a few other odds and ends had to be packed. The Seder was nice and Maya behaved quite well. That is apart from asking for string in the middle of it all because she wanted to tie Ilana securely to her chair. We came home late and all went on a picnic the next day.

There were also several visitors who wanted to see Nava and, when finally everybody left, I flopped down on the couch and begged Pampf to bring me some fresh strawberries with sugar. He did so immediately, though unfortunately he took salt instead of sugar and with the last shred of my self-possession I refrained from spitting in the living room. I only asked him in a strangled voice to remove the offending dish and bring something else.

*

D.M. D.G. Bialik 27.7.78

Shlomit says that whenever she comes home I am making something for the Efronis. Rona says she has to do all her own sewing with almost no help from me. Nava says that owing to the fact that she lives so far away she doesn't seem to belong to the family any more, her feelings also being measured by the amount of sewing done for her.

My cousin Rachel used to say that the mother of a teenager can do nothing right, but apparently since I have no teenagers any more, a mother can't do anything right, period.

*

D.M. D.G. Bialik 22.10.78

The Post Office is striking again and we phoned Shlomit in Chicago. She will cable you and also Monica when she will arrive. The US government is against her staying another month and seeing San Francisco. I hope somebody will be in Stockholm to take care of her when she arrives and although the idea of her standing around in Stockholm all by herself is less frightening than the same in New York, it is an experience which she does not need for her future life.

In between sending Shlomit off, Rosh Hashana, Yom Kippur, Suckoth, a broken boiler (unmendable), babysitting with Lady, who is too big for our apartment, trying out a whole new cookbook, visiting Ma'ayan and Hanita for their fortieth birthdays, we managed to have a few days of vacation.

We spent them in Tiberias being afraid that in other places it might be too cold. Well, there it wasn't and my husband, ever afraid of not being warm enough, took me to bathe in the hot springs of El Hama. It is a place near Tiberias. You drive half an hour along the Jordanian frontier if you wish to visit it. Not that this is dangerous. El Hama is under sea level but somewhat higher than the Kinnereth.

The water is in an open air pool. A sign says that the water is 42 degrees and you are not allowed to stay in it for more than fifteen minutes at a time. You might faint, collapse or die. You are not supposed to swim either. But I did and although I did not collapse I felt terrible because while swimming one inhales all that sulphur and I did not do it again.

When you leave the water you get the illusion that it is cool outside, but this does not last long. After two days whenever Pampf had finished his sulphur baths, we drove on to the Kinnereth to recover and swim in real water. It is not clear what the benefits of the hot springs are. But unless you go there for three weeks I shouldn't think there are any. Lots of people hope that it is good for losing weight. Not that the bodies reclining around the pool give one that impression. In fact Pampf regretted having invested a small fortune in a Playboy magazine, as there was an abundance of female flesh, scantily clad in bra and panties, or wet dresses without benefit of those, all around us. It was not an appetising sight.

As there are few shady places around the pool, people tend to sit in clusters suffering and feeling smug about doing something for their health. One can listen to a lot of conversations all supremely uninteresting. Of course we did not understand everything as there was a lot of Arab and Russian talk flitting through the hot, still air.

If all this sounds a bit like hell to you, it isn't really, as you can get up and go – which if rumours are true you cannot do at the other place.

Hanita's fortieth anniversary was a big do and as Pampf belongs to the original pioneers[*] we received VIP treatment. We sat at a table next to President Navon's which was quite a nuisance as the TV crew tried to film him and we always got the light in our eyes. They did not film us in which case I would have excused the high-powered beams.

*

D.M. D.G. Bialik 4.3.79

I had a busy winter; I redecorated the flat and had guests visiting from the US. Among my other adventures was inviting six guests for dinner, four of whom came a week early when we were just about to get dressed and drive to Nahariah visiting friends. Since the guests came from Ma'ayan we could not very well send them back. I phoned the friends in Nahariah and begged them to come with any other people they might have invited and bring cake and other prepared goodies with them. They did! Our early dinner guests could hardly complain since Pampf had phoned Reuwen twice to fix the right date in his mind. I had had a feeling that there might be a misunderstanding. Both men had laughed heartily at my fussiness. Now there was more laughter, although mine was a bit on the hysterical side until I had a decent dinner on the table.

---

[*] See Appendix

Then I had the flu but got better in time to take care of Maya as her parents wanted to go to Europe. I was told it would be for two weeks only, but the two weeks turned into three as Nava had miscounted the days.

Maya is a very lively girl and I was glad that Shlomit was around now and then to take care of her. No napping time for the little one, as it was she went to bed only at nine thirty, at which time she usually decided that she was missing her parents very much. I had to tell her the truth, namely that they were not available and that I missed them very much too.

Once when left in Shlomit's care she greeted me plaintively with the words:

"I don't get on with Shlomit!"

She did not like my reply that it was out of the question that I provide her with a better aunt. I spared her the clinical facts.

One Saturday morning I looked out of the window and exclaimed:

"Oh, what a beautiful day!"

Maya pushed me aside and asked:

"Where do you see a beautiful day? I see only houses."

We took her to the woods, so she could see the day too.

*

D.M. D.G. Bialik 2.8.79

Rona is now happily married and her new name is Rona Taoz. It was a Yemenite wedding and I can only advise everybody to have one. One does not have to drag the bride and the groom to the Chuppah. They come of their own accord. One does not have to lead the bride seven times around the groom which is usually a very undignified procedure as there is hardly any room for three to walk abreast under the canopy.

One lady remembered that when she was married her mother told her to step forcefully on her future husband's foot so she would have the upper hand in years to come.

In our case Yemenite proceedings were especially appreciated as Erez' parents, who had been divorced a long time ago, came with their respective second spouses and there was room for all three middle-aged couples to stand in comfort and the question of who would have the honour of escorting the bride did not arise. They were married on the eve of the month of Av which the Ashkenazim do not permit. There were still a few religious snags but Motke, Erez' father, arranged everything. We did not inquire too closely as it seems that there was some blackmail, including a donation from a friend, involved.

The rabbis finally agreed that the young couple could be married before sundown. As it happened the rabbi was very busy and came after the sun had set, still the marriage is legal.

Times have changed a lot and Rona is worth 40,000 pounds. You may remember that I as a genitzte Kalle fetched only fifty at the time. Women's lib has still a long way to go and I hope it does although I do not advocate going without a bra after a certain age.

I have tried to bring up my daughters with a sense of their human dignity but I am not sure that Erez is always grateful to me. Especially when there is a dispute about who is going to make tea or coffee in the evening, both maintaining that they have worked all day. Just the other day Erez got up sighing to brew it but turned around first and said to his friend, Shimon:

"Never choose an Ashkenazit, otherwise you too will get up to make the tea while your girl and her mother remain sitting with their feet on the table."

At the time we had our feet on Selma's old suitcase.

The marriage was filmed by a friend who tapped me quite often on the shoulder because I was in his way. Nothing came of the film but not because of me.

The food was marvellous and all prepared by Motke's wife, family and friends. The dancing and singing had to be seen to be believed. It was so full of joy. The Jeckes did not join in but appreciated the merry atmosphere. Maya, almost six, thought it a good idea to get married to Shai, Erez' little brother, since the rabbi was there anyhow. There were two problems; Rona would not give up her flowers and Shai, aged ten, was not willing to renounce his bachelorhood. Maya did not take it to heart and danced till her parents took her home. She managed intricate steps and paces and her partner had to recall her to his presence. Seev, her father, less interested in dancing, enjoyed the food and somebody who did not know he was the brother-in-law of the bride remarked:

"That guy ought to pay for what he is eating!"

The wedding took place in the garden of the American Union College where Motke works as a gardener. We sat outside, enjoying the dry Jerusalem air and the lovely evening.

*

D.M. D.G. Bialik 6.9.79

I had an unexpected visit from a neighbour the other day. They usually do not come, as they are afraid of Speedy, who barks ferociously at all comers. Only one friend comes for an occasional chat, braving the lion in its den. I am not sorry about this state of affairs, although it keeps out the good as well as the bad.

I had been out all morning, had just relaxed over a cup of coffee and was on the point of attacking the housework.

The first thing that hits people in the eye when they enter is Shlomit's outsized and unmade bed. When she came home from abroad she used to make her bed every morning before going to work. I was quite proud of this late blooming of a careful upbringing. It soon degenerated into once a week bedmaking and by now I have lost count of her activities in this respect.

Regrettably the rest of the apartment did not look much better. I had washed the floors on the appointed day but had not had a broom, so the result was not too good. Pampf broke the broom a few days earlier when he had pushed the fridge off its wheels and had tried to push it back with the broom. As was to be expected the stick expired. In spite of my warnings he had also dislodged the stove while he was about it. In the end we succeeded in returning the fridge and the stove back to where they belong. It is beneath Pampf's dignity to wait for the younger generation to come home and help. So I remained without a broom and the floor was not shining.

To make matters worse, I have the unfortunate habit of only dusting when guests are expected. I do not consider a little dust as dirt. We hadn't had guests for two weeks so I had skipped it. The children used to write their names in the dust. As an educational device it was a failure and I pointed out to them that the dust was theirs as much as mine. After looking at the pictures on the wall my guest spotted Shlomit's rocking chair, also a heavy, oversized piece of African hand-made furniture. She sat down in it exclaiming:

"Oh! What a beauty!"

After rocking a while she got up and where her arms had been the wood was suddenly bright and shiny.

At moments like these nothing much can be said. I could only hope that she would be as discreet about my dust as I had been about her cockroaches, of which I had been told. Cockroaches have the advantage over us by millions of years and are a law unto themselves. I have also been discreet about another neighbour's home where my daughters stopped babysitting because they disliked being stuck to the floor by unidentifiable messes.

Everybody has their own preferences about what or what not to clean.

Although I do not talk about these things to my neighbours, I privately strike a superior attitude. Today cleaning day has come around again, but it amuses me more to write a treatise about cleaning than actually do it. After mature consideration, I have decided that Rosh Hashana is too far off to do any in-depth cleaning and I am certainly not doing it twice. Soon we will go to Switzerland for a month and by the time we come back the dust will have settled again.

*

D.M. D.G. Bialik August 1980

I had a letter from Kurt Lewin from, of all places, Bratislava. A first in our lives, he has never written a letter to me before. If he waits another forty years to write the next I might not be alive any more.

I seem to have told you about Rona's wedding. No, I don't know the price of a camel, and even if I did, it wouldn't be the same by the time you got the letter. Bread prices doubled last week. I will spare you the rest of the inflation.

I shall have to write about all the misfortunes that have overtaken us. Shlomit had jaundice and had to stay in hospital. She was quite ill.

I broke my left hand, I also sprained it and had an open wound. The doctors who examined me did not think much of it; neither did I but I would have liked to have it attended to nonetheless, and mentioned it before they put the plaster cast on my arm. I was asked several times where I had fallen, which was in the garden. They were unimpressed and neglected to clean the wound with the result that when they took the plaster off after a week they found a piece of glass in my arm. I was not surprised as I had felt that there was something wrong.

I got a new cast and lived with it for five weeks, during which time we had two young cousins from Germany here for two weeks. They enjoyed their stay although they had to help with the washing up. I became quite proficient with one hand and was able to hang the wash from a window with a peculiar flip of my right hand and holding on with the plaster. Sometimes things fell down but no oftener then when both hands are in good working condition. The cooking went all right too and I learned a few shortcuts that formerly had not occurred to me.

Three days after the cast came off Pampf swallowed a chicken bone which first lodged in his throat and then in his tummy. It eventually disappeared, but he too had to go to the hospital. Soon afterwards he had an infection in his throat that may or may not have had something to do with the chicken bone. Our doctor did not see anything, mainly because she did not look and Pampf had to go to the hospital again for a week. A few days after he came out, the right side of his face had an odd cast downwards which got worse, then stopped, then got the tiniest bit better. He has been in the hospital every two days for check-ups. Everything anybody could think of in the way of examinations was done without finding anything. I shall not give you any details, they are mostly disgusting.

*

D.M. D.G. 5.10.1980

My bank adviser, Rona, has brought me Israeli pounds again instead of the new currency, as there are no shekels available. If rumours are to be believed they are printing them again having burnt the old ones.

Prices in the stores are partly in pounds and partly in shekels and with the inflation the way it goes, you can't ever be sure what they mean. I have suspended payment at the grocer's for the time being till things clear up a bit and also because I don't like him.

*

D.M. D.G. 3.8.81

It was nice to hear from the Kalters that you are still alive and kicking. So are we mentally kicking at Mr Begin and his misgovernment. We really suffer when we see and hear him on TV. I have been told that most of the people who voted for him are illiterate, as all the papers are against him but I can't give you a first hand opinion as I do not indulge in the masochistic pastime of newspaper reading. TV is quite enough for me and we have to pay for that too.

Our immediate plans are a trip to the US, formally okayed by the embassy, who at first seem to have had their doubts about me. After seeing Pampf's multiple visa they granted me one too. They were probably impressed by his earnest Zionist's face and the fact that he is the import manager for International Harvester.

The trip is occasioned by the fact that Jack has his sixtieth birthday and my niece, Tammy, is getting married. On our way back we shall stop in Copenhagen, take a car and tour the south of Sweden. Stockholm is too far. That's why you get a letter that you haven't earned. We want to meet you and the Kalters somewhere south of Norrköping.

For the wedding proceedings I will have to take a dress with me; a problem, as I hate shopping for dresses. I have decided to take the one I bought for Rona's wedding. Nobody in the States has seen me in it and several people have told me it looks nice. Well, they would hardly walk up to the mother of the bride and say: "My God! What an awful dress you are wearing!"

It is not the latest fashion but some people might think it is in Israel and who am I to disabuse them of such thoughts? Shirley wrote that she will not allow me to go to the synagogue in pants and if she remembers that I had the same dress with me last year but did not wear it she is too nice a person to remark on it. Not like a friend of mine who when seeing me in a perfectly presentable but aged pants suit, remarked:

"This still looks very nice, how long have you had it?"

I'm not sure if I wrote about the additions to the family. Nava has a nine month old daughter, Amit, and Rona a six month old baby boy named Noam. When they are all here together, with Maya who is now seven, you can't hear yourself think. Nava and daughters visited us two weeks ago. Naturally Rona and family appeared as often as possible and also, naturally, at mealtimes. Knowing this in advance I had cooked a lot before they came. What I could not know was that Nahariah would be shot at in earnest that same week and Menahem and Ilana would seek shelter here, as they have none of their own. They stayed about the same time as Nava, which was a week.

Once when eight people sat down to dinner, not counting the babies who also sit and take up a lot of space but do not really eat, the door opened and Shlomit arrived bringing a girlfriend from the Army for the night.

Everybody ate and slept somewhere. Shlomit and friend found the atmosphere congenial and stayed the whole next day too, telling me from meal to meal that they would remain for another food offering. I had some help but people did not take their tasks seriously. Nava, who had to string beans, cut off only one end and left them whole; so did I and I got some astonished looks.

*

D.M. D.G. 25.2.1982

I think I wrote you two letters and I hope your not answering is due to laziness and not illness or freezing weather or both. We had no real winter, the rains started only around the end of January. Till then we had sunshine and were very unhappy but I don't expect you to understand that.

Pampf was in Bruxelles and Milano on business where the weather was pleasant and came home to torrential rain. His suitcase was wet even on the inside. He was not pleased either but it is better than blue skies forever.

Since the library fired me, partly because they want to reduce the staff and partly because I did not smile sufficiently at our mayor, I am now a student of ceramics at the university in Haifa. I am quite glad that I was fired and enjoy my studies. The university, as you may know, is way up on Mt Carmel and I am always astonished and incidentally very glad when I arrive there in one piece. Pampf is afraid that I will fill the apartment with big ugly sculptures but I am not advanced enough for this and am obviously the last person who wants a lot of sculptures to dust, handmade or otherwise.

Speedy was run over by a car but escaped with a dislocated leg. The doctor's bill came to 400 shekels. I would gladly have paid more if he had been able to go out by himself.

I have always had visions of growing old gracefully, still with a good figure, silvery hair, elegantly dressed, etc. etc. You have read about such people in books. I find it extremely difficult with a resident dog, an almost resident grandson, two granddaughters who come for frequent visits with their parents, aunts and one permanent and one changing uncle. Although it now seems that Shlomit has found what she has been looking for as we hear no more discussions about whether or not he is the right one and if not how to get rid of him. Even Maya complained in the presence of one of the boyfriends that she could not be expected to remember all their names and would Shlomit please keep the current one?

Erez has finished his studies and is looking for a job; Shlomit is studying English and the Bible to get her matric. Rona just arrived alone for dinner, her husband and son had already eaten at his mother's.

*

D.M. D.G. 27.7.82

Thank you, although belatedly, for your prompt letter depicting Gert with a fever in bed and Speedy with a dislocated leg. I am keeping the drawing to show people what a dislocated leg looks like.

Things around here are as hectic as ever and I can't imagine how I ever found the time to go to the library to work. At the moment the ceramic course is all I can manage apart from this crazy family.

Several months ago things were going quite smoothly and I started to tidy up all the cupboards and dressers to get everything organised, now that we are, theoretically at least, two persons and a dog, and the dog whatever else his faults may be, does not need any cupboards. Then the wallpaper hanger suddenly appeared and put wallpaper up and my idyllic cupboard cleaning came to an abrupt end.

Speedy did not mind the guy who hung the wallpaper, a very nice bloke who fishes in Elath when he is not busy wallpapering. He is also apparently fond of dogs as Speedy got him trained in no time to open the door for him whenever it pleased him to go out or enter.

Pampf then talked about having doors and window frames painted. He has done this for the past ten years but this time I took him seriously enough not to return our books to their shelves. Luckily, because the painters really arrived. They painted the doors, the windows and screen frames and made quite a mess, but I was told that it could have been worse. It usually can. They finished on a Friday. Pampf and I went out for lunch and prepared to rest and start on the dirty work afterwards. It was at this point that we received a phone call from Ilana and Menahem that Nahariah was being shot at again by Katiushot and could they come over and sleep at our house?

"Of course!" we said and hurriedly made the guest room ready. We also had to put the doors back, among them the one to the toilet which presented us with some difficulties and almost led to a divorce. I advised Pampf to wait for Menahem and do the job with his, a man's, help. He refused, he prefers me as a helpmeet after all. They stayed several days and then war broke out. All the kids came for visits. Haim, Shlomit's boyfriend, was called up. They plan to get married in October. By now he is home but may be called up again at any moment. Seev was called up too but he had had an accident two years ago and was not deemed healthy enough to be shot at.

By the time the house looked normal again it was time to prepare for Nava's visit with Maya and Amit for the summer holidays. They came a week later than expected so we ate the food I had prepared in advance and I had to improvise during their stay. Amit, not yet two, is not housetrained and Nava is quite unhappy about that, as Maya at her age was clean during the day. Nava decided to let the kid walk about without benefit of her diapers so as to be ready in an emergency to have the potty inserted under her behind. Unfortunately this does not always work, partly because Nava is busy talking to the other members of the family. On the first day little Amit emptied her bowels on the porch and then sat on Pampf's favourite chair. There was quite a bit of yelling and cleaning to be done. Next morning, a Saturday, Pampf got up early to make breakfast for the whole family and Amit climbed into his empty bed wetting it out of all proportion to her size. I had to wash a lot of sheets, scrub the mattress and then, thank God, Nava gave up her training program and put diapers on the kid.

Naturally there was a lot of to-ing and fro-ing between the Taoz family's and our house and at the end of this ten day vacation, Shlomit, Haim and Seev came too. I had made the house more or less childproof and can't find anything any more.

Shlomit packed most of her belongings to take with her and auctioned off the rest to her sisters and nieces. There were leftovers that nobody wanted and by the time everybody left, the house was in such bad shape that there were several rooms that you literally could not walk into. When I had almost finished sorting things out I got a phone call to say that Nava and family were coming again. By that time Rona, pregnant, was moving to another apartment which is not on the fourth floor without an elevator, which is difficult for her to manage. So apart from feeding people I also took care for a few endless hours of the two babies and the dog who comes and goes continually when they are here.

Pampf played 'Go' with Maya behind closed doors. They know what is good for them. The dog was sick and had to get shots which made him pee all over the place. That's when we had visitors from the US. My brother-in-law's first wife with her third husband. They came for dinner and invited us back to Haifa for a drink. When we came home we found that the dog had slept squarely and fairly in the middle of our beds and had had an attack of pishing. You can imagine the ensuing workload.

We want to take a vacation but with Rona expecting a baby soon, Shlomit getting married, Nava proposing a visit, and all this apart from the ongoing Lebanon war about which you can read in the paper, it is not easy.

This war is called "Shlom Hagalil" which roughly means peace for the Galil, it has the same aim as the Litani fighting, to get the Syrians and the PLO out of Lebanon.

*

D.M. D.G. 15.10.1982

We are home from Switzerland where we spent three weeks with Lea and Benjamin from Ashdod. We started from Basel in an extremely small car; I had to take my shoes off before getting in, otherwise there wouldn't have been room for my feet. We drove to Stansstad, Tesserete, Ronco supra Ascona, La Chaux de Fonds, Moutier, Baden and back to Basel with a few other towns thrown in. We visited the Isola Bella in the Lago Maggiore which was a big disappointment to me, as it was all tourists' claptrap and its beauty seems to have vanished. Not at all as I remembered it when I had been there with my parents.

For part of the way we had a very bad odour in the car. Among the suitcases, bags and parcels that four people are apt to carry with them the origin of that awful smell was hard to detect. It plagued us, and especially Lea and Benjamin who were sitting nearest for several days till we finally decided to unpack the whole car in Montreux and the culprit, an aged cheese, was found. Benjamin with his head held high, ashamed of having an evil smelling thing like that in his possession, disposed of it at quite a distance from the hotel as well as our car.

Since Pampf did almost all of the driving and Lea needed a smoke whenever we stopped, Benjamin and I were responsible for accommodation. In Ronco we contacted the owner of a restaurant as we were told that she also had rooms, apartments and a hotel at her disposal. She took us to an apartment house and we followed her over a pretty rocky road up and down the mountain with me always anxiously asking if we could get there by car. She got quite impatient and assured me that if she said it was near a road, it was. Later on I had to concentrate on my breathing and did not ask any more stupid questions. We arrived at the apartment house from above, it was built into the rock and had among others the perfect flat for two couples with a good road at the base. The lady who was quite a bit older than we were put the house in order for her guests as quickly as she had run up the mountain. The house also boasted a swimming pool and a terrace for sunbathing overlooking Lago Maggiore at its best.

While Pampf and I were taking our well earned rest, Lea and Benjamin went out and bought detergent to wash all the dishes in the flat as they did not trust whoever had washed them before. This was very nice of them and we took the detergent with us in the car wherever we went. In Basel, however, I decided that it was not mine but theirs and I proceeded to return it to them. Lea, being somewhat nervous about our return trip, refused to accept the small parcel. Not wanting to burden myself with any unnecessary weight I dropped the offending package in a waste basket at the airport, half expecting a fusillade from the Swiss soldiers who were watching us closely, arms at the ready, from above. When Lea asked later about the soap I explained loftily that I had thrown it away.

We were also lucky with our rooms at a hotel in La Chaux de Fonds. The owner, a former chef, had bought a place outside the town with three rooms for guests and a big restaurant where he cooked to his heart's content. The rooms were huge and we did a whole week's washing immediately. The food was excellent, the host agreeable and we would have stayed longer but our rooms had been booked some time before. The landscape around the town was marvellous. The clock museum well worth visiting.

On the 19th of September, Rona's baby daughter, Lior, was born. On the 22nd we came home, and also on the 22nd my niece, Tammy, arrived for Shlomit's wedding which was on the 30th.

I wore the same dress, slightly changed, as at Rona's and Tammy's wedding and was told that this time I looked much more elegant. I had new shoes and a new necklace.

Shlomit is now Mrs Haim Cohen and very happy. The wedding was very nice only the music was too loud, as is usual in this country. It was at the school were Haim works and one could go outside and sit in the garden. Neither at Nava's nor at Rona's wedding did I eat much and I decided that this was my last opportunity. So while Pampf made the rounds to see that all the guests were satisfied, I sat down in lonely splendour at the head table and fed my ulcers. They have a tendency to act up at weddings.

For the next weeks I was busy with the ever growing family and their incursions into my home, kitchen and larder. I took with equanimity the fact that Maya broke half a bottle of wine and half the phone, Amit a light bulb, and also that part of the fridge fell out, but became slightly ruffled when I found that some of the children had borrowed my floor rag and not returned it which made it difficult to clean up.

A Great Sorrow

I've just reread all the letters of condolence that I received. All were from the heart in their grief about Pampf's dying. He had been ill on and off for five years, in and out of hospitals, taking medication and gasping for air.

"Don't let the kids know, don't let anybody know!" he told me.

In the spring of 1985 Esther and Eck invited us to stay with them near Nice in a rented apartment. The doctors not only consented to our going, they made a journey to France and Switzerland sound like an all-time cure for emphysema and other ailments. When our car was parked a little too far from the travel agency in Haifa Pampf had trouble walking back to it and I became doubtful if we should go. But he had his heart set on the trip and we made it; almost from the hospital to the airport.

We remained with the Künstlichers for a week and although Pampf was frail and tired we were all glad to have this time together. Then we rented a car and drove on the Route Napoleon to the Swiss border and from there to Zürich. As far as we could we enjoyed the scenery, the sunshine, the quiet, the hotels, the food and being with one another. The doctor had not told Pampf that some of the pills should be discontinued after a week and later taken again. He had swallowed them regularly every day and only when he read the small print and stopped taking these particular tablets did he feel a little better and less sleepy.

On our last day in Zürich we went to the zoo and in spite of my objections Pampf insisted on walking up and down the mountain looking at more animals than I thought strictly necessary.

"I can't spoil myself like that. I have to move!" he exclaimed walking on.

He had a heart attack next day at the station and I rushed to a pharmacy in the Bahnhofstrasse to bring him nitro-glycerine which he knew would help him. Pampf himself looked up which platform we were to use. But once there he insisted on taking the train on the opposite siding. After an initial protest I was afraid to argue, he had just taken strong medicine and looking at the clock I was sure that we would get to the airport in time even if we travelled first in another direction. Luckily an officially clad person came by and pointed out the train to Kloten. I retrieved our luggage from the wrong train and put it on the right one. Only when the train moved and the conductor had seen our tickets and approved Pampf grinned and admitted to being mistaken.

On the flight home he had to be given oxygen twice but refused a wheelchair on arrival.

The customs officer in Ludd held up his hand to stop us but when he saw Pampf's face he took his hand down again and let us go through without a word. Erez, who had come to take us home, was shaken when he saw how haggard Pampf looked and when we discussed visiting Shlomit first he said:

"I'll take you anywhere you want to go!"

Pampf wanted to see his youngest daughter, her husband and his youngest grandson. Roi had been born a little over a year earlier. He also wanted to give them their presents. I was adamant; visiting was fine, unloading and unpacking out of the question. After a lifetime of never going anywhere without taking a gift Pampf could not bring himself to come for once empty handed. He may also have felt too tired after the trip. We drove home and half an hour later he asked me to call the emergency station. By now it was late evening. Two doctors came and sent for an ambulance at once. Pampf would not let me come with him, he stood in the doorway pushing me back:

"You stay here, you can't do anything at the hospital, you'll just sit around all night. Go to bed and rest. I'll phone you in the morning!"

Unable to remain in one place, I unpacked and cleaned the apartment. An anxious week followed. I stayed with Pampf as often and as long as I could but the head nurse in the emergency ward would send me out time and again. Pampf had always to ask one of the male nurses to please call me back.

One day when Pampf was evidently suffering great pain I tried to get the attention of a nurse or a doctor which in the end I could only do by entering the doctors' room where one of them told me that he knew Pampf was in bad shape and started to quarrel with the head nurse as to who had given me permission to enter their sanctum. I was close to tears. Luckily the head of the ward on his way home threw a perfunctory look into Pampf's room, saw the state he was in and in seconds I was thrown out again and the whole apparatus for emergency examination was put into motion.

I felt as if I had been through a wringer. One would think that being in hospital is the best possible place for a sick person to be, but not there.

Again, Pampf did not want me to tell the kids how serious his condition was or let them or his brother come as long as he lay in the emergency ward. At the end of the week he was pronounced well enough to leave that section and I phoned Walter to say that he could come and visit next morning.

I drove home and was just about to eat some soup when Nava stormed into the apartment. She rushed to the phone; she had left Maya and Amit alone and wanted to know if Seev had arrived home from work in the meantime.

"I couldn't stand it any more!" she said. "I had to see for myself what is going on."

We sat down together to eat and I had hardly begun to tell her that her father was feeling better, when the phone rang. It was the hospital.

"Are you Mrs Weil? Will you please come immediately!"
Erez took us to the hospital. I did not trust myself to drive. I was stunned. Rona was in Tel Aviv studying for an exam that would be the next day. Erez drove straight back to his children and Nava and I spent the night outside the barracks which is the emergency ward for heart attacks. Pampf was in a coma. When he became conscious early in the morning, we were allowed to see him. The doctor told him:

"Your wife is here!"

I had taken his hand in mine and Pampf pressed it. Then his face changed and the doctor sent us out again. Half an hour later on the 21st of June my husband died.

II

Erez came to take us home and the whole process of notifying the family and arranging for the interment began. Many came to Pampf's funeral. The children, his brothers, Jack had come from Chicago... friends, neighbours, chaverim from Ma'ayan, colleagues from work. Some I did not know, many I had not seen for a long time, it all became a blur.

There is nothing solemn about a funeral here. The whole train of people had to wait for the grave to be readied, the body lay on a stretcher without a coffin and Pampf's hand fell out from under the covering, it was a horrible moment, it still looked so alive. The cantor held out his hand as soon as he had finished singing. He had just performed a good and necessary deed and wished to be paid.

Erez hadn't listened to me when I told him that one has to bring money to a funeral and I had been told not to bring my purse. He had to borrow from a friend.

Not having a purse, I also had no keys. Seev had locked the apartment, pocketed the keys and taken his mother back to Haifa after the funeral. Erez had to climb over the roof and the porch to open the door for us. Jack sat on the stairs and cried and I went to console him although at the back of my mind I had a faint feeling that it should be the other way around.

The children remained and we sat Shiva for a week according to Jewish custom. People came to visit during that week. They visited me, they visited my daughters. The house seemed always full, the phone seemed always to be ringing. Walter and Jack came often. We had to eat; my sons-in-law did the shopping and I cooked. Some of the children's friends sat down at the table with us, I was never quite sure how many there would be. It was June and hot, and we offered cold drinks to everyone. Neighbours brought cookies and cake and would have brought whole meals if I had consented.

After a week I remained alone and the rage started; the rage at Pampf's death, the rage at his dying like that and without having seen his family. The rage that all his possessions were there and he wasn't. The unfairness of it all. Then the doubts began. Had I done the right thing in letting him travel to Europe? Should I have overruled his decision of not letting the children come to see him? Had I done enough? Should I have remained at his bedside day and night? Would any of that have helped?

Lies and Fredl came to Israel that autumn and I learned more about emphysema from Lies than from any doctor. Her brother-in-law had died of it. There is no cure and it is a slow death.

The rage has long since gone. The doubts and the grief remain ten years after my husband's death.

III

As an antidote to grieving and feeling guilty I cleaned and scrubbed. I scrubbed all the cupboard doors and promised myself never again to do this particular job. I sorted out all of Pampf's belongings and gave the children what they might use and then I dreamed that Pampf had come back and asked where all his belongings were. I choked, I had no answer, a nightmare!

I started to clean the apartment on Saturdays to overcome the loneliness of the day that we had used for swimming and lying on the beach in summer and going on outings whenever the weather was fine. The entrance door broke down, then the fridge and the washing machine. The bank wanted me to settle accounts. I had to cope and I did.

Cuni, a widow herself, said to me once;

"You have to decide whether you want to live or not! It's very hard!"

Noam came over on his own several times in the afternoon to sit with me now that I had no husband. He asked many questions as children will do and in his own way tried to comfort me.

Being alone slowly became my normal life but even today I catch myself thinking:

"I have to tell Pampf about this," whether it is a new baby or a new traffic light or news about friends.

More Letters

D.M. D.G.   10.6.86

    First an explanation: This letter is written with heat (not that I am angry) on thermal paper which is very sensitive. I have a nightgown with the words on it: "I'm very sensitive!". It is, of course, American and has nothing to do with this letter. The paper dislikes heat, dampness and light and I thought Stockholm would be a good place for it. Don't put medicine on it or oil, don't rub it with a hard object as it might develop colour because of the friction. Don't put it in the car when the sun is shining. All or any of this would ruin the letter, although why you should try to experiment in this way is beyond me.
    I have 30 degrees heat in my apartment at eight o'clock in the evening and shall not touch the paper myself only maybe after midnight. I can feel my brain melting.
    We will now proceed to the real letter.
    My congratulations to Monica and Daniel. I hope they will be very happy! Here, you have to be very careful whom you marry. Divorce for women is too difficult and for men too easy. A man can, if the rabbis allow it, and they do so for the most extraordinary reasons, take a second wife and let the first wife fend for herself.
    Seev has returned from Australia, Rona and Shlomit are in the throes of their last exams, Erez is working a lot of overtime and Haim wishes to study as soon as Shlomit has finished. She is expecting again.
    Pessach came around as usual and there were eighteen people for the Seder. With five children running around, with

people bringing pots and pans into the kitchen and remaining to chat, things became hectic. Just as we were trying to sit down Speedy came home bloody but unbowed. Pampf always took care of the medical aspects of our family and I have no idea how and where to start. Though he once treated me with vitamin C, which might have been good for a horse, and gave me something against seasickness instead of sleeping pills, I trusted him implicitly.

Luckily, Yael, Nava's girlfriend, came for the Seder and she has lots of experience with dogs and did all the dirty work in spite of her pretty dress while I held the dog down.

It had been arranged that Amit, now five, should sleep at Rona's, the Cohen family and Maya with me, and Nava and Seev at above mentioned girlfriend's house. When all had taken to their respective beds, Rona brought Amit back because she would not stop talking and her own children could get no sleep. She brought her, naturally, without the mattress that I had sent over in the afternoon. With Maya's help I put the kid to bed. The Cohen family were fast asleep; they have always been a very tired bunch of people.

Next day everybody assembled here for breakfast and a picnic that I was supposed to have prepared, God knows when. People tried to help but asked too many questions. Ilana, another of Nava's girlfriends, came over and brought four kids who I believe were all her own. She planted herself firmly in front of the fridge and looked surprised when I threw her and everybody else out. The picnic went well, till at the very end Noam and Lior wallowed in a mud puddle and Erez refused to take them home in his car. I gave them the dog's towel which I keep for emergencies in my car to wrap them up in.

The other night I came home to find three very tall policemen in front of my house. They were not easily recognisable as such and I had doubts about going home. Still I did and when they started asking questions I asked for identification as one of the things they wanted to know was if I lived alone. One policeman was outraged but the second said that I was well within my rights. Although when I took out my glasses to look at the identification even he became indignant.

Actually there is Speedy but although he has a mean bite I doubt if he could do something serious about burglars. They had just apprehended two of them trying to get into the house, though whether they were interested in the upstairs or downstairs apartment the police wouldn't tell me.

*

D.M. D.G. 30.10.86

My biggest news is that Shlomit is expecting twins next month and she could not get a job in view of this event. I am supposed to go and help whenever they arrive, and I am not exactly looking forward to it but am not supposed to say so. I know that other grandmothers would bubble all over with joy. I'm probably just lazy.

Seev has founded his own company and decided never to go anywhere without his family again. Nava, on the other hand, is willing to let him go now and then, not for too long, to let off steam. He is an expert in cooling systems and air conditioning for trucks and other vehicles.

I had an interesting vacation in the States, Canada and Switzerland. I flew from here to Saginaw via Amsterdam and Chicago, stayed a week at Bill's and went on a three week tour with him and Shirley to Ontario, New York State, Vermont, Hampshire, Maine, Nova Scotia, Prince Edward Island, New Brunswick, Quebec, Ontario, Michigan. We travelled 6382 km, or 4114 miles. One day we had breakfast in Vermont, lunch in New Hampshire and dinner in Maine where we met Cuni, my cousin from Budapest, Werner and Margot, my cousin and his wife from Atlantic City, and a friend of theirs from Germany. Werner wanted to reduce my food consumption to two meals a day.

"This", he said, "should be enough for anybody!"

Since Bill was paying my expenses, I objected and told him:

"It is our custom in Israel to eat three times a day!"

Actually we eat more, but in an emergency I can do with three meals. He later remarked:

"I am awfully sorry. I did not know that you had ulcers and a legitimate reason for eating more often."

"Apology accepted!" I answered. "But I really don't think I need a legitimate reason for eating when hungry."

As he was forced to sit at the table for a third meal because everybody else did, he ordered a bowl of soup and then proceeded to eat more rolls with butter than anybody else.

We travelled together for a few days, taking a ferry to Canada, and had a lovely time when decisions had to be made. Breakfast the first day in Maine was to be at 10:30. I refused point blank. I always wake up at six and Cuni, who wakes up even earlier, kept me company at a very early breakfast. We had a long chat over our coffee and afterwards a refreshing nature walk as it is called in the US. We then went to my cousin's room which she shared with the German lady, who opened the door for us clutching a very small towel in front. When she saw me she stood up straight instead of rushing back to the bathroom, held out her hand and said in a strong voice:

"Guten Morgen!"

It was a memorable and very German experience.

On our trip we visited the amusement park in Toronto and saw lots of Italians there. We had a false fire alarm at the hotel, luckily false otherwise I would not be writing to you as it took us a long time to realise what that awful noise was. We slept three to a room because it is cheaper and since Bill was so tired that he fell asleep with his clothes on, Shirley thought that he should go and find out if there really was a fire. In the meantime several huge fire engines had assembled in front of the hotel. Bill complied with our wishes but stated:

"You realise, of course, that they won't let me come back if there is a fire!"

Bill came back with good news, but the hotel forgot to inform people officially.

We took a boat trip through the Thousand Islands, which are a lot nicer than the salad sauce. We saw a play in Gananoque which was surprisingly good. I lost $5.75 on the ferry to Nova Scotia, and we celebrated Shirley's birthday with a lobster dinner in a church restaurant. This is how they get the money for the leaking roof nowadays. I took almost five rolls of film, Bill took fourteen and we all had a thoroughly good time.

Back in Saginaw we had just missed the flood and travelling in canoes through the streets. Tammy's and Tom's vegetable garden was flooded and peppers and tomatoes could not be used. But Tom sold a lot of carpets as the inhabitants of Saginaw had had the sewage flow back into their houses and their carpeting had to be ripped out.

From Saginaw to Chicago to visit Marilyn and Jack for three days which was not a great success. I read three books while there, which I can do more comfortably at home.

From Chicago to Zürich for a rest and then home for Erev Rosh Hashana. I had been told on the phone that the family dinner would be at my house, but not to worry, Rona would do the cooking. What I had not been told was that the Taoz family, owing to redecoration schemes of their own, was living at my apartment. On the way home we collected Speedy at Shlomit's. He has by now had another tooth drawn at high cost and the vet will soon kiss my hand when I get there.

The things I left at Nava's house are still there, I only insisted on getting my driver's license and my credit card back and these were sent through Rona's bank. I could not ask for shoes and other apparel. The bank after all is not the parcel post.

Although I do not get unnecessarily upset at our politics, having the dwarf, Shamir, flitting across my TV screen all the time is about the limit.

*

D.M. D.G.   1.4.87

Thank you very much for the picture of the coming generation, your granddaughter, Maria. One can see very well that you are only too pleased to be wound around her little finger.

Did I ever write you that once I had Amit in my arms in the swimming pool and looking into my bathing suit she asked why I had a behind in front? She also told me confidentially that Mona, her kindergarten teacher, had the same.

At table, when everybody but Amit got a knife, she exclaimed with every sign of joyful anticipation.

"When I'll have hair on my pipi, I'll get a knife too."

Grandchildren! Be ready!

I had a long, wet and busy winter. Busy because of Shlomit's twins. Long like everyone else's and wet because apart from the rain several pipes broke, the main tap got stuck and one could not shut off the water, and the repairman had no intention of working in or under water. He made a hole from what would be the attic if it were a little bigger to the bathroom which let the water run off and I had a lovely time cleaning.

The twins are male, not identical, named after Pampf, Assaf (Josef) and Eran (Ernst). They are, objectively seen, very cute. I have always viewed my daughters and their offspring objectively and shall continue to do so.

I spent two weeks with Shlomit before they were born because Haim was working late in the evenings. Then I went home and came again when they actually arrived to prepare for their homecoming. For the Brith Mila I also worked although all I had to do for the event was drive one of the twins to the hall. The other twin was in another car. I hate driving my grandchildren at this tender age, especially in Hod Hasharon where everybody who gets into a driver's seat is instantly overcome by some madness not often seen even in Israel. They do not repair the roads there and think that potholes contribute to the beauty of the landscape and help to keep foreigners like me out.

I stayed for another two weeks and was then allowed to go home for a weekend. At home I discovered that I could not speak and had a temperature of over 39°, I, who with a fever of 37°, am mortally sick. I was told that this was typical for bronchitis which I then had for more than three weeks. During this time Shlomit had only three hours sleep in twenty-four and received me with open arms when I reported back for duty. She exclaimed on the phone from the depth of her being:

"Thank God!"

Haim, too, is pleased and said I could come whenever I wanted and since I fit in so well with his nearest and dearest I could stay for two years. Even considering all the circumstances it was still a nice statement. After that I went back and forth in different states of exhaustion. Once I was so tired I did not even wake up when Roi stood next to my bed screaming his head off with earache.

Since I have been home Shlomit came with all the children for a one week visit and I got a big bunch of flowers from a grateful father for his vacation. When they all left I locked myself in, disconnected the phone and slept till the next morning at 10:30 and Shlomit went green with envy when she heard about it. Well, I was young once and for several years got up every night all to do with Rona and Shlomit. Nava never wanted anything but sleep at night. Shlomit is planning to come again, probably after Pessach.

I wish you a nice Seder and may come and visit you in September.

So long

D.M. D.G. 24.11.87

I am home again and can only think with longing of the days now becoming a dim memory, when I was spoiled by friends and relatives from Stockholm to Budapest.
The train ride from Stockholm to Helsingborg was eventless and Esther and Eck picked me up at the station. A day later Shirley and Bill arrived and Eck took us through the glassrike with an overnight stay and a visit to the paper factory in Lessebo. Next day we had lunch on Öland and came back to Helsingborg. Saying goodbye and many, many thanks to our hosts, we took the train to Oslo where, according to weather reports, it had rained buckets. After Göteborg the train hemmed and hawed and the conductor came to our compartment and made something of a speech. Bill kept nodding his head and agreeing. After the guy left I asked:
"Did you understand what he just said?"
"No, I didn't."
"So why did you nod?" This was, I think, a good and relevant question.
The train came to a halt and we tried to look out but could not see much. Suddenly the conductor came back, regarded us with exasperation and explained to us partly in English, partly in sign language, that we were in Moss, that the line to Oslo was flooded and the train could not get through. We would have to get out and continue by bus. We raced to the buses on the double with all our luggage. I was almost run over by another bus which would have been a pity. Not only did we make it, we even got seats.
After the long train and bus ride we were hungry and had a meal of sorts at the station which was probably the most expensive and lousiest we ate on the whole trip.

We had opted for a hotel a 'little bit out of town' because Oslo is not all that big to begin with. By the time we took a taxi we were not in the best of moods, the long journey topped with insufficient food had taken its toll. We were driven out of the station, through Oslo, out of Oslo, up a mountain, down a mountain, up another mountain where the driver finally deposited us near the entrance of the hotel, and although I gave him a nice tip he did not bring any of the luggage in.

The weather had been bad here too and there was no electricity. We got a candle with our keys. Having trudged around with my suitcase to the train, from the train, to the bus, and to every other place we had had to go I refused to budge and demanded help. The young lady at the reception smilingly picked up my and one other suitcase as if there was nothing in them and raced to our room. I had trouble keeping up with her. The room was very nice and by the time I was ready for bed the electricity had come back on.

When we had arrived we had met an American lady, very pleasant but fat, so that even I recognised her next day in broad daylight. She and her husband had come by car and gave us a lift into town and the first thing we did was ask at the station how we could get out of Oslo again. We were told it was possible but nobody knew how. We had to be satisfied with this information, walked around the town and took a tour through four museums. I had enough with three and rested my tired knees a bit. Enough is enough is enough. We took the train back to our eyrie in the mountains, or so we thought. This train could not get through either and a bus took us to a station higher up where another train took us almost to the hotel and then we walked. Our appetite for dinner was excellent.

By common consent we remained at the hotel all next morning as it seemed useless to go into town. We spent the time with the American couple who told us that he had been stationed in Italy and before returning to the US they were taking the grand tour through Europe, each one snapping pictures right and left. There was one place they had to visit again as the pictures had not come out. They also gave us a prolonged and detailed description of prostitution in Napoli during and after World War II up to the present day.

Having had enough sex, we took a taxi to the station where Shirley and I watched people doing other things and incidentally our luggage. Bill walked about till it was time for us to board yet another bus from a very muddy field. A few people had to stand and some shouting went on as it seemed not quite clear to everyone where the bus was going. Suddenly one man yelled a destination and was told that this was not his bus. He got off, taking his luggage with him which was unloaded from the compartment underneath and consisted of a full-sized bathtub. Everybody in the bus released their anxiety by laughing madly. When our bus left I saw that man still standing forlornly in the mud next to his tub.

We drove away and I pointed out the Royal Castle to Bill who, without turning his head, said:

"I already took a picture!"

Oh! Oh! Oh! Un autre chateau!

As was to be expected, the train was late in Göteborg. Tiring of my suitcase, I took a taxi back to the station next morning and sent my suitcase to Augsburg where we were invited to my great cousin's wedding. In spite of Shirley's and Bill's dire predictions it awaited me on arrival. From Göteborg we took the ferry to Fredrikshaven but did not stay in Denmark because of the different currency.

We went straight to Hamburg where a deep depression overcame me which I walked off next morning partly in a museum and partly in the biggest Hamburg store. In the museum I saw a map of Europe and the Middle East but although my home country was on it the name Israel was not. This did nothing to assuage my gloom. Shirley and Bill went to Lübeck and Shirley bought me some lovely roses to make me feel better. Next day we went to Flensburg which I knew, and believe to be a little bit Danish.

The day after it was time to travel again and I convinced my relatives not to go sightseeing in the morning in order to avoid getting to Augsburg around midnight. We took the morning train and arrived at a normal hour, in time to have dinner with Ferry and Beate, the parents of the bride.

The cousins took us to our hotel and when Shirley stepped into the car, Ferry, being a very nice man, opened the door for her and carefully lifted her long coat into the car so it would not get dirty. Shirley is the victim of a rigid puritanical education and the minute she felt a hand on her coat she screamed as if she were being raped and poor Ferry, quite stunned, let go of the coat and left it and Shirley strictly alone.

On the wedding day we had champagne at Ferry's house. There were quite a few people milling around and in the excitement and euphoria one female relative was locked up and Ferry had to go back and release Dagmar from the apartment.

The wedding was ecumenical as the bride is a Catholic and the groom a Protestant. This made the wedding longer, as both religions had to have their say, but the music was nice. We were in a Catholic church and there were boards for kneeling but few people did.

When it was finally over I was good and frozen. How do they expect people to be religious when they give comfort in such an ice-cold atmosphere? I do not remember being cold in a synagogue when going there as a child with my mother. At least orthodox Jews can sway back and forth, keeping warm, which kneeling Catholics can't.

We then stood in line to congratulate the newlyweds. We had done this before but getting nearer to the couple I had pointed out to Bill and Shirley that, although not good at recognising people and not knowing the groom from Adam, the bride looked very unfamiliar to me. It really was the wedding before the one we were supposed to be attending.

We had a wonderful time drinking lots of lovely wine and dancing half the night. I think my dietician is wrong in forbidding me to drink alcohol. In spite of my new shoes and my old knees I felt no pain at all. For fear of people getting too drunk wine was free but anybody who wanted something stronger had to pay for it.

It is also the custom in Bavaria to abduct the bride and the bridegroom has to buy her back. The family stipulated that the bride could only be abducted inside the building because too many of these abductions had ended in a ditch or worse due to drunken driving.

Bill, Shirley and I were introduced as: "My cousin from the States, his wife and his sister." One Bavarian gentleman, somewhat inebriated, sat next to me and protested how he had always loved the Americans but one could not always say so, one did not always know whom one was talking to. And I thought to myself:

"You have no idea whom you are talking to now, better shut up!" But I smiled politely.

Shirley who hardly drinks at all, now drowning in German with a funny accent at that, took to the good wine like a fish to water. When she filled my glass twice to the brim I knew she had had enough. Because usually when I drink she watches me like a hawk and goes: "Tsk! Tsk!" at me.

When the wedding guests started marching around I walked out taking my cousin with me for a breath of fresh air. Too much Bavarian Gemütlichkeit is not for me.

Next morning I took the train to Budapest and had ample time to think about the wedding, the wine, the dancing and the fun we had had. At the Hungarian frontier came the rude awakening. Well, not rude. Everybody was extremely polite. First somebody came to ask if I had a passport. He did not wish to see it, just to be sure. Another official came and asked if I needed a visa. No, I had applied for one in Stockholm. The next official asked to see the passport and the visa. I was then asked for my ticket and it turned out that I had to pay from the frontier to Budapest as my Eurailpass was not good for Hungary. Then two people came and searched the train. Then one more official came and asked if I had anything to declare.

After that things were easy and I got to Budapest without a hitch.

Cuni awaited me with a baggage cart and took over. She received me as if I were a cross between an aged aunt and her beloved daughter. The only thing she was strict about was sightseeing. I had a hard time convincing her that if I am standing on one hill, looking down on Budapest and see another hill opposite with an ugly statue, there is no point in going to the other hill with the ugly statue and looking down at Pest and Buda.

I saw a lot, among other things the synagogue and where Cuni had stood taking care of children when the Russians arrived. We met a couple from Tel Aviv also visiting the synagogue who could not understand what an Israeli who doesn't know Hungarian is doing in Budapest.

There I was everywhere introduced with gusto as an Israeli, whereas in Germany people are wary about mentioning Jewish roots however small, apart from the newlyweds who had been willing to tell everyone about theirs with pride and who would soon be on their way to Israel and me for their honeymoon.

And then I came home: Nava was going to move the next day, so I fled in the early morning to have breakfast at Shlomit's. The whole Cohen family had gotten up at five o'clock and looked it. Shlomit takes care of two other kids five days a week. This being Friday was not one of her working days.

When she awoke to the possibilities that my coming had for her, she rushed Roi into his clothes and pushed the kid and Haim out of the house, shoved the twins in my direction, took my car and went shopping. I cooked a meal for us in the meantime. Later I discussed my homecoming with Rona on the phone but when I arrived the house was empty although there were signs of recent occupation. It turned out that Rona and family were moving back into their apartment, having again lived at my house because of another of their redecoration schemes. They were naturally busy so I made dinner for the lot.

Later that week Ilonka and Wolfgang from Augsburg came after spending five days with Shlomit. For the past thirteen days I have shopped, cooked, led sightseeing tours and given sightseeing counsel and may now live my own life again. Well, not quite, in case I forgot to tell you, Nava is expecting twins. They are due in December.

*

D.M. D.G. 30.12.87

Here is the big news from Israel. Nava's twins have arrived safely. They are called 'boy' and 'girl' as their parents haven't given them names yet. The babies are still in hospital because the boy has hepatitis and Nava commutes from her sixth floor apartment to the hospital. The lift at their apartment house is out of order and she sometimes stays at the hospital from one feeding to the next to save her legs. Seev and Nava at times park one car in the evening at the hospital because in the morning all parking spaces are occupied. Then Seev takes Nava there in the morning and she drives her car back when she has finished.

"Oh, you poor darling!" I said to her.

"Ima! Nothing of the kind, I am not poor at all," she answered. "You should see some of the babies there. I am very lucky indeed!"

I went to stay with them yesterday to be of help and take care of Amit who comes home from school when the apartment is empty. I met her near her school and she took me to the new house to which they moved to have enough room for the twins. She could not open the entrance door and told me that we could get in through the back. I did not argue, being loaded down with parcels and luggage. It turned out that going through the back door was quite a distance. We went around the house and downstairs and inside the house upstairs where we reached the elevator which was as I mentioned non-functioning. Amit went up to see if her mother was home because her car was there. She wasn't and we climbed together to the higher regions loaded like packasses in the Himalayas. And there I remained.

Next day: Amit has returned from school and is too tired to eat. Nava and Seev have gone to the hospital to bring the babies and life here will be back to more or less normal. I go home tomorrow, there really is not enough room for me.

It is raining, it is cold, it is winter and even in Israel winter is not always pleasant. I can sing a song about that since at home I have burst pipes again, an oil heater that is not heating, a wet spot on the ceiling of the guest room, and a few other items that have to be seen to. And quite frankly I wish I were there to see to them because at home, in spite of all my troubles, I have an electric blanket to sleep on and a Spanish convector to keep the room warm and other little comforts like quiet in the night. No stray persons walking about at ghastly and ghostly hours, as happened last week at Shlomit's.

The babies are home; they are sleeping and perfectly sweet, but will probably change at night into two screaming little devils.

I wish you a very good New Year. It is now forty-five years since we escaped to Sweden. What a long time and how life has changed since then!

*

D.M. D.G. 11.4.88

The whole family assembled here for the Seder. Shlomit came two days early so that her kids could get used to their new surroundings. They did so very well and in record time. The twins are now one year and four months and Roi is four years old. He was greeted with the greatest pleasure by Rona's children who kissed and squeezed him. All my grandchildren have this liking for their younger cousins and the smaller and more defenceless these are the more they are kissed and cuddled.

I had cleaned and shopped and cooked and childproofed the house out of all proportion. I had tried to find out early from Shlomit if she needed anything special and got her shopping list the day before the Seder. Being a good mother I shopped again and encountered a great traffic jam going home from the supermarket. I drove in the opposite direction through a side street and with the help of a decent traffic light made it back.

Having finished the work, I even had a nap and thought that everything was under control. It was then that a great screaming attracted my attention. Eran had fallen off a bench and broken a tooth out with the root. He had reason to scream. He was taken to the sickfund where nothing was done but the parents were calmed down and given instructions how to feed the child. This is the kid who eats anything and weighs two kilos more than his twin brother who is not exactly starving himself either.

The table laid, the food ready, we now awaited the Efroni family with mother-in-law and cake. When they finally came and everybody had greeted everybody else and all the paraphernalia for two babies had been brought in, it was time for their feeding. They are three months old. Some of the other kids and some of the grown-ups helped themselves to food, and watching the scene I had the feeling that I am not as strong as I once was and might not be able to go through this particular experience often again.

Next year one more baby will grace the Seder table, Rona is pregnant but not with twins. Whilst two babies were being burped the reading of the Haggadah began and Roi went to sleep on the couch. People sang and recited and I was afraid that the line where it says "und jetzt wird nach Belieben gespeist!" had been overlooked. But no, we could finally eat. Seev exclaimed that the food this time was good and Erez helped bring in the dishes and cut the meat, something I never do when the house is full. As soon as we had eaten Noam went to sleep on the second couch. Slowly but surely everybody went to bed. Lior started to scream and was taken home by her parents with a sleeping brother and one of the cousins. Nava and Seev took the babies and went to Selma's house to sleep there. They forgot the baby food and had to come back. Everyone else, including Seev's mother, was deposited around the house in different beds and Maya helped me clean up the mess. Then the two of us retired to my bedroom and looked at old snapshots.

Most people came next morning for breakfast which was an American 'help yourself' affair. Some kids went out to play, some grown-ups went back to bed. It was very quiet for about ten minutes and then some of Nava's girlfriends came, bringing some of their kids. News was exchanged and fresh coffee served. After that nobody wanted even to hear about lunch, so I had a small unkosher snack by myself and retired to my bedroom. At three o'clock people were hungry again and I served a hot meal. Afternoon coffee was served at Rona's house, but before we could all move Eran started to throw up and continued to do so for the rest of the day and the night. Assaf was moody too and next morning Shlomit and I took the kids to a doctor. Assaf was pronounced healthy but possibly jealous and Eran and Shlomit were sent to hospital for observation. Roi and Assaf remained with me. Haim came back from work to take his family home and when everything was packed and the children deposited in the car it would not start. I rushed around to get cables for starting it because mine are in Tel Aviv in Seev's car.

By now Eran is well again and I have been cleaning the house for two and a half days, removing Mazzos and Mazzo kneidl from tables, floors, walls and some unmentionable places. Next year Shirley and Bill and a new grandchild will be added to the above mentioned personae.

P.S. We are so deep in botz (mud to you) that there does not seem to be any way out. The fanatics on both sides are getting the upper hand and everybody outside the government knows exactly what we should do.

Our soldiers have quite often the order not to shoot and we have American policemen writing to the Jerusalem Post that during the unrest in Detroit they had orders to shoot to kill. Maybe Arab lives are more precious than Americans' of whatever colour. No more of this, I hope you are well.

*

D.M. D.G. 1.8.88

The kids were here and unplugged the freezer – my God what a mess!

I visited them and am now back in my quiet home where I am not awakened early in the morning by two diapered persons yelling, "OMAAH, OMAAH!" into my reluctant ears.

*

D.M. D.G. 14.9.88

Shlomit's twins are two very loveable and extremely active boys. They open every door and every closet and one of my big kitchen cupboards is now permanently stocked with things they may play with and that I do not need, especially not in the kitchen.

The other twins are quite as active and although they do not yet walk, they get everywhere they want to go only a little slower. Little number ten, Rona's daughter Lihi, will soon be crawling around here too.

I bought traps to be put in the kitchen, not for small children but for small cockroaches who have shown signs of wanting to settle here again.

*

D.M. D.G. 6.1.89

I am not really an envious person, but having put my feet into every museum I could, so to speak, lay my hands on, while I was in Switzerland missing a Schiele exhibition by a few weeks is really too bad. I hope you enjoyed it. I ploughed through every museum in sight, even the Beatus Höhle sports a little one.

Jack was here with wife, two sons and one daughter-in-law. We visited the cemetery. Rona came with the kids and I gave them a meal of sorts as it was neither lunch nor dinnertime.

In answer to your question, of course I wrote poetry when I was young but I did so in German, and some of it I even like today.

Politically, things are getting worse all the time. It is also cold, sometimes wet and my doctor sent me to have tests and an

ECG. The ECG was fine, the machine wasn't. Neither was the nurse. First the chit from the doctor got lost, then the nurse did not know how to operate the machine, so she called another nurse, they put all the cables on top of me and spoke about taking 'IT' apart. I insisted they do not take me apart. I was told to be quiet. When the machine had warmed up whilst I froze and was being rubbed with cold water, they stuck little metal things on to my body which fell off. I mentioned this to the two nurses who had not been quite sure where to put the metal pieces in the first place. They both turned on me and told me to relax and shut up. As always, things could be worse but not much. Maybe I'm healthy! I'd have to be to stand up to this treatment.

P.S. Rona and family are now members of the country club in Acre and Noam has complained to Lior that she has all the fun since she can enter the ladies' showers and see all the big busts, whereas he is confined to the men's shower room where nothing interesting is on display. They usually go with another family and Noam has asked Lior about the other lady's bosom. Lior stretched out her arms and said:
"My hands are not big enough to show you!"

*

D.M. D.G. 17.7.89

Thank you for your good wishes for my birthday. The occasion got lost between Pampf's memorial day and the children's end of year festivities. I never invite my elderly relatives when there is a chance that the young families might arrive and they would have to suffer the little children. After all, we are not Christians.

I haven't had much time this spring. Shirley and Bill were here for Pessach, and the whole family congregated at my house for the Seder. Shlomit came here for a summer vacation with her three boys and assorted other grandchildren appeared for meals and such, and in my spare moments I drove them wherever they wanted to go.

*

D.M. D.G. 10.2.90

Thank you for the beautiful picture of Nacka. I am sending you one from Saltsjoebaden. Sweden is more beautiful than Switzerland, especially for parched Israeli eyes. Still I prefer going there because the Swiss know how to make tourists comfortable and it can't happen to you there that you follow a sign to a restaurant for several kilometres and at the end you not only find that it burnt down some time ago, but that there is nothing in the way of food anywhere near. And God, were we hungry.

I went to Ashdod in a raging storm. One should sometimes listen to the weather forecast, but I arrived safely anyhow.

*

D.M. D.G. 22.4.90

Pessach and the Seder are always good for new experiences. Only Nava and family came but when we were ready to sit down, Mor and Itai, the twins, were missing. They had come provided with tricycles by their thoughtful parents and had taken the opportunity thus offered to widen their field of activity. They were helped by Lior, now seven, who took them to the nearest playground. It took thirty minutes to get them back. Then Seev and Amit decided that they were not dressed for the occasion and my nerves became slightly frayed.

I am going to Spain and Portugal in May and to the States in September and have a very bad conscience about spending so much money on myself. I have been advised to put my scruples in the washing machine.

*

D.M. D.G. 15.7.90

Thank you for your good wishes. My birthday was a busy day. All the kids came and I tried to work less and ordered the food at the Chinese take-out. Haim came with me and took one of his kids and luckily his car. Eran had not been feeling too well and on the way back he was sick over the food which was wrapped extremely well, thank God. Haim cleaned the packages and the kid and Shlomit cleaned the car. Dinner was a little late.

Over the weekend a glass, a vase, and a picture frame were broken and the overloaded electric network expired so that we sat for ten minutes in the dark with a lot of screaming children.

One of the kids turned the freezer off. Apparently they thought that I had liked that the last time. I saw the mess only three days later! This time I called the electrician and he rearranged the electrical outlets so that the freezer is now on a porch where children are not allowed and grown-ups seldom go. At present it is empty, I am saving money for my trip to the States.

One of the grown-ups broke my fan, one of the kids peeled off some of the wallpaper and then tried to pull an electric cord out of the wall. This is where I came in. I gently detached Mor's hand from the cord and wallpaper. She was deeply offended anyhow and cried for the next forty-five minutes in a very monotonous voice.

When you opened this letter you probably thought you would read something about Spain and Portugal. I am coming to it. They were both interesting, scenic and very photogenic. The Spaniards were not very friendly when we were together as a group, they were much politer when we went out for lunch on our own. They knew less English than the Portuguese and all of them were weak in arithmetic. One had to watch them.

In Barcelona I was given an occupied room on the 6th floor which was very inconvenient as I had just arrived from Tel Aviv and needed a private bathroom most urgently. The clerk had read the room number wrongly, which I pointed out to him but was disbelieved.

From Barcelona we flew to Malaga, stayed in Torremolinos and had to leave by taxi and train because there was a bus drivers strike on. We missed Gibraltar and went straight to Sevilla. The train broke down on the way and we moved into another, carrying our luggage. Guided tourists are not supposed to carry their suitcases but in Spain this was very difficult as we were usually too early or too late for the people whose work this was. In Sevilla the bus driver and the bus awaited us at the station. He had gone through the picket line under police protection. We too had been offered this chance but had declined to take advantage of it. To have stones thrown at us in buses, we need not go to Spain.

Apart from Sevilla we saw Cordoba, Lissabon, Estoril, Cascais, Cabo da Roca, the westernmost cape of Europe, Sintra, Nazaré, Obidos, a veritable jewel, Batalha with a most beautiful cathedral, Leiria, Salamanca, Avila, Toledo with two beautiful synagogues, and Madrid – our last stop, where we even had a little time to ourselves and could do what we wanted for two whole days. We saw the Flamenco, heard the Fado and danced on a boat on the Guadalquivir drinking Sangria which we mixed ourselves. It was a trip full of wonderful sights and I decided that I had to see both countries again one day, taking in the views in a more leisurely manner. I even had a gentleman friend who paid for my taxi rides. He is over eighty but not much. At the end of the trip I knew more Spanish than our guide, which was not difficult because he knew none.

Franco's grave, in the Valley Of The Dead, is in a most beautiful place overlooking a grandiose landscape. That is not surprising, seeing that he had the whole of Spain to choose from. It is also a memorial for all those who fell during the civil war in Spain. The tapestries, we were told before entering, were made by prisoners. I lost any wish I might have had to view the huge hall and left to eat an ice cream.

As my friend Eva remarked so aptly:

"I am neither a Catholic nor a fascist, what am I doing here?"

Maya is leaving at the end of the month for Europe, including Russia and Lithuania. Partly to dance with her group of folk dancers, partly to sightsee. It is a great opportunity for her but I wish she were already safely home again.

My family is very hard working and none of my sons-in-law are available for small repairs. What I need is, of course, a boyfriend who is handy with a drill and preferably not over eighty.

Be well D.

*

D.M. D.G. 28.10.90

I travelled again, a month in America and two weeks in Switzerland. The last night or what there was of it I slept at Nava's. She drove me at two o'clock in the morning to the airport and when she came home was afraid to get out of her car as this is the hour of the thieves. The usual waiting in Ludd, flight to Paris and more waiting. Then the plane to Detroit with another delay which I used to take a bus to the prescribed gate only to have to march back almost all the way to my starting point.

It was then announced that my flight to Flint was cancelled and we were offered a bus. A two hour drive instead of twenty minutes on a plane. Not trusting my ears or my English I turned to my neighbour who, after the initial shock had worn off, confirmed what I had heard. From Flint Shirley and Bill drove me to Saginaw and after twenty-five hours travelling I finally entered the Berton abode. Once, for a moment, I had the impression that I might collapse but nothing came of it.

After two days' rest we moved on. We went to Canada to see a play in Stratford, not especially but because it was on our way. Bill drove nearly six hours to get there, we did some sightseeing on the way, found a restaurant for dinner and when I sat down in the theatre I was ready to drop.

The theatre was a big hall with wooden benches slanting upwards on three sides of the stage. A couple and a young man sat behind me and the lad's feet were at the height of my ears. He stamped and shouted loudly. When I could bear it no longer I turned around and asked more firmly than politely:

"Will you stop that noise?"

He answered in a very friendly way:

"Sure, Lady, I will!" He was as good as his word.

Five minutes later the three of them were on stage. They and especially the young man were the stars of the evening. The play was involved and not as funny as I had been led to believe. I had trouble keeping my eyes open and just a few moments after I decided to shut them for a little while, I felt some movement in front of my face. The young star was standing there trying to give me one of the flowers that he dispensed to the public. It was the first time in my life that I absolutely needed to close my eyes during a performance and the first time I received a flower from an actor.

Trying to keep me awake Shirley went out during the interval and bought ice cream. When she came back I asked;
"Where is it?"
"It's in my purse."
"Well, take it out!"
"You are not allowed to eat in here."
"No one will see us, it's already dark!"
"No! You can't do that! Give me something to put under my purse so it won't melt on my knees."

I gave her the program. When we came out, by the feel of it there was no ice cream left.
"Throw it away! You can't eat that stuff any more!"
"Not on your life!" Shirley was determined. "If you knew what I paid for it you wouldn't talk like that."

We slurped it up and when Bill, who had had a beer and a nap in the meantime, picked us up at the theatre we were slightly hysterical and had trouble telling him why.

We travelled roughly 2,500 miles visiting Moura, our school friend from Florence, in Canada, and my youngest nephew, Rob, his wife and five loveable children in North Carolina. In between we were in Washington and saw the Smithsonian - unforgettable; had entrance cards for the Senate and Congress where many talk and few listen. We went to Mount Vernon, Washington's little villa and Monticello, Jefferson's smallhold, designed by himself. These people were rich on a grand scale. Having been guided through the White House and Mount Vernon, I decided to take a self-guided tour, thus advertised at the entrance, in the gardens of Monticello which included sitting on a bench and enjoying my surroundings. There I was pounced upon by a lady who told me in the fifteen minutes that

I sat there, her own and several other life stories, including somebody's complicated operation, what her mother had said on her deathbed and other stimulating titbits.

We drove over the Outer Islands of North Carolina, slept in a motel in Devil Kill Hill, seeing Nagshead and the place where the Wright brothers experimented with their flying machines. The islands are flat and sandy with clusters of high grass, grey wooden houses on stilts, and the ocean moving rhythmically around them.

In Europe I spent two weeks in Switzerland and was told in Chur that I had been given the biggest room in the hotel, God knows why, and when I left the lady at the reception said:

"Oh, you had the biggest room!" (It wasn't that big.) "Did you like it? Did you sleep alone?"

Well yes, actually I did, but what a queer question!

Now I am back again in time to get my gas mask for the next war. If rumours can be trusted, the gas in Iraq comes from Germany, so do the masks. We are not allowed to open them, as this is detrimental to their well being. One can't wear glasses underneath the mask and it is troublesome to put them on without.

And how do we know when to use them? Who can know what kind of bombs will be dropped? If they are the regular kind, you hurry downstairs into a shelter if available. If gas is what they want to kill you with, you go upstairs as high as you can. I have no problem as my air raid shelter is my bathroom and I can't get on to the roof. One is supposed to have a battery-operated radio permanently noising into one's ear and, so one hopes, ALL will be told you.

We are a long way from beautiful gardens and snow-capped mountains with sunshine and a few clouds judiciously scattered here and there in a blue sky.

In the meantime Rav Kahane has been murdered. I can't say I grieve for him, nor do I know anybody who does. Many a better man has been murdered with less provocation. It is said that no one is irreplaceable, on the other hand I was taught, and it might be from the Bible or the Talmud, that every person is unique. So let's piously hope that in this case religion is on our side.

*

D.M. D.G. During the Gulf War

Thank you for your letter and the postcard. It is nice to get mail from abroad, all my other letters are from the bank. You ask about my limp. I broke my hand, why should I limp? The last time I broke a hand I was told to go home and wash dishes. This time I didn't even ask. I also took off the plaster cast by myself with permission of the doctor, of course. There was no one else. I was just in time to seal off the little room near the entrance with ugly brown tape, and deposit my sculptures on my bed.

The first night when the sirens sounded, Rona's mother-in-law rang to tell me that Rona was alone with her three children. I went over to help and somehow or other, after the all clear signal, all five of us ended up in the big double bed. The other nights I remained at home.

Some people get phone calls from the US from relatives telling them: "You will have an air raid immediately, go to your sealed room!" And by the time they put the receiver down the sirens are sounding. Many boast about the number of phone calls they get from abroad, the more inconvenient the time the better. A phone call might have done me some good as I slept through two alarms. The sirens in Bialik are somewhat weak.

We too keep phoning each other and asking how everybody is holding up, and there are lengthy talks with grandchildren who cannot be visited. The only convenient time would be on

Saturdays but we have Scuds coming in as early as seven in the morning. I would hate to be caught alone on the road. Erez, who often comes home late from work, just goes on driving and when stopped during an alarm by the police, once explained that he would certainly not sit on a dark road in the Galil near Arab villages with the chance of getting a knife in his back.

We had two Scuds yesterday night but nothing was hit. Five minutes after one of them fell, Shlomit called, it was announced that it fell south of Acco.

Having been told that one should not sit next to or opposite an outer wall I later chose the toilet as the only room where this is possible. There I sit with my phone, my pocket computer, my gas mask and, most important of all, my radio.

Announcements are made in Hebrew, English, French, Russian and Amharic. The contents of the different languages do not always match. At least the first three, I do not have to worry about Russian and Amharic, neither of which I understand. The military speaker, Shai Nachman, has a very calming voice and is the one to release us from our discomfort. He has been called the 'Valium of Israel' and a song has been written about him.

The Ministry of Education had nothing prepared and all children in educational institutions were sent home. When schools started again but kindergartens didn't, Nava took the twins with her to school. Shlomit distributed mail with one or other of the children when Haim was not available and he usually wasn't. Young mothers had a really hard time.

Shlomit's children refused to put on their gas masks and were paid to do so by her. I think ten agoroth was the going rate. Rona was luckier than most with two grandmothers around the corner.

Seev has been called up and is quite glad to earn some money as business has almost come to a standstill. Oranges and flowers are not picked. Vegetables not harvested. The Arabs from the so-called occupied territories can't come here and work. The intifada is still with us and curfews are the order of the day on the other side of the green line. After six o'clock in the evening everybody stays home. It is said that some Arabs danced on their roofs as the Scuds kept coming but later decided to stay inside for safety reasons.

An Arab doctor from the Nahariah Hospital had a piece of Scud damage his house and asked his Jewish colleagues what he had done to deserve that.

I have been invited, with my brood, to the States and to Germany, but so far only Shlomit would be willing to send her children away because they drive her nuts. Many children did not go out for two weeks, spending their time in front of the TV watching children's movies or the news about the Gulf War, called 'Desert Storm'.

Mor and Itai when asked if they knew why they were home said firmly:

"Because we are sick!"

*

D.M. D.G. 10.3.91

I wish you both a happy birthday and a good New Year. Owing to circumstances I never turned the pages of my calendar.

Having got over the Scud stage we are now embarking on the much more dangerous road of peace in the region. And what a government to do it with! Apart from peace there are many other problems that massive immigration brings with it.

Two people died directly from Scud attacks, thirty-five died on the road during that time. The proportion of the wounded is similar. A few elderly people choked to death in their gas masks not knowing how to handle them. Teachers who fled the country and did not come back in time or are still abroad are supposed to get fired, but the Histadruth disapproves. Mail is coming in again very slowly. Nurses and doctors are on and off strike. The nurses want pay for overtime during the war. I don't know exactly what the doctors want; they wrap things up.

I had my own little accident when I had to brake suddenly one hundred metres from a traffic light and was bumped from behind by the next car. I managed to brake again and avoided damaging the car in front. As I got out the man who hit me greeted me with a cordial, "Good morning."

"What!" I said, not being used to politeness between hitter and hittee, also not at my best at seven thirty in the morning. After this exchange of pleasantries I let him write down the requested information and have since been told that this is wrong.

Some people give completely fictitious names and addresses but he has been found. He was as honest as he was friendly. His insurance company will have to pay a slightly inflated bill, but they have enough money. The garage made a nice buck and I was the only loser. The hitter went merrily on his way but I was without a car for two days.

Since my bus comes but rarely, I flagged down a taxi, realising at the last moment that the driver and other passenger were Arabs.

Ever since those women were murdered at the bus station in Jerusalem I have had a spray against dogs in my purse. Hiding my hand under my coat I took hold of it feeling ridiculous and too old for this kind of adventure. When more passengers filled the car, most of them Jewish, I put the spray back with relief.

Prior to the war there was not enough money to keep the kindergarten open on Fridays. Parents had to pay extra or care for their children at home. Now, as compensation for shutting down said institutions during the war, they will be kept open all week till the end of the year. Many people, not believing in peace, have left the sealed rooms sealed. Yours truly among them. It is quite a bit of work to rip off everything and in many cases the paint comes with the tape and who wants to spend money on painting the house just now?

You should come and visit us before the next war.

*

D.M. D.G. 14.9.91

Erez will go on a business trip to the States and go to Sweden to honour his karate teacher. He will visit you too, be prepared.

This year I will take Maya with me to Switzerland and France for a month before she has to go to the Army. It is her eighteenth birthday present. Her other grandmother is very pleased and asked:

"And what will you buy her?"

"Nothing!" I said. "I think the trip is quite expensive enough."

"But surely if she wants something you will buy it for her."

Well I won't and if I know Maya she won't ask for anything. There are more grandchildren waiting to be treated well. It is the considered opinion of many Israelis that 'Abroad' is one great store house where one goes to buy and buy and buy.

I wish you would address cards and letters to my POB. I have been asking this from friends and relatives for more than two years with limited success.

*

D.M. D.G.   9.12.91

Thank you very much for taking care of Erez, he was very enthusiastic about all of you.

I can't imagine that I did not write fully about my change of address. I live in the Date Street and some fool started to send some of my letters for no reason at all to the Fig Street. There a responsible man picked them up and phoned me, and I drove to Fig Street to retrieve my mail. We both complained to no avail at the Post Office. This went on for months and months. I then had the fabulous idea to bring dates and figs to the Post Office to show them the difference but was convinced that they would only remember that they got both and wouldn't recall where I live. The idea to really look at the envelope would probably not occur to them. I bought two boxes of dates and wended my way to the office where they sort the mail.

Everyone was pleased and I was assured that I would get my letters from now on at my real address. You can guess what happened next. I got a phone call a day later that there was more mail lying around for me in the Fig Street again. I could not help myself but laughed out loud, whereupon the man in the Fig Street with whom I had had many a conversation and a few meetings accused me of not taking life seriously enough.

So I hired a POB and told him so. I gave him a plant with pretty flowers at the bank where he works, thanked him for his endeavours and said goodbye.

You seem to have the wrong impression about my trip to Europe with Maya. She is eighteen and did as she was told, and whenever she was uninterested in her surroundings she listened to Israeli songs on her walkman. She had brought an ample supply of tapes in her sponge bag and came on a four week trip with no soap, no shampoo, no face cream, no body lotion, no toothbrush because she couldn't find it, and no toothpaste (why bring toothpaste if you haven't got a brush?). She is a very clean young lady and apart from a brush, which she bought, borrowed everything from me.

Before I left Rona and family came to say "Goodbye!" Lior immediately entered the bathroom and washed her hair leaving it wet and hairy. Lihi and Noam ate Popice dribbling all over the place and Erez examined what kind of food I had still standing around.

Shlomit received the car for the duration and drove me with one yelling twin to Nava's where I spent the night.

Mor and Itai fell asleep at eleven o'clock, Seev and Maya came home around twelve. Nava and I saw a movie till one o'clock. I was then given a bed and Maya started packing, discussing in extremely loud whispers important things like whether to take chewing gum with her mother. The dryer worked with part of a zipper in its insides that nobody can get out. This piece of metal made irritating noises at odd moments. I had hardly fallen asleep when I had to get up again and was taken to the airport.

Maya came almost without a coat and only decided at the last moment to take a thin jacket belonging to her father. She felt quite cold when we went in a cable car to the Diavolezza, and as I took her picture sitting in the snow she asked me to hurry, reminding me she was not made of concrete.

We took a trip to France with a Swiss tourist company and saw a lot of places we were not supposed to see, and did not get to see some we were because the driver took many a wrong turn, and his colleague, a young girl with a map on her lap, was no help. Apparently she could not read it and was unable to direct him.

Coming back we had a big entourage, Seev and the Cohens coming in full force to take us home. Shlomit asked immediately for a tissue to wipe the twins. Seev asked for tissue to wipe off some ice cream he had eaten. Haim asked for tissue to wipe his nose. Shlomit could not find the keys to my car. Thank God I have spare keys for everything. She found them later in a pail underneath some rags. She had washed the car. Good kid, but forgetful.

When you take the departure together with the homecoming, is it any wonder that, like clockwork, I need a vacation every year?

*

D.M. D.G.   K. Bialik, end of January 92

I have bought a computer together with the Ginossars and a friend of theirs and we got a sizeable discount. As Gad says we are still young enough to enjoy it. I ask a lot of questions of Gad, Sara, Shlomit and Norman, a friend in Rosh Hanikra who has had a computer for years. I am always hoping for clear answers because reading the computer literature is extremely boring in any language, at least for me because, even if I understand what I read, it is seldom what I want to know.

With Norman's help I now have Einstein so I can write, and Scrabble so can I play against the computer. Norman also gave me Hangman, but I do not enjoy it. Hangman is a word game and the first word the computer asked me to guess was "zyzzyva". Naturally I did not know it. It is a tropical weevil. I have come across weevils in English literature but never known what they looked like. Now to my great astonishment I found that it is a Kornwurm in German and probably quite small although hardly appealing.

I have big news for you. I received a letter from Joachim from, of all places, Elath. He seems to have problems with events that took place about fifty years ago. I wrote a short note and will write him more fully later on. On the 2nd of January it was my mother's hundredth birthday and would have been our fiftieth wedding anniversary had we stayed married.

I wish you a happy New Year. Come and visit me, look at my art...

*

D.M. D.G. Spring 1992

 Maya is in the Army and apparently quite happy. She calls me quite often and also writes but has trouble sending letters. In Switzerland this activity had to be watched, especially after she sent our hotel room key which looked like a credit card to an unknown destination in the mail and we had to ask for a new one.
 I had a long letter from Joachim. Apparently we are embarking on a correspondence which was not what I had had in mind when I wrote an explanatory letter about why I had left him all those years ago.
 It seems that I have developed a split personality. I told Maya ten good reasons why I did not need a new jacket at the time and two days later went out and bought one. When asked how long ago anything was I am prompt with the wrong answer. I always have to add the years since Pampf died. I find that I discount those I have been living alone.
 About Joachim too, I think as if he were two different people. Before and after.
 I have started to paint again and you will be astonished to hear that I have sold two of my paintings and now dream pleasant but unrealistic dreams of getting rich at this late date.
 Subject to Luise and Alfred Kalter's approval, I will come to Sweden in August and/or September and hope to see you. I will also see Joachim, a meeting that I look forward to with extremely mixed feelings. We will meet in Copenhagen. Joachim wants the meeting to be on neutral ground and I don't want an audience.

*

D.M. D.G.   Autumn 92

I am home again and you will want to know how my meeting with Joachim went. We met in my hotel room where he had put some beautiful roses and when he stepped in the shadowy figure that he had been for all those years, composed of unhappiness, grudges and a bad conscience dissolved like a black and white still on TV that suddenly comes to life and colour and all that seemed important was that Joachim was alive and well. And so, to my utmost confusion and amazement, instead of the simple "Hello" that I had intended, I heard myself say:
"I am glad you wrote."
It was of course not me talking but my alligator brain taking over. You may know that scientists have found that underneath the more modern layers of our mind we have a small brain from the time when we belonged to the lower orders. It may have been a crocodile's but I prefer to think of it as belonging to an alligator. I am glad that its German grammar is perfect because if I had said: "I was so glad that you wrote," it would have been a bold faced lie. You may recall that I was not the least bit pleased about his letter when we talked on the phone months ago. I spent the first half hour of our meeting in even greater bewilderment than I had expected.

We walked a lot, we talked a lot, we were also silent, each of us busy thinking about the past. We saw the Andersen Museum and went to see the Louisiana. All of this sounds easy but really was quite difficult and sometimes distressing.

A question that had disturbed me over the years on and off I asked now. Why had Joachim taken me to dinner more than once in a posh hotel, full of Nazis in wartime Berlin? He looked astonished.

"We were hungry!" he answered, as if this explained everything. My trust in him must have been boundless.

We talked about more important issues where I had thought that his actions had been ungenerous, but it did not really seem to matter any more. We had both lived our lives, I had had no regrets. I had liked my time in France, I had been happy with Pampf and had become an Israeli which I think suited me better than being an acclimatised Swede.

Having resigned myself to not growing old gracefully, as life in Israel and ten grandchildren seem to be a hindrance to this, I had thought that I might grow old without any further emotional and mental stress. I was wrong. As I told you, living alone one is more vulnerable.

Being wined and dined in Copenhagen by Joachim at my age, or any other age, was very flattering and he did it well. We decided to stay in touch. This journey into the past was not my idea and I can hardly blame myself for the unexpected outcome. Our relationship in the past was romantic, and owing to circumstances in Nazi Germany, dramatic. It is now surprising and highly unusual.

Epilogue

Kurt, by now a well-known conductor, viola player, and teacher, had visited me in Israel for two weeks a few years before. Now Joachim, Kurt and I decided to have a reunion for the fiftieth anniversary of our escape. We thought first of Copenhagen where we might visit Larsen's grave together with his son. But the men decided it would be too expensive for me to come to Europe in winter for such a short time and they would altogether prefer coming to Israel.

It could not be on the exact date but neither Kurt nor I care about such things, especially not after fifty years, and even Joachim admitted it would be better to meet on a different date than not to meet at all. Nava and I picked them up at the airport and after some refreshments at her house I drove them to my home. We had a wonderful week, visiting Sara and Gad, Ilana and Menahem, seeing some sights, talking a lot, reliving our memories and being astonished how different some of them were.

We set aside one evening for our reunion dinner which the men served. It consisted of salmon, fresh white bread, two bottles of champagne, and one of vodka freshly imported from Sweden and Denmark, with the tape playing soft music. They arranged everything while I had the evening off from duties and took a nice long shower. Joachim sprinkled parsley evenly on to the salmon, watched by a head shaking Kurt, and lit some candles to make everything as festive as possible. That the breakfast crumbs were still on the table disturbed no one. And with the help of one more bottle of wine Joachim and Kurt also overcame the tensions that had developed over the years between them since they are so different in their nature and disposition.

Kurt left after one week and Joachim stayed on and at the ripe old age of almost seventy my life is taking a new turn.

Glossary

Aliyah	Immigration to Israel
Aliyah Beth	Illegal immigration to Israel
Ashkenazim	European Jews but not those who were evicted from Spain. They are called Sephardim, Spaniards. They moved from Spain to the countries around the Mediterranean. Many also to the Netherlands and England
Bar Mitzvah	Boy's confirmation
Chanukah	Feast of Light and the Maccabees
Charimsel	Pancake for Pessach
Chaver, Chavera, Chaverim, Chaveroth	Friend or member of a kibbutz (male, female, plural male and plural female)
Chuppah	Canopy
Chutzepedick	Sassy
Davar	Jewish newspaper
Es ist nicht asoi wichtig	It isn't that important
Genitzte Kalle	Second-hand bride
Ghafirim	Arab word for auxiliary policemen – Jewish settlement police
Hachsharah	Preparation for agriculture in Israel
Halachah	Religious law
Hanita	A kibbutz on the northern border

Katiushot	Rockets
Keffiah	Arab head-dress
Kosher	Ritually clean
Kreppchen	Filled noodle dough
Madrich	Instructor
Mazzeklösse	Dumplings made of Mazzo meal
Menorah	Candleholder for Chanukah
Nargileh	Water pipe
Pessach	Commemoration of the Exodus from Egypt
Pitta, Pittot	Arab bread
Purim	Festival in memory of the deliverance of the Persian Jews
Sabra	Native born Israeli
Scheitel	Wig worn by pious women to hide their hair so no other man would find them pleasing
Shlichim (Shaliach sing.*)*	Delegates
Seder	The readings of the Haggadah about the Exodus from Egypt with a festive meal
Simchat Torah	Last day of the feast of the tabernacle to express our joy over the Bible
Suckoth	Huts which were built for the Tabernacle festivities
Tel Litwinski	Name of an Army camp
Yom Kippur	Day of Atonement
Youth Aliyah	Organisation that was founded by Henrietta Szold to send youngsters to Palestine and give them an education for a future life in agriculture. Later giving help to underprivileged children.

Appendix

The kibbutzim that were founded before the State of Israel came into being were settled on land that was bought and paid for by the Keren Kayemet l'Yisrael. The monies came from donations especially for this purpose.

The young settlers, with the help of members of already established kibbutzim, would set up a watchtower, a fence and tents in one day. Then the volunteers usually left.

Hanita, on the border of Lebanon, was an especially dangerous site and some of the volunteers remained longer. My husband was among them. He was the only driver of the tender bringing in provisions, taking the dirty linen to the laundry in Nahariah, or taking people to the hospital if needed.

It was a very strenuous job and once he was so tired that after ordering strawberries with cream in Nahariah he woke up with his face in his plate.

Here are three letters he wrote to his mother's cousin and her husband, Erna and Arthur Kahn in Jerusalem, from that time.

Hanita, April 10th, 1938

Dear Erna and Dear Arthur,

You are probably very angry with me for not writing much earlier, but since you live so far away this does not unduly distress me. I am sure you've read all there is to read in the *Davar* and know everything about Hanita.

I am driving our new Ford tender and four Ghafirim ride with me. We accompany everybody to Nahariah together with our armoured car. Last week our convoy was attacked. The Arabs shot at us for two hours but hit only the cars. At the beginning, the Ghafirim fired back from the tender and I felt like driving gangsters in a movie.

According to the management here we are all heroes and I look at myself twice daily in the mirror to see what a hero looks like. Any inferiority complexes that I had have vanished and I am now aware of my manly strength and fortitude. However, we are being kept from getting too uppity by the military education we get.

Apart from that I am fine, cigarettes and food are first class. For the past two nights I have slept in a real bed with pyjamas, till then only with my boots on.

I always escort our big shots, Ussishkin, Ben Gurion, and Berl Katznelson with the tender when they go back to Haifa or Nahariah.

I hope very much that you will write to me. That is if you think your hero worthy of receiving a letter from you.

Regards and kisses, also to Uncle and the boys.
                              Your Ernst.

*

Hanita, April 19th, 1938

Dear Erna and Dear Arthur,

I was very glad to get your letter. I had just come back with my tender from Acco, where I had to make a report about the incident on Saturday. Because people are stupid and will not listen, four people died.

Seev A., who worked with me on my tender, was one of the eight people who rushed to help the attacked. I had just gone to my tent to rest a few minutes (I work Saturdays too!) when the alarm came. I jumped on to the tender and came down. We met two people who had been able to escape. I put my foot as hard on the accelerator as I could to get there as quickly as possible. After about eight hundred metres we drew fire. I hardly heard the bullets, concentrating only on my driving.

Command: Stop!

From 95 km down to 0.10m is what I had to do. That the car did not overturn is a miracle.

We get out of that box and start shooting. The Arabs are surprised and retreat. Funny that one is so cool in spite of everything. We calmly aim and fire. Today we learn the results: four dead, two wounded on the Arab side. One of them is on my conscience.

Suddenly we hear Seev call. He is on the other side of the road and wounded. He has already tied up his leg and we put a bandage on. One of the guys gets into the car with me and we drive full speed to Nahariah. There they bandage him again and send him to Haifa by truck. You can imagine my mood when I heard of Seev's death, probably of shock...

In Nahariah I look at my car. Two bullet holes behind my head, one under my behind, one behind my back and one in front of my feet. Here they introduce me to guests as an exhibit.

The British police who came later in three armoured cars are afraid and leave. I am still surprised how eight people could stand up to more than a hundred. Today we were told that we may get more rifles and an armoured car which I hope to drive. Although I have a steel helmet now, an armoured car is safer. My parents know that I am here, I don't know who told them, but it can't be helped any more.

In spite of all this fighting we don't neglect our agriculture and I really prefer driving peacefully with a load of hay.

This week we'll move to higher ground. We have been holding the Arab house for a week now, I would love to come and visit you but my tender has no second driver and I can't leave for the time being. It would be nice if you could visit me but it is strictly forbidden at the moment. It might be possible for Arthur to come if he can get a certificate from the Jewish Agency.

I would have loved to write you a more cheerful letter but I am really not in the mood for it. Still, don't think that I am downhearted.

I now get more letters from Ma'ayan and you will be interested to hear that I have a new girlfriend. As you know I specialise in 'love at a distance'.

That's all, love and kisses from one of the heroes of the Upper Galil.

Your Ernst.

*

Hanita, April 28th, 1938

Dear Erna, Dear Arthur,

I received your regards through Meckler and heard that Arthur might be able to come.

Dear Erna, please get me the following things and give them to your beloved husband.

1. Two pairs of short khaki pants, 80 cm around the middle and 40 cm long.
2. Two khaki shirts with short sleeves, 95 cm around.

Please choose good material, I have to wear the stuff every day. Other than that I don't need anything. You could send me a nice book if you have one.

I had mail from my parents today. Father seems to be making an all-out effort to get out of his store. I am sorry for the old man, he really does not deserve this. Hopefully he is sensible enough to get out of Germany as soon as possible. I would also like to know what will happen to my grandparents.

I wish I could come and visit and go with you to the cinema. But there are not enough drivers.

Ma'ayan is almost empty. Ten people are doing guard duty in Kfar Hachoresch without pay, eight are on the northern frontier as Ghafirim, two in Hanita. That's twenty out of a settlement of fifty. Do you get visitors from Ma'ayan? What do you hear from Waldi, is he still sitting in the desert? How is Uncle, you write neither about him nor the boys?

I filmed quite a few good scenes here. Maybe I can sell them.

Love and kisses, Ernst.

Dear Arthur, if you can't come, please mail the shirts and shorts.